CRACY IN ARGENTINA

F

DEMOCRACY IN ARGENTINA

Hope and Disillusion

LAURA TEDESCO

University of East Anglia

FRANK CASS
LONDON • PORTLAND, OR

First Published in 1999 in Great Britain by
FRANK CASS PUBLISHERS
Newbury House, 900 Eastern Avenue
London, IG2 7HH

and in the United States of America by
FRANK CASS PUBLISHERS
c/o ISBS, 5804 N.E. Hassalo Street
Portland, Oregon, 97213-3644

Website: www.frankcass.com

British Library Cataloguing in Publication Data

Tedesco, Laura
    Democracy in Argentina: hope and disillusion
    1. Democracy – Argentina 2. Representative government and
    representation – Argentina 3. Argentina – Politics and
    government – 1983 – 4. Argentina – Economic conditions –
    1983–
    I. Title
    321.8′0982

ISBN 0-7146-4978-3 (cloth)
ISBN 0-7146-8094-X (paper)

Library of Congress Cataloging-in-Publication Data

Tedesco, Laura.
    Democracy in Argentina: hope and disillusion / Laura Tedesco.
        p.   cm.
    Based on author's thesis (Ph.D.) – Warwick University, 1994.
    Includes bibliographical references and index.
    ISBN 0-7146-4978-3 (cloth). – ISBN 0-7146-8094-X (pbk.)
    1. Democracy – Argentina. 2. Argentina – Politics and
    government – 1983– 3. Argentina – Economic conditions – 1983–
    I. Title.
    JL2081.T43   1999
    320.982′09′-048 – dc21   99-29120
                                                              CIP

Printed in Great Britain by
MPG Book Ltd, Bodmin, Cornwall

To Olga, Piro, Adriana, Ricardo, Lucila, Marcos and Francisco

To Richard

Contents

List of Tables   viii

List of Abbreviations   ix

Acknowledgements   xi

Introduction   xiii

1   A Brief Historical Background of the Crisis of the Argentinian State   1

2   The 1976–83 Military Dictatorship and its Economic Legacy   23

3   A Failed Attempt to Resolve the Crisis, 1983–85   62

4   The Deepening Crisis, 1985–87   102

5   The Downfall, 1987–89   132

Conclusions   168

Appendix: Argentina's main economic indicators   181

Bibliography   189

Index   205

Tables

1. Wage bill as a share of national income (1974–81)   27

2. Inflation rate (1974–81)   28

3. Real wages per sector (1974–81)   28

4. Industrial activity: main branches (1975–80)   35

5. Industrial employment (1975–80)   36

6. Percentage of poor population of
    Greater Buenos Aires (1974–82)   41

7. External debt (1976–82)   44

8. Gross Domestic Product (1981–89)   149

9. Price indices (1984–89)   150

10. Fiscal deficit as a percentage of GDP (1984–89)   150

11. External debt (US$ million) (1984–89)   150

12. Total debt as a percentage of GNP (1984–89)   151

13. Interest paid as a percentage of GNP (1984–89)   151

14. Real wages by sector (1984–89)   151

15. Purchasing power by sector (1984–89)   152

16. Unemployment and underemployment rates (1981–89)   152

17. Income distribution (1974–89)   158

Abbreviations

ABRA	*Asociación de Bancos de la República Argentina* (Argentinian Republic Banks Association)
ADEBA	*Asociación de Bancos Argentinos* (Argentinian Banks Association)
AOT	*Asociación Obrera Textil* (Textile Workers Association)
BCRA	*Banco Central de la República Argentina* (Argentinian Central Bank)
CAC	*Cámara Argentina de Comercio* (Argentinian Chamber of Commerce)
CEPAL	*Comisión Económica para América Latina y el Caribe*
CES	*Conferencia Económica y Social* (Economic and Social Conference)
CGT	*Confederación General del Trabajo* (General Confederation of Labour)
CONADEP	*Comisión Nacional de Desaparición de Personas* (Argentina's National Commission on Disappeared People)
CONINAGRO	*Confederación Intercooperativa Agropecuaria* (Agrarian Confederation of Cooperatives)
CPI	Consumer Price Index
CRA	*Confederaciones Rurales Argentinas* (Argentinian Rural Confederations)

ECLA	*Economic Commission for Latin America and the Caribbean*
ERP	*Ejército Revolucionario del Pueblo* (People's Revolutionary Army)
FAA	*Federación Agraria Argentina* (Argentinian Agrarian Federation)
GEN	*Grupos Económicos Nacionales* (National Economic Groups)
GNP	Gross National Product
GOU	*Grupo de Oficiales Unidos* (United Officials Group)
IMF	International Monetary Fund
INDEC	*Instituto Nacional de Estadísticas y Censos* (National Institute of Statistics and Census)
ISI	Import Substitution Industrialisation
LIBOR	London Inter-Bank Offered Rate
MTP	*Movimiento Todos por la Patria* (Movement All for the Fatherland)
OPEC	Oil Producing and Exporting Countries
SMATA	*Sindicato de Mecánicos del Transporte Automotor* (Union of Automobile Mechanics)
SRA	*Sociedad Rural Argentina* (Argentinian Rural Society)
UIA	*Unión Industrial Argentina* (Argentinian Industrial Union)
UOCRA	*Unión Obreros de la Construcción de la República Argentina* (Construction Workers Union)
UOM	*Unión Obrera Metalúrgica* (Metal Workers Union)
VAT	Value Added Tax
WPI	Wholesale Price Index

Acknowledgements

The writing of this book has been a long process. It is based on my PhD thesis submitted at Warwick University in 1994. I would like to thank all those who throughout the years have been related, in one way or another, with this project, mainly Atilio Borón, Julio Faúndez, John King, Peter Burnham, Charles Jones and John Holloway. I would also like to thank those who have helped me to improve the book with their advice and comments: Richard Youngs, Paula Alonso, Rut Diamint, Olga Arratibel San Miguel, my MA students in FLACSO/Buenos Aires, and an anonymous reader at Frank Cass. Finally, I would like to thank all interviewees in both Argentina and England for their useful comments.

For their financial help throughout these recent years, I must also thank the University of Warwick, the British Council and the *Consejo Nacional de Investigaciones Científicas y Técnicas (CONICET)*.

I left Argentina in August 1991 to come to England to do my PhD. Domingo Cavallo's Convertibility Plan was 4 months old and the memories of hyper-inflation were still fresh in people's minds. In 1983, as everybody else in Argentina, I believed that a new era was beginning. I was overjoyed with the return to democracy and was naive enough to believe that *con la democracia se come, se cura, se educa* ('with democracy one eats, one is cured, one is educated'). But disappointment soon set in. In writing this book my aim has been to help both myself and others to understand why the amazing experience of living under democracy after seven years of military dictatorship ended in hyper-inflation, looting and disenchantment.

Introduction

*Con la democracia se come, se cura, se educa [with democracy one eats,
one is cured, one is educated]*
(Alfonsín's slogan, 1983 electoral campaign)

*(Con la democracia) Creo que se come, se cura, se educa, pero no se
hacen milagros [I believe that with democracy one eats, one is cured,
one is educated, but miracles do not happen]*
(Alfonsín, 1992, p. 48)

Raúl Alfonsín's government initiated a new era in Argentina. It faced serious challenges: to consolidate democracy and achieve economic development in a country devastated by military dictatorships, human rights violations, a lost war, high inflation, and a huge external debt. With the arrival of democracy, the hopes and expectations of Argentina's society were high. Five and a half years later, hope had been replaced by disillusion.

Raúl Alfonsín's government is mostly remembered for its chaotic final months. This book looks at this period with the aim of understanding not only the reasons for Alfonsín's downfall but also for the implementation of far-reaching reforms during the 1990s. It argues that the genesis of the 1990s reforms must be understood through historical analysis. Raúl Alfonsín's government was the last and most dramatic period of a long crisis of the Argentinian state. Seen in this historical context, Alfonsín's period in office can be understood as crucial for laying the foundations for the resolution of this crisis of the state through the establishment of a new equilibrium between social classes. These new social relations constituted a consolidation of the new democratic regime, but also a deepening of the logic of the 1976 military dictatorship's *disciplinamiento social.*[1] Alfonsín's government consolidated democracy, but in a context of increasing poverty. Political inclusion was established simultaneously with the imposition of domination by economic and social exclusion.

This book examines the interrelation between the economic and political factors underlying the fall of Alfonsín's government. It does so by analysing the Alfonsín government from a historical perspective: the 1983–89 government saw the culmination of a long crisis of the state. It was a period when class struggle was exacerbated, class alliances were being re-created, factions fought for position within their respective class, and Argentina's social relations underwent fundamental change. The outcome of this struggle produced a reshaping of the state and its social relations, which conditioned Argentina's democratic development and the nature of the economic restructuring which followed.

This book provides a historical analysis of the crisis within the Argentinian state. It argues that Argentina during the 1980s was not only experiencing a democratisation process but also, and more importantly, an exacerbation of the crisis of the state. In order to analyse the causes and consequences of this exacerbation, the book studies the influence of three actors on Alfonsín's government: the trade unions, the Armed Forces and international creditors. This permits an understanding of the underlying class struggle, taking into account the importance that Argentina's historical and political evolution had given the Armed Forces and the trades union movement. The book analyses how the events which took place under Alfonsín prepared the way for Carlos Menem's economic policy. It seeks to answer some questions regarding the restructuring of the 1990s, arguing that the answer to those questions must be found in the period of the first democratic government and its inability to deal with and resolve the crisis of the state.

In the remainder of this introduction, the state and its crisis are conceptualised. This is followed by an analysis of the international context and, more specifically, the international shift to monetarism. The third section discusses some of the peculiarities of the Argentinian case.

CONCEPTUALISING THE STATE AND ITS CRISIS

There is ongoing debate over the definition of the state. The state is a concept, an abstract idea of domination. As Miliband (1969) puts it: 'the state is not a thing'. It is a concept which has been developed according to its own historical conditions. The argument of the book follows from a particular conceptualisation of the state. The state is understood here as a historical form of class domination (Holloway and Picciotto, 1977, p. 77).[2]

The state dominates through institutions, values, norms, law, and, mainly, social relations.[3] The first four elements are expressed through the state apparatus: the government,[4] the administration, the military and the police, the judicial branch, local government and parliamentary assemblies (Miliband, 1969). The last element, social relations, is shaped by class structure. The latter is the outcome of the relationship of different groups to the production and distribution of wealth.

The balance of power between classes shapes the state's social relations. These social relations are dynamic, as there is a constant tension between classes to either maintain or improve their respective economic and political positions. In response, the state is also dynamic, assuming different characteristics at different moments in time. The capitalist state assumes different forms: developmentalist, populist, bureaucratic-authoritarian or neo-liberal. These are simply different forms of class domination, different structures of power relations between classes. The developmentalist state dominates through the image of development from above and for all. The populist state dominates through the image of the state as organiser of, and provider for, the working class. The bureaucratic-authoritarian state dominates through the idea of normalisation, reimposition of order and repression. The neo-liberalist state dominates through the image of the state as guarantor of democracy, law and order, efficiency and provider of the legal framework to permit the market, civil society and the individual to flourish.

The continual dynamism of social relations is reflected in periodic crises of the state. Crisis is neither solely 'economic' nor solely 'political'. The concepts of 'economic' and 'political' are specific to capitalism, since 'the relations between slave and master or serf and lord were indistinguishably economic-and-political relations' (Holloway, 1992, p. 160; and Anderson, 1979). The concepts of 'economic' and 'political' are fetishised categories which reflect the superficial fragmentation of capitalist society. Although crisis presents itself as economic, it expresses the structural instability of capitalist social relations, 'the instability of the basic relation between capital and labour on which society is based' (Holloway, 1992, p. 159).

Each development of the state must be seen as a particular manifestation of the crisis of the capital relation. Crisis of the capital relation inevitably involves a restructuring of social relations which take specific economic and political forms (Holloway and Picciotto, 1977). Crisis involves a process of struggle. The outcome of this struggle determines the nature of the new pattern of accumulation. Thus, crisis is a crisis of the capital relation; a crisis of a historically specific form of class domination; a crisis of accumulation which involves the totality of capitalist social relations. Crisis is composed of both breakdown and restructuring, and 'between crisis-as-rupture and crisis-as-restructuring there is a whole world-history of struggle' (Holloway, 1992, p. 164). The outcome of this struggle reshapes social relations and may open the way for the emergence of a new state.

There are periods of time during which the tension between classes is controlled – the state's domination not being under any direct threat and/or the form of social relations being generally accepted by all actors. This control can be secured either by an accepted-by-all image of domination or by repression. However, the tension can increase when either the image of domination is no longer accepted by all actors, or the means of repression lose their effectiveness. A crisis of the state can begin when the tension increases and the balance between classes is distorted. The magnitude of the crisis will depend on the reason behind the increase in tension. An increase in tension is not necessarily sufficient to set off a crisis of the state. The tension could be reduced by different types of concessions. The old balance could then re-establish itself or a new one emerge without a crisis or period of struggle. However, on other occasions, such concessions may not be enough and, in order to regain a balance, a fundamental restructuring of the state and its class relations must be applied.

THE INTERNATIONAL SHIFT TO MONETARISM

It is necessary to highlight that the capitalist state is not an isolated actor. It acts and reacts to stimuli from both within and outside its own body. The state is part of an international system of states. The world market must be understood as a single totality constituted by many national economies. These national economies with their social relations are under pressure from both the national and the international sphere. Therefore, the state is not only shaped by the internal tensions between social classes but also by the external tensions which shape the international system of states.

After the Second World War a new international economic order was established. The Bretton Woods system of fixed exchange rates regulated the movement of money between nation states. To some degree this insulated the national state from the global movement of capital. This relative insulation provided the basis for the state-oriented policies of the post-war period. Richard Nixon's suspension of the dollar's convertibility in 1971 destroyed a central pillar of the Bretton Woods system. The system finally collapsed with the decision in 1973 to let exchange rates float. After the oil price shocks of 1973 and 1979 there was a process of adjustment on an international level, followed by a period of expansion based on the liberalisation of capital movements and the deregulation of the major financial markets. These modifications led to a fundamental shift in power relationships. On an international level, the rise of market forces increased the power of international investors, creditor countries and the two major financial institutions – the International Monetary Fund and the World Bank. The main losers were those countries heavily dependent on foreign capital.

While the Bretton Woods system was based on the idea of co-ordination of the international economy by governments, its failure gave rise to the notion of the market as the most efficient regulator of the economy on national and international levels.

These international changes triggered changes on a national level. During the 1970s, Keynesian policies were abandoned and replaced by monetarism. While Keynesianism emphasised full employment, monetarism emphasised price stability and monetary regulation. Economically, monetarism's central theme is 'the need to maintain monetary stability to ensure the smooth operation of the market and the achievement of a full employment equilibrium' (Clarke, 1988, p. 323). In general terms, monetarism prioritised monetary regulation as a means of achieving price stability. The economic role of the state is 'to confine accumulation within the limits of the market by restructuring the growth of the money supply' (Clarke, 1988, p. 328). This economic aspect was complemented by the eradication of the institutional structures of Keynesianism and the restructuring of the state as the means of imposing the rule of money and law. Thus, the political institutions of Keynesian class collaboration were reformed.

Monetarism attempted to exploit and intensify the divisions within the working class in order to reimpose the rule of money (Clarke, 1988, p. 355). Money replaces the state as the agent of restructuring; the rule of money is imposed on capital and on the state by the banks and the financial institutions. The monetarist restructuring of the state and its class relations is an attempt to 'resolve the political crisis of the state by trying to disengage the state politically from the economy so as to depoliticise economic policy formation' (Clarke, 1988, p. 27).

The 1980s witnessed the process of struggle between the collapse of inward-looking strategies and the emergence of outward-looking strategies. This was a struggle over income distribution, rather than for radical transformations. It was a struggle over the nature of the welfare-state and the continuing validity of Keynesianism.

The 1990s have seen the results of this struggle: the implementation of new social relations and a new type of domination. An economic retreat by the state was implemented as the guiding principle of policy and this perpetuated the structure inherent in the structure of social relations upon which the state is based. Importantly, the prime purpose was neither to enhance the efficacy of development polices nor to transform income distribution but to maintain the class structure of domination. Market efficiency was more a means to this political end than an end in itself.

To summarise: the theoretical framework of this book rests on a view of the capitalist state as a historically specific form of class domination. The analysis of the development of the capitalist state must be located in its historical context. The development of the state must be seen as a particular manifestation of the crisis of the capital relation. Class struggle influences the historical form of the state. In this sense, the economic policy of the capitalist state is primarily an outcome of both domestic and international class struggle. This framework overcomes the artificial divide between 'economics' and 'politics'. This fetishised separation is caused by the constitution of the proletarian as both property-owner and citizen, a specific feature of capitalist society. The coexistence of the classless status of citizen and the class character of capitalist society is the origin of the division between 'politics' and 'economics'.

Regarding the concept of crisis, the assumption is that although crisis is often experienced in an economic form, it inevitably involves a restructuring of social relations. Crisis expresses the instability of the labour–capital relation which is the basis of capitalist society. Thus, this book is guided by the assumption that the crisis of the capitalist state means a breakdown and a restructuring of the capital relation. In the context of the globalisation of capital, the restructuring of the capital relation means a restructuring of the state and its relationship to the global economy. The 1970s and 1980s witnessed such a restructuring throughout the international system. With the triumph of monetarism over Keynesian policies this restructuring means, ideologically and politically, the imposition of the rule of money.

These theoretical assumptions provide a framework within which the attempt to restructure the Argentinian state by both the 1976 military dictatorship and the 1983 democratic government can be understood, emphasising the interaction between economics and politics rather than analysing these as two separate spheres. This framework helps to place the 1983–89 government in its historical context as a period of struggle situated between the initiation of a restructuring of the state (under the 1976–83 dictatorship) and the resolution of that process (under the Menem government).

THE INFLUENCE OF THE MILITARY DICTATORSHIP'S LEGACY UPON ALFONSÍN

The crisis of the Argentinian state saw its first manifestation with the 1930 military coup and the military's attempt to exclude the middle classes – represented, at that time, by the Radical party[5] – from the political scene. The emergence of Peronism[6] and its inclusion of the working class as a political and an economic actor was another manifestation of the crisis. The crisis brought a movement away from the established class-equilibrium and, in 1930 and 1955, a reversal of the social inclusion achieved in 1916 and 1946. From 1955 to 1976, neither the Armed Forces nor the political parties could control a politically mobilised working class which was demanding the restoration of full political rights through the inclusion of the Peronist party in general elections. This period was important for the structuring of the party political system. Argentina's politics were governed by the Peronist/anti-Peronist dichotomy: while the majority of the Armed Forces became representatives of anti-Peronism,[7] the trade unions took up the mantle of Peronist ideology.[8] This scenario undermined the role of the political parties (Cheresky, 1998, p. 47). Argentina's party political system lacked both a party which represented the bourgeoisie – a role taken up instead by the Armed Forces – and a strong and institutionalised party linked to the trade unions, there being, instead, strong trade unions linked to a weak Peronist party. The Peronist party was banned and thus the trade unions became the only channel of representation for the politically activated working class. Throughout these years the trade unions gained significant autonomy not only from their main leader, Juan Perón, but also from the workers (Halperín Donghi, 1994a, p. 42). More-over, the Radical party was divided and unable to gain the support of the majority of the electorate: it was seen as collaborating with the Armed Forces and their proscription of Peronism rather than defending democracy. Thus from 1955 to 1983 Argentina's political party system was virtually replaced by the Armed Forces and the trade unions as the main representatives of, respectively, the bourgeoisie and the working class. During Alfonsín's government these two actors struggled either to maintain or regain their historical power.

From 1976, the military dictatorship attempted to resolve the crisis of the Argentinian state by implementing economic structural reform combined with state terrorism. The consequences of this attempt dramatically influenced the first democratic government. In 1983, after seven years of military dictatorship, Argentina was on the verge of international isolation. Systematic human rights violations, tensions with Chile and a war with Great Britain made Argentina's foreign policy problematic.

The outbreak of the external debt crisis, with Mexico's default of 1982 and Argentina's own difficulties in repaying interest, showed that Argentina's economy was undergoing a profound crisis far worse than the old, and well-known, balance of payments difficulties. The huge external debt constrained Argentina's economic growth and the whole range of the Radical government's economic policies. A monetarist restructuring of the state was imposed on debtor countries through IMF 'conditionality' loans. While the Radical government initially opposed such a restructuring,[9] it later gradually began to implement the IMF's requirements. The external debt crisis, together with the Malvinas adventure, meant that the government needed to rebuild Argentina's international relations urgently, since it would need support from the international community to cope with its financial problems.

Domestically, the consequences of the military dictatorship were also dramatically influential. The role of the political parties during the Malvinas (Falkland Islands) war, supporting the Armed Forces' adventure, had weakened their already limited role in Argentina's politics. During the dictatorship and after the war, human rights organisations were almost the only organisations able to mobilise civil society. Their slogan during the war highlighted the fact that the Armed Forces' 'dirty war' could not be forgotten through another war: 'the Malvinas are Argentinian and so are the disappeared people'.

The mobilisation of the human rights organisations meant that the incoming government could not ignore the Armed Forces' 'dirty war' and its consequences. The attempt to bring the military to trial complicated the relationship between the Radical government and the Armed Forces. The government was unable to implement its own policies towards human rights violations, preventing a definitive solution to this problem. In addition, the failure to resolve this problem intensified internal unrest within the Armed Forces, fostering the breakdown of the Army's hierarchy.

The relationship between the government and the *sindicalismo Peronista* was marked from the beginning by the fact that, since the emergence of Peronism in 1946, Raúl Alfonsín was the first presidential candidate to defeat Peronism in free elections. Due to this, the Peronist trade unionists came to distrust him, and he in turn distrusted the unions. He believed that the *sindicalismo Peronista* was responsible for the 1966 military coup against the Radical President, Arturo Illia.

After the 1983 electoral defeat, the Peronist party underwent a period of internal struggle and reconstruction[10] which meant that it did not function as a strong opposition party until 1987, when the *Renovación Peronista* won the mid-term elections. Therefore, the *sindicalismo Peronista* acted as the main opposition to the government.[11] The main scene of confrontation was not the Congress but the streets, with 13 general strikes, social mobilisations, and hundred of thousands of labour conflicts. The political mobilisation of the working class was very high throughout this period.[12] The Radical government unsuccessfully attempted to control and demobilise the unions. The trades union movement was able to block government policies, becoming the ultimate barrier to the restructuring policies adopted by the government.

In summary, the 1976 dictatorship attempted to restructure the state and its class relations by implementing economic structural reform and state terrorism. The consequences of the economic structural reform and state terrorism constrained the margin of manoeuvre of the 1983 democratic government and lent distinctive features to the crisis of the state. The main economic constraints were the huge external debt and the impoverishment of the working class. The main political constraints were the need to bring the military to trial while avoiding a direct confrontation with the Armed Forces and the need to achieve cohabitation between a Radical government and *sindicalismo Peronista*.

In order to analyse the crisis of the Argentinian state during the democratisation process, it is thus essential to look at these three actors: the government, the Armed Forces and the trade unions. To understand fully Alfonsín's fall and its consequences, this book analyses the interaction between the Armed Forces, the trade unions and the government's economic policy. They constantly interact as obstacles to resolving the crisis of the state. The Armed Forces, the trade unions, international creditors and the bourgeoisie were able to block government policies without presenting a viable alternative for resolving the crisis. This book is an attempt to analyse the crisis of the state and its resolution by studying the interrelation between these actors.

The book suggests that the Radical government, although unable to resolve the crisis of the Argentinian state, was able to set out on the path towards consolidating democracy through its policies on human rights violations, which undermined the political role of the Armed Forces. Despite three military rebellions and far-reaching concessions to the Armed Forces, Alfonsín's government achieved the political demobilisation of the Armed Forces, thus modifying a historical feature of the crisis of the state. This was Alfonsín's main achievement.

THE OUTLINE OF THE BOOK

This book analyses the crisis of the Argentinian state during the period of the 1983–89 democratic government. It argues that there was a crisis of the state in Argentina which deepened during the

1983–89 democratic government and prompted the restructuring during the 1990s.

Given the importance of appreciating the historical context conditioning Alfonsín's government, the book begins with a historical account of the economic and political situation in the 1950s, 1960s and early 1970s. It highlights the development of the crisis of the Argentinian state which ultimately led to the 1976 military dictatorship.

The second chapter analyses the economic structural reform applied by the 1976 military dictatorship. The main objective of this reform was to discipline society. The chapter highlights the main legacies of this reform for the incoming democratic government. It also studies the causes of the collapse of the military dictatorship and the transition process, in order to discover how the collapse and the transition would influence the democratic government.

The third chapter analyses the first two years of Alfonsín's government. It studies the first policies applied by the government to tackle the main legacies of the dictatorship, namely the policies towards the external debt and the domestic economic strategy, and the policies towards the unions and the Armed Forces. It shows that the government attempted to constrain the unions by controlling their internal elections. As this strategy failed, the government sought to achieve a social and economic agreement with the unions. However, in turn this strategy also failed. Regarding the Armed Forces, the government tried to apply its 'due obedience' proposal but this also came to grief, owing to the pressure of the Judiciary and human rights organisations since they believed that 'due obedience' was a hidden amnesty. Thus, the government was not able to execute its preferred policies towards the Armed Forces. Lastly, the chapter deals with the treatment of the external debt, the most significant issue in the economic sphere. It also analyses the reasons for the failure of the first economic strategy of the democratic government. In summary, it shows how the failure of the external debt negotiations and of the domestic economic strategy prepared the ground for the launching of the *Austral* plan.

The fourth chapter studies the development of the crisis from the launching of the *Austral* plan to the Radical party's defeat in the 1987 legislative elections. It describes the main objectives and features of the economic reform. It also assesses the subsequent economic plans which were applied after the failure of the *Austral.*

In the context of such economic reform, the chapter analyses the attempts of the government to control the unions. It analyses the main causes and consequences of the appointment of Carlos Alderete, from the Light and Power Union, as Labour Minister. By this time, Argentina had undergone its first military rebellion. The chapter examines the development of the crisis in the light of these three main events: the launching of the *Austral*, the temporary agreement with the unions and the first military rebellion.

Chapter 5 analyses the last two years (1987–89) of the Alfonsín government when the economic crisis was at its peak. While in this period the degree of confrontation with the unions declined, the government was faced with two military rebellions and a significant guerrilla attack on an army unit. This prompted speculation that another economic crisis would end in a political crisis and, as before, in a military coup; however, the 1989 general elections and Alfonsín's resignation were peaceful events. The chapter examines the increasing economic crisis and the role of the unions and the Armed Forces as historical barriers to the restructuring of the state. The chapter also charts the main economic and political consequences of Alfonsín's government.

The final chapter concludes with the development of the crisis of the Argentinian state under the democratisation process and explains why the crisis could not be resolved by the 1983–89 government, and why it could begin to be resolved by the 1989–95 government.

NOTES

1. Canitrot (1981, p. 132) emphasises that the 1976–81 economic programme had a political objective: the *disciplinamiento social* (social discipline) which means the weakening of the working class that had become politically powerful through the Peronist party.
2. After a very careful examination of some theoretical approaches to the state it was argued elsewhere that the more comprehensive and helpful conceptualisation of the state is that which contains two of its main aspects: its historical development and its relation to social classes. This analysis of state theory is not reproduced here since the study of state theory is not the main aim of this book. For more details see Tedesco (1994). For other accounts see Miliband (1969), (1973) and (1983), Poulantzas (1973) and (1978), Hall (1986), Krasner (1978), Dahl (1956) and (1961), Jessop (1990) and Skocpol (1980) and (1985).

3. The state applies its different types of domination through images, as will be shown.
4. In this work the state is understood as a more abstract concept and is defined as a form of domination. The government is just one of the institutions of the state apparatus. In common language these terms are used synonymously. Here, however, the distinction is maintained throughout the text.
5. The Radical party, founded in September 1889, had as its main objectives the demand for honest elections, real representation and the establishment of universal male suffrage. In 1916, after the Saenz Peña law of 1912 that guaranteed a secret ballot and universal manhood suffrage, Hipólito Yrigoyen, leader of the Radical party was elected President. His successor, Marcelo T. de Alvear, was also from the Radical party. Yrigoyen was elected President again in 1928. In 1930 the first military coup ended with 14 years of democracy. After the appearance of Peronism in 1946, the Radical party could only win elections from which Peronism was proscribed. In 1957 the Radical party split into two new parties: one led by Arturo Frondizi, *Unión Cívica Radical Intransigente*, and the other by Ricardo Balbín, *Unión Cívica Radical del Pueblo*. In 1958 Frondizi, with the support of Peronism, became President. In 1962 a military coup interrupted Frondizi's presidency and called for elections in 1963. Arturo Illia, from the *Unión Cívica Radical del Pueblo*, won the elections. Due to the proscription of Peronism and Perón's advice to his followers to abstain, with only 25 per cent of the total vote cast Illia was appointed President. In 1966 a military coup interrupted his presidential term. In 1973, Raúl Alfonsín organised an internal movement of the Radical party for the presidential nomination for the approaching elections. The *Movimiento de Renovación y Cambio* lost the internal elections, and so Ricardo Balbín was nominated presidential candidate for the Radical party. He lost the general elections. Alfonsín tried to push Radicalism to the left to oppose the struggle begun by President María Estela Martínez de Perón (Isabel) to left-wing trade unions, but Balbín opposed him. Under the 1976 military dictatorship, Alfonsín became an ardent defender of human rights. Balbín died in September 1981 and, after internal elections, Alfonsín became the presidential candidate for the Radical party in the 1983 general elections. For more detailed accounts see Rock (1975), Wynia (1992), del Mazo (1959), Luna (1958), Puiggrós (1957) and Alonso (forthcoming).
6. Peronism emerged as a consequence of Colonel Juan Domingo Perón's policies in the Secretariat of Labour from 1943 to 1945. Perón, from his position, benefited the workers economically and socially. This made him the 'natural' leader of the workers' movement, which until 1943 had been very weak. Perón also promoted the unionisation of workers, making the trades union movement the arbiter between the workers and the state. Besides, through unionisation the workers achieved more social benefits and became politically organised. For more details on the emergence of Peronism see Potash (1969), James (1988), Corradi (1985), Lewis (1992), Luna (1973), (1982), Peña (1973), Laclau (1973) and Fayt (1967).
7. A sector of the Armed Forces was Peronist but, in overall terms, they

represented anti-Peronism. It can not be forgotten that Peronism was brutally repressed within the Forces, as in the case of General Juan José Valle and his followers, who were executed after a rebellion in June 1956.

8. As said, Perón promoted the unionisation of the working class. By organising the trades union movement, Perón also became its main leader. This gave rise to a 'Peronist trades union movement' (*sindicalismo Peronista*) which remained, in principle, loyal to Perón but achieved significant autonomy from its leader during his 18 years of proscription, with some leaders promoting 'Peronism without Perón'. For an analysis of Peronism and the trades union movement, see Matsushita (1983), James (1988) and Torre (1988), (1989), (1990a) and (1995).

9. Alfonsín was a supporter of the Welfare State, which he defines as a state that intervenes in the economy in order to achieve growth as well as an equilibrium in income distribution. The public sector is seen by Alfonsín as responsible for ensuring equal opportunities and accessibility for basic social services (Lázara, 1997, p. 313).

10. For more details see Unamuno *et al.* (1984), De Ipola (1987), Maronese *et al.* (1985) and Moncalvillo and Fernández (1986).

11. As explained above, this was more a traditional feature of Peronism rather than an exception. Indeed, when Juan D. Perón was exiled in Madrid, the *sindicalismo Peronista* had more control over the working class than the Peronist party. While the party was proscribed and neutralised, the trades union movement did find the way to make its voice heard (Cavarozzi, 1997, pp. 20-1). In this period the *sindicalismo Peronista* gained significant autonomy from the party, its leader and the workers. It is not the aim of this book to consider to what extent the trades union movement was, and still is, *the* representative body of the workers. The trade unions are studied here because, from 1955, they assumed the political and institutionalised representation of the workers. The movement attempted to replace the Peronist party and became a significant player in Argentina's rather unique party political system. In this context, as said, the trades union movement gained autonomy from the workers and its representative function became debatable.

12. For instance, there were 465 sectoral strikes from 1 July 1985 to 30 June 1986 (Lázara, 1997, p. 350).

1

A Brief Historical Background of the Crisis of the Argentinian State

The objective of this chapter is to set the scene for the analysis of the 1976 military dictatorship, explaining the historical origins of the crisis of the Argentinian state. The chapter is divided into three sections. The first deals with the recent political background, explaining the causes and consequences of the crisis of the Argentinian state. It analyses the emergence of Peronism, *sindicalismo Peronista*, and examines the political role of the Armed Forces. It highlights the reasons why, historically, in Argentinian politics, the Armed Forces and the trades union movement played an influential role. The second section explains Argentina's recent economic development, preparing the ground for the study of the 1976 economic structural reform. The last section concludes by analysing the development of the crisis of the Argentinian state and outlining its main features in 1976.

THE POLITICAL BACKGROUND

The Emergence of Peronism and Sindicalismo Peronista

In 1930 the first military coup ended 14 years of democracy in Argentina. The 1916 Radical government had signalled the incorporation into the political sphere of the middle class.[1] The coup was the first manifestation of the crisis of the Argentinian state since it excluded the middle sectors from political involvement. This process began with the 1929 world crisis and its effects on Argentina's economic structure (Halperín Donghi, 1994b, pp. 93–116). After 1916, it seemed that Argentina had achieved a modern and mature democracy. However, the economic structure and the hegemonic role of the agrarian bourgeoisie – which had not been modified by the democratic government – turned out to be inadequate to cope with the Depression. Although the Radical party did accept the hegemonic role of the agrarian bourgeoisie, the latter felt threatened by a political order which it did not control, combined with an unfavourable international situation. The military coup showed that Argentina's democracy was unable to change the social relations established by the economic structure. The 1930 coup was, in this sense, a return to the past. The reincorporation of both the middle and the working classes had to await the arrival of Peronism.

In 1943, after a succession of conservative governments had been in power since 1932, as a result of electoral frauds,[2] a nationalist sector of the Armed Forces[3] took over. The GOU (*Grupo de Oficiales Unidos* – United Officials Group), a secret military society, organised the coup. The main aim was to overthrow President Ramón Castillo and the presidential candidate Robustiano Patrón Costas, who would have been elected by another electoral fraud (Potash, 1969). The objective of the coup was, thus, to end the 'electoral fraud era' (*década infame*), and its political conservatism. One of the main participants of the 1943 military coup was Colonel Juan Domingo Perón. He was gradually increasing his power and by 1944 was, simultaneously, Vice-President, Minister of War and Secretary of Labour (Potash, 1969, p. 248).

From his position as Secretary of Labour, Perón encouraged the unionisation of the working class. The labour movement which existed at the time of the 1943 military coup was divided and weak. There existed four labour organisations: the anarchist *Federación Obrera Regional Argentina* (Argentinian Regional Workers' Federation), the syndicalist *Unión Sindical Argentina* (Argentinian Syndical Union), and the *Confederación General del Trabajo* – CGT – (General Confederation of Labour) 1, controlled by socialists, and CGT 2, controlled by communists. In 1943 only 20 per cent of the urban labour force was organised, the majority of them from the tertiary sector. The great majority of the industrial labour force was, thus, outside effective union organisation (James, 1988, p. 9). Construction, food-processing and wood-working had been organised by the Communist Party, while textiles and metal-working, which had been the vital areas of industrial expansion in the 1930s and the 1940s, were not unionised. 'Of 447,212 union members in 1941 the transport sector and services accounted for well over 50 per cent of membership, while industry had 144,922 affiliates' (James, 1988, p. 9). In this context of weak unionism, there were wide wage differentials, seasonal unemployment, and general low pay. Perón encouraged unionisation. He released union leaders from prison, opened government posts to union men, provided many short-term benefits to the workers and added a large welfare dimension to the activities of the state (Corradi, 1985, p. 58). He established a 40-hour week, a minimum wage, medical insurance, rights for dismissed employees, and annual paid holidays (Lewis, 1992, p. 140). He also integrated the trade unions into a single massive national confederation. In November 1944, Perón dissolved the communist CGT 2 and ordered all trade unions to join the CGT 1 (Lewis, 1992, p. 141). Perón also enacted the Law of Professional Associations which established that:

> No union could claim legal status unless first granted recognition by the Secretariat of Labour. Without such recognition, it could not sign a legally binding contract, represent its members in labour courts, or own property. Only one union was allowed in each economic field. In theory, the government was supposed to recognise the largest unions as the most representative. (Lewis, 1992, p. 141)

Perón was also concerned with rural labour. He promulgated the *Estatuto del Peón* (Statute of the Rural Worker) which regulated minimum wages for rural workers. The Statute required farmers to provide decent housing, medical services, warm clothing and wholesome food for the rural workers (Lewis, 1992, p. 142).

Through these measures Perón integrated the working class into the political and economic scene and recognised its civic and political rights within society. A plot within the Armed Forces against Perón resulted in his arrest on 13 October 1945.[4] There are few events in Argentinian history that can be compared with 17 October 1945. Even now it is unclear who was behind the organisation (Luna, 1982) but from very early in the morning, thousands of workers came to Buenos Aires to demand Perón's release. Félix Luna captures the atmosphere of 17 of October:

> Well, there they were. As if they wanted to show all their power, so

that nobody could doubt that they really existed. There they were all over the city, shouting in groups which seemed to be the same group multiplied by hundreds. We looked at them from the side walk, with a feeling akin to compassion. Where had they come from? So they really existed? So many of them? So different from us? Had they really come on foot from those suburbs whose names made up a vague unknown geography, a *terra incognita* through which we had never wandered ... During all those days we had made the rounds of the places where they spoke of worries like ours. We had moved through a known map, familiar: the faculty, Recoleta for the burial of Salmún Feijóo, the Plaza San Martín, the Casa Radical. Everything up till then was coherent and logical, everything seemed to support our own beliefs. But that day when the voices began to ring out and the columns of anonymous earth-coloured faces began to pass by we felt something tremble which until that day had seemed unmovable. (quoted by James, 1988, p. 78)

After 17 October 1945, Argentina was never the same: the working class had appeared as a political actor. Because of the social demonstration in the *Plaza de Mayo*, Perón was released. He went to the balcony of the House of Government and made his first speech to the thousands of people waiting for him. This would become a tradition during Peronist governments. After 17 October 1945 Perón won the 1946 and 1952 general elections. A military coup in 1955 overthrew Perón's government and obliged him to flee from Argentina. His return was prohibited for 18 years.

Peronism was characterised by the incorporation of the workers into the political scene and their organisation as a labour force. Perón extended political and social rights to the workers. Perón and his wife, Eva, were seen as their protectors.

One of Perón's main objectives was to create a *comunidad organizada* (organised community), and to organise the working class (Smith, 1980, p. 81). He argued that unorganised workers 'present a dangerous panorama because the most dangerous mass ... is an inorganic one. Modern experience shows that the best organised working masses ... are those which can best be directed and led in all spheres' (Smith, 1980, p. 81). Perón emphasised the role of the unions as the representatives of the working class. The trade unions were incorporated into a Peronist movement and 'were called upon to act as the state's agent *vis-à-vis* the working class, organising political support and serving as conduits of government policy among the workers' (James, 1988, p. 11). Between 1946 and 1951 total union membership increased from 520,000 to 2,334,000 (James, 1988, p. 9). In addition to the organisation of the trade unions, real wages for industrial workers increased by 53 per cent between 1946 and 1949, and the share of wages on the national income increased from 40.1 per cent to 49 per cent in the same period (James, 1988, p. 11).

The Peronist years saw the emergence of *sindicalismo Peronista*[5] (Peronist trades union movement). As indicated, Perón, from the Secretariat of Labour, promoted the unionisation of the workers. In July 1943, the government established that labour organisations could not be involved in politics or spread ideas 'contrary to Argentinian nationality' (Lewis, 1992, p. 141). This gave Perón the power to intervene directly in union affairs. He removed and arrested trade unionists who opposed him and replaced them with his followers. He was able to do so due to the weakness of the trades union movement. Thus, by 1945, the leaders of the textile workers, meat packers, railway, metallurgical, bank, telephone, printing, sugar and construction workers were loyal to Perón (Lewis, 1992, p. 141). This was the origin of *sindicalismo Peronista*; after the Peronist era most trade unionists were still loyal to Perón. Indeed, the *Peronización* of the trades union movement had significant compensations for workers and trade unionists. Perón gave them a voice in Argentinian politics and greatly improved their political, social and economic situation.

Although after Perón's fall, the social situation changed, Argentina was never the same. Despite Perón's exit, in reality, the working class could not henceforth be ignored by Argentina's governments. In addition, the Armed Forces, through the 1955 military coup, became the representatives of the upper bourgeoisie since it had lost its traditional and broader influence based on the 'electoral fraud system'.[6] Therefore, after Perón's fall, the Argentinian political scene had changed dramatically, the Armed Forces and the working class having become its new, most influential actors. While the working class remained loyal to Perón, the majority of the Armed Forces were deeply anti-Peronist. Thus, from 1955 on, the Armed Forces tried to *desperonizar* Argentina.

The Political Role of the Armed Forces

Desperonizar Argentina was the main objective of the *Revolución Libertadora* (Liberating Revolution) of 1955, namely, to free the private sector from state controls created under Peronism and to purge all Peronist influences from national politics prior to returning to civilian rule (Smith, 1980, p. 99). President Lt General Eduardo Lonardi (September–November 1955) and his successor Lt General Pedro Aramburu (1955–58) aimed at depoliticising the labour movement by breaking the Peronist union bosses' hold on power. Lonardi began the process by removing the Peronist General Secretary of the CGT, Hugo Di Pietro, and replacing him with two younger Peronists who were willing to negotiate with the new regime in order to defend labour's gains (Lewis, 1992, p. 227). Under Lonardi's presidency there was a general strike called by the CGT due to Lonardi's removal of all union officials in order to call for trade unions elections. After the strike, Lonardi restored them all (Lewis, 1992, p. 228). However, Lt General Pedro Aramburu, who replaced Lonardi, made no attempt to negotiate with the trade unions. Armed raids of Peronist unions increased, and when the CGT responded with a general strike, Aramburu sent in troops to seize its offices (Lewis, 1992, p. 229).

General elections were scheduled for February 1958. Peronism was proscribed and the Radical party was divided into two factions: the *Unión Cívica Radical Intransigente*, which nominated Arturo Frondizi as its presidential candidate, and the *Unión Cívica Radical del Pueblo*, with Ricardo Balbín as presidential candidate.

Perón was then in Caracas. Frondizi made a secret pact with him. Perón agreed to instruct his followers to vote for Frondizi, who would, if elected, restore the Peronist party, the Law of Professional Associations to its original form, lift the control over CGT activities, release all Peronist labour leaders from jail, drop all criminal charges against Perón, and re-nationalise the banking system (Lewis, 1992, p. 238). Frondizi was elected President with 45 per cent of the total vote cast, while Ricardo Balbín from the *Unión Cívica Radical del Pueblo* received only 29 per cent (Wynia, 1992, p. 32). From his exile, Juan D. Perón was still dominating Argentinian politics. However, Frondizi did not fulfil his agreement with Perón, especially in the economic sphere.[7] In addition, Frondizi's strategy to co-operate with organised labour was not very successful, mainly owing to the decline in real wages and periodic action by the police and military to repress strikes (Smith, 1980, p. 103). Thus, Frondizi could not retain the workers' support. Indeed, Frondizi's decision to allow Peronist candidates to run for the March 1962 mid-term elections resulted in an important victory for Peronism which obtained the governorship of Buenos Aires province and 31.5 per cent of the total vote cast (Smith, 1980, p. 103). The result of the elections was not accepted by the Armed Forces, which removed Frondizi from the presidency and replaced him with the President of the Senate, José María Guido.

The Guido administration was marked by internal conflicts in the Armed Forces. Two factions emerged: the *colorados* (red ones) which combined 'extreme economic orthodoxy and inter- nationalism with near-fanatical anti-Peronism' (Smith, 1980, p. 104). They favoured a doctrine of total vigilance over national politics, the postponement of elections and the complete purge of Peronism from all aspects of national life. The *azules* (blue ones) favoured a quick return to constitutional rule. They were led by Lt General Juan Carlos Onganía who stood for the 'military's "spirit of self- preservation", defined as the defence of its corporate interests, internal cohesion, and autonomy from the political struggles raging in civil society and in the rest of the state apparatus' (Smith, 1980, p. 104). The dispute between the *azules* and *colorados* led to unprecedented armed conflicts in September 1962 and April 1963 when the *azules* obtained a definitive victory (Smith, 1980, p. 104).

With the *azules'* victory the demand for general elections was realised. For the 1963 general elections, Peronism was proscribed and Frondizi was in prison, thus, the *Unión Cívica Radical del Pueblo* won the general elections with 25 per cent of the total vote cast (Wynia, 1992, p. 32). Blank ballots, mainly cast by Peronists, accounted for 17. 5 per cent of the total vote cast and Frondizi's party, 16.2 per cent (Smith, 1980, p. 101).

The elected Radical President, Dr Arturo Illia, was opposed, from the very beginning of his term, by the CGT. The CGT argued that Illia had been elected by fraudulent and illegitimate means, namely, the proscription of Peronism. Labour opposition was manifested through a prolonged series of general strikes, occupations and demonstrations against the government. During 1963, there were 143 national strikes; in 1964, 265; and in 1965, 291 (Smith, 1980, p. 100). Illia's main goal was the re-establishment of full political rights. Therefore, for the 1965 mid-term elections, although Perón was still proscribed, the Peronist party was allowed to present candidates. It won 34.5 per cent of the total vote cast while Illia's Radical party obtained 28.6 per cent (Smith, 1980, p. 101).

The Armed Forces were sure that the 1967 elections would result in a Peronist victory. In order to prevent the return of full democracy and of Peronism, the Armed Forces, once again, overthrew a 'democratic' government. However, the 1966 military coup was different:

> This would not be merely another repetition of the familiar coups of the intervene-and-exit variety, turning power to the most 'reliable' civilian politicians. The army's internal memoranda reveal that something quite different was being planned. According to the leading theorists of the *doctrina azul* (blue doctrine), since 1955 all the major non-Peronist political parties had been given their chance to create a stable democratic government, overcome the social stalemate, and modernise the economy; all had failed. Consequently the next military intervention had to be a 'revolution' to sweep aside the entire 'corrupt' system of political parties and competitive politics, and not merely a coup to replace an individual president or a particular political party. (Smith, 1980, p. 109)

The Armed Forces did not understand that to create a 'stable democratic government and to overcome the social stalemate' Peronism could not be ignored. The working class was the ultimate barrier to any attempt to govern Argentina. Any solution which excluded the workers and/or their leader, Juan D. Perón, would fail. As indicated earlier, before the emergence of Peronism, the middle sectors and the workers were excluded from Argentinian politics. Peronism meant a restructuring of the state and its social relations. It mainly meant the full inclusion of the workers as a political and social force. The 1955 military coup was an attempt by the Armed Forces and the upper bourgeoisie to restructure the state and its social relations by depoliticising and demobilising the workers. In 1966 the Armed Forces imposed a new kind of military coup, with different objectives, in order to break down the institutionalised power of the working class. However, the latter proved too powerful and the Armed Forces' strategy failed.

The 1966 military dictatorship has been defined by O'Donnell (1988, p. 31) as a Bureaucratic Authoritarian state (BA), that is a 'defensive reaction by the dominant classes and their allies to crises involving a popular sector that has been politically activated and is increasingly autonomous with respect to the dominant classes and the state apparatus'. The principal social base of the BA state is the upper bourgeoisie, in a class structure defined by O'Donnell (1988, p. 31) as subordinated to the upper echelons of a highly oligopolised and transnationalised bourgeoisie. The main objective of the BA is the political deactivation of the popular sector, the reimposition of 'order', and the stabilisation, 'normalisation' in O'Donnell's words, of the economy. The BA state is a system of political and economic exclusion of the working class. From O'Donnell's point of view, the political activation of the popular sector was seen by the bourgeoisie and the Armed Forces as a threat to the capitalist system in Argentina.

From 1966 to 1973, the Armed Forces tried to achieve two main objectives: the imposition of what they understood as political and social 'order' and the stabilisation of the economy. The first President of the 'Argentinian Revolution' (as the new military government was called) Commander-in-Chief Lt General Juan Carlos Onganía tried to achieve the second objective by appointing as Minister of the Economy a man from the upper bourgeoisie, Adalbert Krieger Vasena.[8]

Regarding the trade union movement, the military dictatorship did not have a specific strategy to *desperonizar* it. The government chose to 'divide and conquer', 'meeting labour protests head-on and ruthlessly suppressing them, at the same time inviting selected unions to ally themselves with the government as long as they refrained from protesting its policies' (Wynia, 1992, p. 83). As a result of this strategy the CGT was divided into two bodies: *CGT de los Argentinos* (Argentinians' CGT) and *CGT–Calle Azopardo* (CGT–Azopardo Street); the former was much tougher in negotiating with the military government (O'Donnell, 1988, p. 149). The existence of the CGT was becoming a real problem for Onganía and his economic policy due to the increase of trade union demands through strikes.[9] But the beginning of the end of Onganía's presidency was signalled by the so-called *Cordobazo*. The antecedents of the *Cordobazo* were confrontations between university students and the police. On 15 May 1969, during a protest against increases in cafeteria prices in the Corrientes province, a student was killed; another student died in a demonstration in Rosario (Wynia, 1992, p. 83). On 28 and 29 May, in Córdoba (one of the largest and richest cities in Argentina with one of the oldest universities), students, workers and other middle sectors 'launched a mass uprising. Assailed by rocks, Molotov cocktails, and an inflamed multitude, the police retreated, and the insurrection took over most of the city, focusing its attacks on targets whose symbolic implications escaped nobody: property of the government and of transnational corporations' (O'Donnell, 1988, p. 159). After the *Cordobazo*, the idea of order and the government's authority lacked credibility. Likewise, guerrilla activity soon emerged. On 29 May 1970, former President, Lt General Pedro Aramburu, was kidnapped and later killed by *Montoneros*[10] (the revolutionary wing of the Peronist Party). This buried completely the idea of order and the authority of the 'Argentinian Revolution'.[11]

All these events indicate that the military dictatorship was unable to control the institutionalised power of the working class and to prevent the emergence of armed urban guerrillas. The seizure of state power by the Armed Forces, as a response to the political crisis, failed to tackle the real barrier to the resolution of the crisis, the institutionalised power of the working class.

After Onganía's resignation, Lt General Roberto Levingston took over as the second President; he intended to 'nationalise' the 1966 military dictatorship. Under his presidency, the Radical party, the Peronist party and some other political parties agreed, in a document called *La Hora del Pueblo* (The Hour of the People) on an urgent return to democracy (O'Donnell, 1988, p. 207). In addition to the emergence of political party activity a second *Cordobazo* in March 1971 – known as *Viborazo* – marked the end of Levingston's term. Moreover, economic problems and lack of support from the upper bourgeoisie – which had never agreed with Levingston's return to 'economic nationalism' – unleashed a coup by Commander-in-Chief Lt General Alejandro Lanusse (Lewis, 1992, p. 286). Lt General Lanusse tried to organise – particularly by negotiating with Peronism – a return to democracy. In 1973, after seven years, the Armed Forces left the government without achieving any of its objectives; order, social peace and economic stabilisation were all absent from Argentina in the early 1970s.

As the 1966 military dictatorship was unable to demobilise the working class, it was not surprising that a Peronist candidate won the 1973 general elections. In March 1973, the Peronist candidate for President, Héctor Cámpora, won the general elections with 50 per cent of the total vote cast. After 18 years of exile, Juan D. Perón returned to Argentina on 20 June 1973. On 13 July, Cámpora and the Vice-President, Vicente Solano Lima, resigned to allow new general elections to be held on 23 September. Juan D. Perón and his new wife, María Estela Martínez de Perón, won the elections with 62 per cent of the total vote cast (Wynia, 1992, p. 60). Perón's presidency unsuccessfully attempted to reach a social pact between the government, the trade unions and the business organisations.[12] It seemed that, after 18 years of exile, Perón no longer controlled Argentinian politics. In his absence, there had been important changes. A harsh internal struggle had broken out within the trade unions, different factions each claiming to be the successor of Perón's leadership.[13] The left-wing Peronist youth section had obtained an important role under Cámpora's presidency. Now they came into conflict with Perón in an effort to maintain their influence. Perón could no longer control the internal struggles in either the Peronist party or the trades union movement.[14]

After Perón's death in July 1974, his widow's government had to deal with these continuing power struggles. In addition, José López Rega, the Minister for Social Welfare, had now formed a neo-fascist paramilitary group, the *Alianza Argentina Anti-Comunista – Triple A* – (Argentinian Anti-Communist Alliance) which had the objective of '"ideological cleansing" (*depuración ideológica*) to eliminate *zurdos* (literally, left-handed persons) and Marxist "infiltrators" who had entered the Peronist Movement' (Smith, 1989, p. 228). The struggle of Triple A against the *Montoneros* and the Marxist *Ejército Revolucionario del Pueblo* (People's Revolutionary Army) led Argentina to violence on a scale previously unknown.

O'Donnell (1988, p. 142) defines the pre-1976 situation as 'a crisis of social domination with serious challenges to the coercive supremacy of the state apparatus'. A crisis of social domination is a crisis of the state as an apparatus, but also, 'in its primary aspect as a guarantor and organiser of social domination' (O'Donnell, 1988, p. 26). This type of crisis is defined as the 'supreme political crisis', it is a crisis of the state as a form of social domination (O'Donnell, 1988, p. 26). There was, indeed, a crisis of the state. However, the

emergence of this crisis was not in the 1970s or the 1960s. The
emergence of the crisis of the Argentinian state began in the 1930s
when the Armed Forces, for the first time, overthrew a democratic
government. The emergence of Peronism in the 1940s deepened the
crisis and made the restructuring of the state and social relations
more difficult due to the rise of the institutional power of the
working class.

Once again, although just three years earlier the Armed Forces
had failed in their attempt to impose order and stabilise the
economy, on 24 March 1976, they took office through a *coup d'état*.
Essentially, the main objective of the 1976 military dictatorship was
the imposition of *disciplinamiento social* (social discipline) (Canitrot,
1981, p. 132) – the attempt to discipline society through subordinating the working class in both the political and the economic
spheres.[15] This *disciplinamiento social* was imposed through
economic structural reform and state terrorism.

In contrast to the failure of the 1966 military dictatorship, the
1976 dictatorship did achieve some of its objectives. The political
demobilisation of the working class, albeit on a temporary basis, and
the defeat of the armed urban guerrillas was achieved through the
implementation of state terrorism, the establishment of concentration camps, and the 'disappearance' of 30,000 people.[16] Fear was
one of the best political allies of the Armed Forces. In addition, the
economic structural reform achieved the economic subordination of
the working class, and transformed Argentina's economic structure
to make it impossible for any future government to embark on a
'return to the past' (Smith, 1985, p. 74). Thus, the objective of the
military dictatorship was the imposition of a *disciplinamiento social*
which was to last longer than the dictatorship itself. Before
analysing the 1976 military dictatorship's efforts to achieve this
disciplinamiento social, it is necessary to explain Argentina's
economic development from the 1950s to the early 1970s.

ECONOMIC BACKGROUND

The Peronist Economy

Peronism not only changed Argentina's social and political scene
but also its economic structure. Helped by the accumulation of

reserves during the Second World War, the Peronist government stimulated activity in non-saleable goods and services, the production of marketable goods expanding as a result of the opening up of international trade immediately after the war (Gerchunoff, 1989, p. 63).

One of the main priorities of the Peronist government was a redistribution of income in favour of workers. In the manufacturing industry, the real wage per worker increased by 72 per cent between 1950 and 1954; 80 per cent of this increase took place during the first three years of the Peronist administration (Gerchunoff, 1989, p. 64). In 1954 a basket of basic food items cost an Argentinian industrial worker 14 hours of labour as compared with 25 hours for an Uruguayan industrial worker, 40.5 hours for a Brazilian, and 74 hours for a Peruvian (Lewis, 1992, p. 208).

The second notable aspect of Peronism was the expansion of the economic role of the state. Total state expenditure jumped 87 per cent between 1939–44 and 1945–49; by 1955 the increase was only 16 per cent (Smith, 1980, p. 76). State investment increased by 248 per cent between 1946 and 1950 (Smith, 1980, p. 76). These increases were the result of the new presence of the state in public services (railroads, shipping, energy, communication) and in areas that traditionally were developed by foreign capital (foreign trade, insurance, banking), as well as the opening up of new public-sector activities such as airlines (Smith, 1980, p. 76). In addition, the state, through loans from the *Banco de Crédito Industrial* (Industrial Credit Bank), promoted specific industries such as housing construction, regional meat-packing plant, agricultural machinery producers, regional electricity co-operatives, frozen-food factories, and the purchase of diesel vehicles (Lewis, 1992, p. 185).

Finally, the third most notable feature of Peronism was the nationalisation of foreign trade. The newly created *Instituto Argentino de Promoción de Intercambio* – API – (Argentinian Institute for the Promotion of Trade) 'received international market prices for Argentina's exports in hard currencies and then turned around and paid rural producers in *pesos* at well below the world market price' (Smith, 1980, p. 77). The generated surplus was to finance industrial investment and urban consumption. This state-managed transfer from the rural sector to urban labour served to finance industrialisation with income redistribution. However, after 1949, the decline of the terms of trade together with bad droughts in

1951 and 1952 reduced the volume and purchasing power of exports. Thus, the transfer system was, in fact, put into reverse. In order to increase incentives for rural producers, the state began to transfer surplus generated in urban areas to the agricultural sector (Smith, 1980, p. 78).

During Peronism, there was a double process of industrial fragmentation and centralisation of production. This resulted in an increase in the number of manufacturing firms from 86,400 to 151,800 between 1946 and 1954 (Smith, 1980, p. 78). The fragmentation occurred in the light industry sector while the centralisation was in the more dynamic intermediate and heavy industry sectors (basic metals, vehicles and petrochemicals) 'which increased both their proportion of industrial GDP and their share of industrial employment' (Smith, 1980, p. 78). Thus, the industrial bourgeoisie became divided between a large number of small and medium-sized companies and a small group of firms, organised as corporations, which had considerable capacity to achieve monopoly or oligopoly rents due to their capacity to fix prices. The latter group did not feel protected by Peronism, and thus it formed a temporary alliance with the *Pampeana* bourgeoisie (Smith, 1980, p. 78). The basis of this alliance was, mainly, support for the liberalisation of state controls. This alliance was the social basis of the 1955 military coup.

The 1955–66 Economic Strategies

The politically unstable period of 1955–66 witnessed the increase of foreign capital inflows. In the 1950s, foreign investment started to control the most dynamic branches of industry and consolidate the strategy of import substitution industrialisation (ISI) which had started in the 1930s. From 1958 to 1966, US$630 million in new foreign investments arrived. The share of US capital was 55.2 per cent of the total foreign investment. More than 90 per cent of all US investment went into chemical, petrochemical, transportation, metallurgy, machinery, electrical equipment and petroleum industries (Smith, 1980, p. 90). This resulted in a further concentration and centralisation of capital.

> Looking at data from the Industrial Census of 1963 (by which time the biggest spurt of foreign investment was largely completed), one finds that while transnational firms comprised only 0.5 per cent of all

industrial firms (666 out of 143057), they accounted for 25.1 per cent of total industrial production and 75.1 per cent of production in the ten most important industrial branches, measured in terms of value added. The transnational firms, together with a somewhat larger number of big locally-owned firms (many of whom also had significant linkages with transnational capital through portfolio investment, technology, management interlocks, etc.), formed the more advanced elements of a process of diversification of entrepreneurial leadership, and thereby comprised the dynamic core of the modern internationalised bourgeoisie expanding its dominance over the entire urban economy. (Smith, 1980, p. 91)[17]

This internationalisation of the economy was made possible through the dismantling of state control over foreign exchange, prices and wages, favouring the imposition of 'market rules'. As a result, wages declined from 48 per cent of the GDP between 1950–55 to 38 per cent in the early 1960s (Smith, 1980, p. 93).

Economically, the most significant period between 1955 and 1966 is that of Arturo Frondizi's presidency. The main objectives of Frondizi's *Desarrollismo* ('developmentalism') was that Argentina had to '1) pursue a strategy of "deepening" its economy in order to construct an integrated industrial complex centred on basic industries (steel, chemicals, paper, machinery, etc.); 2) free itself from the international division of labour under US domination; and 3) develop large-scale, highly capitalised agro-industrial enterprises' (Smith, 1980, p. 102). A list of investment priorities was drawn up which included the extraction of petroleum and natural gas; development of chemicals and petrochemicals; steel production; the extraction of coal and iron; and the automobile industry (Petrecolla, 1989, p. 110). These priorities were to be financed by foreign investment. The sanction of the law 14780 gave foreign capital rights equal to those of national capital. Almost no sector of activity was excluded from the entry of foreign capital. The latter could participate in import substitution industries, in the promotion of exports, or in the promotion of development activity to 'increase the growth of the country' (Petrecolla, 1989, p. 110).

At the very beginning of Frondizi's presidency there were significant wage increases; however, in 1960 a restrictive wage policy was put into effect. Collective bargaining agreements were signed for two years, during which a wage increase of 20–30 per cent was authorised, less than the price increases, which went up over 30 per cent from 1959 to 1961 (Petrecolla, 1989, p. 113). This, together with attempts to reduce the number of state employees, caused a confrontation with the trade unions. For instance, in August 1961, the Minister of the Economy, Roberto Alemann, announced that 75,000 railway employees were to be laid off, 'several lines would be closed down, and the working day would be increased from three and a half to six hours' (Lewis, 1992, p. 262). The railway workers struck, and remained out until December when the reorganisation plan was abandoned. Thus, Frondizi, despite being elected through Peronist votes, could neither control nor demobilise the workers. They were the ultimate barrier to any non-Peronist restructuring of the state.

As noted earlier, Frondizi was expelled from the government because he allowed Peronism to run in the 1962 mid-term elections. Since José María Guido's administration was in office only 562 days, it could not implement any significant economic changes. The economic strategy was characterised by liberalisation of the exchange market, reduction in government spending and greater monetary control (De Pablo, 1989, p. 135).

The 1963–66 Radical administration was marked by recession, a large foreign debt and fiscal deterioration. The foreign financing of 1960–61 added to the foreign debt which had been growing since 1955. 'The resources gap, equivalent to the total of all current account deficits, reached US$2000 million, which meant that between 1955 and 1962 the foreign debt annually financed 16 per cent of all imports or 1.7 per cent of demand' (Guadagni, 1989, p. 150). By 1963 the foreign debt was US$3,000 million with an annual service of US$800 million (Guadagni, 1989, p. 150). As a result of this situation, Illia's administration attempted to keep a positive balance on the current account. The key to the solution of the foreign debt problem is to be found in the favourable behaviour of the balance of trade which, as a result of a constant growth in exports, went from a deficit of US$813 million in 1960–62 to a surplus of US$1,480 million in 1963–66 (Guadagni, 1989, p. 152).

At the beginning of Illia's administration, real wages increased. The government announced that in 1965 wages for the public sector would rise by 15 per cent. However, a harsh campaign from the trade unions, mainly through general strikes and occupations of work places, obliged the government to grant an increase of between 25 and 30 per cent for the first months of the year. Thus, by the end of 1965, the wages of state employees rose by 50 per cent while the inflation rate was 20 per cent (Guadagni, 1989, p. 159).

Illia, like Frondizi, allowed Peronism to run in the 1965 mid-term elections. This, together with the growing opposition of the trades union movement, provoked the 1966 military coup. Illia's administration was economically successful, mainly due its management of the external debt problem. However, the 1955–66 period was characterised by the incapacity of governments to control the trades union movement and to demobilise the workers. Thus, the crisis of the Argentinian state was expressed, from 1955 to 1966, in a political form rather than an economic one.

The Economic Strategy of the 'Argentinian Revolution'

As noted earlier, the objectives of the 1966 military coup were different from the objectives of other military coups. As already quoted, the military government intended to be 'a "revolution" to sweep aside the entire "corrupt" system of political parties and competitive politics, and not merely a coup to replace an individual president or a particular political party' (Smith, 1980, p. 109). Economically, the 1966 'Argentinian Revolution' attempted to stabilise the economy by reducing the role of the state.

Adalbert Krieger Vasena, Onganía's Minister of the Economy, emphasised the control of inflation by the reduction of government expenditures, trimming state employees, raising taxes and increasing public service rates. He decreed a total wage freeze until 1968 and price guidelines (Lewis, 1992, p. 282). Krieger Vasena attempted to launch a strategy of dependent industrialisation based on the expansion of foreign monopoly capital. The objective was first to stabilise the economy and, within this framework, eliminate distortions and increase productive efficiency, and then generate industrial expansion with the aid of foreign capital (Corradi, 1985, p. 89).

Foreign capital did go to Argentina. By 1968 US investment in Argentina totalled US$1,148 million (Corradi, 1985, p. 90). This process, added to the one begun in the 1950s meant the denationalisation of capital and the liquidation of small and middle-sized industries. In addition,

> The new investments were characterised by a high organic composition of capital. The logic of their drive was to increase the weight of constant

capital made up by machines and raw materials, but not in wages, which
tended to increase with the new advances in mechanisation. The upshot
was a decline in the capacity of the industrial sector to absorb labour:
the marginalisation of the working class that had been integrated into
the system during a phase of labour-intensive exploitation. (Corradi,
1985, p. 90)

In this sense, the 1966 military dictatorship differed from other
Armed Forces' attempts to politically stabilise Argentina. This time
the Armed Forces attempted to demobilise the workers by
subordinating them in the economic sphere. In this sense the 1966
military dictatorship and Krieger Vasena's economic strategy were
antecedents of the 1976 military dictatorship and its economic
structural reform. However, the 1966 experiment was destroyed by
the *Cordobazo*, suggesting that the military dictatorship could
neither control nor politically demobilise the workers and civil
society. On the contrary, the 1966 military dictatorship witnessed
two *Cordobazos* and the emergence of the armed urban guerrillas.

   Finally, the military dictatorship called elections which were
won by the Peronist candidate. From 1955 to 1973 the Armed
Forces attempted to destroy Peronism and to control the workers.
The *Cordobazo* and the electoral victory of the Peronist candidate in
1973 highlight that not only had the military lost power but, worse,
they had lost it to the political movement they had set out to banish.

The Last Peronist Attempt

In October 1973, when Juan Domingo Perón took office, he
attempted to make a *Pacto Social* (Social Pact) between the trade
unions and the business sector under the aegis of the state. The *Pacto
Social* was based on a price freeze and one wage increase of 13 per
cent. This resulted in an increase of the share of wages to 46 per cent
of GNP, which represented more than four percentage points,
reaching one of the highest levels of the previous ten years (Di Tella,
1989, p. 218). The Social Pact aimed to expand the domestic market,
redistribute income in favour of the workers, achieve full employment, open new foreign markets (especially among the socialist
countries) and promote manufactured exports (Smith, 1980, p. 537).
The state would regulate foreign investments and international
transfers of technology, promote small and medium-sized

companies, and consolidate the public sector through limited nationalisation of foreign trade and some banking activities (Smith, 1980, p. 538).

In December 1973 there was an attempt to introduce some price flexibility which met with opposition from the trade unions which argued that price flexibility was a violation of the Social Pact. Wages were then increased by 20 per cent from March 1974. After this increase, prices began to rise (Di Tella, 1989, p. 220). To make things worse, the European Community closed its market to meat imports. 'The surplus of the previous year's current account was reduced to about US$200 million and, if the second part of the year is compared with the first, the change is even more dramatic, as it went from US$400 million surplus to a deficit of nearly 300 million' (Di Tella, 1989, p. 220).

As indicated earlier, Perón's third presidency was marked by the confrontation of different sectors within Peronism, mainly, the trade unions and the revolutionary youth wing. Perón himself could no longer control them. During Perón's exile, the trades union movement had achieved a high degree of autonomy from its former leader. Even Perón was opposed by the trade unions when he attempted to implement price flexibility. Perón, like Frondizi, Illia and, to a lesser extent the 1966 military dictatorship, granted wage increases in order to placate the trade unions opposition. The trades union movement proved, then, to be the strongest barrier to any restructuring of the state. Even Perón, who was supposedly the only man capable of governing Argentina, was defeated by the opposition of the unions and the activity of armed urban guerrillas which were part of the Peronist movement, namely, the *Montoneros*.

After the death of Perón in July 1974, the Social Pact was abandoned. Perón's widow, María Estela Martínez de Perón, and her powerful Welfare Minister, José López Rega, dramatically changed the orientation of the government. They looked for the support of the business sector and the Armed Forces. The government's programme was to eliminate the armed urban guerrilla by means of paramilitary groups – the so-called *Triple A* – to eradicate left-wing groups in the universities and schools, and to reduce wages in order to favour the business sector (Di Tella, 1989, p. 221).

In June 1975 the Economy Minister, Celestino Rodrigo, 'announced an IMF-style shock treatment (i.e. a 50 per cent devaluation of the peso coupled with equivalent increases in public-sector prices, etc.) in a desperate attempt to stabilise the economy' (Smith, 1989, p. 229). The so-called *Rodrigazo* was an attempt to produce a real devaluation and to increase public tariffs through a shock, in order to correct the disequilibrium of the balance of payments and the fiscal imbalance (Damill and Frenkel, 1990, p. 7). Fanelli and Frenkel (1989, p. 9) point out that 'the main features of the 1975 crisis were a fiscal deficit that averaged 15 per cent of GDP, a spurt of inflation which led the economy to the brink of hyper-inflation and a marked disequilibrium in the current account accompanied by massive capital flight'.[18] As a consequence of the pressure of the CGT, through negotiations with the government and afterwards the organisation of strikes, the government authorised a 140 per cent adjustment in nominal wages. 'From June to August consumer prices jumped 102 per cent. Production fell off sharply, and financial speculation reached astronomic levels. The state itself was one of the principal losers, facing an unprecedented fiscal crisis: the fiscal deficit for 1975 reached 17 per cent of the country's gross domestic product' (Smith, 1989, p. 230). In the first three months of 1976, the Peronist government tried to implement a stabilisation plan, but it failed again. A 100 per cent devaluation of the peso, an increase of 90 per cent in publicly controlled prices, and an increase of 20 per cent in nominal wages were the main measures of the plan. The results were 'in March, consumer prices shot up 38 per cent, while wholesale prices rose 58 per cent' (Smith, 1989, p. 230).

This economic crisis soon became a political crisis. The state was under pressure to restructure economic and social relations but it was unable to do so. The unions were, by this time, a barrier to any restructuring. As Clarke (1990, p. 27) points out, the response to this crisis is the restructuring of the state and of broader class relations. This response in Argentina took the form, politically, of an authoritarian government.

CONCLUSION

Peronism and its full incorporation of the working class into the political scene put the class domination of the Argentinian capitalist state in danger. The Armed Forces, seizing power, attempted to restructure the state and its class relations. However, from 1955 to

1976, all their attempts failed. The institutionalised power of the working class was the ultimate barrier to such a restructuring.

This political instability unleashed an economic crisis since neither the Armed Forces nor the democratic governments of the period could stabilise Argentina's economy or achieve long-term economic growth. By 1976 the crisis of the Argentinian state was evident in both political and economic terms. Thus, the seizure of state power by the Armed Forces attempted to restructure the state and its class relations politically by demobilising the workers, militarily by defeating the armed urban guerrillas, and economically by implementing a structural reform to make impossible any attempt to 'return to the past'.

The crisis of the Argentinian state was caused by the institutionalised power of the working class which put the class domination in danger. This is not to say that Argentina was on the brink of a 'social revolution', rather it is to say that the working class could not be controlled by the state. Argentina's working class did not attempt to attain a 'social revolution'; its only objective was to maintain the achievements of 1946–55. Peronism, while bringing the working class into Argentina's political scene, made any 'revolutionary' attempt impossible, since it established the perception that the state can benefit the working class.[19]

The 1976 military dictatorship attempted to resolve the crisis of the Argentinian state by implementing a monetarist restructuring of the state.

NOTES

1. For a detailed account of the 1916–30 period see Luna (1958), del Mazo (1959), Ciria (1964) and Galletti (1961).
2. For an analysis of this period see Potash (1969), Luna (1958), Ciria (1964) and Puiggrós (1968).
3. Between 1930 and 1955, with the exception of 1943–45, the Armed Forces were not directly involved in governing Argentina. From 1955 this tradition changed dramatically, see Cavarozzi (1997).
4. For a detailed account on this plot see Luna (1982) and Potash (1969).
5. For a historical account of the emergence of *sindicalismo Peronista* see Matsushita (1983), James (1988), Godio (1989) and Godio *et al.* (1988), Cavarozzi (1984) and Torre (1988), (1989), (1990a) and (1995).
6. From this time, the Armed Forces saw themselves as the 'protectors' of democracy. After 1955, and especially after 1959, Peronism and communism were viewed as 'anti-democratic' and the Armed Forces

promoted their role as the 'guardians' of democracy (Cavarozzi, 1997, p. 39).

7. Frondizi's economic strategy is explained below.

8. Adalbert Krieger Vasena 'had served as an adviser to and a member of the boards of directors of several large corporations, including TNC (transnational corporations) subsidiaries, and was well connected with international organisations and banks' (O'Donnell, 1988, p. 72).

9. There were 68 national strikes in 1967; 50 in 1968; and 93 in 1969 (O'Donnell, 1988, p. 291).

10. For an excellent historical account of the *Montoneros* see Gillespie (1982).

11. Basic references for this period are Potash (1971), Rouquié (1983a), Perina (1983) and Cavarozzi (1984).

12. For more details on the attempt to reach a social agreement see De Riz (1981) and James (1988).

13. See Palermo and Novaro (1996) and Halperín Donghi (1994a).

14. For more details on this period see De Riz (1981), James (1988), Di Tella (1983), Landi (1978) and Bonasso (1997).

15. In fact the objective of the military dictatorship was not only to subordinate the working class but also to restructure the bourgeoisie (Cavarozzi, 1997, pp. 75–84).

16. This is the number commonly given by the organisations of human rights. The *Comisión Nacional de Desaparición de Personas* (CONADEP) – National Commission on Disappeared People – had heard evidence of 8,960 cases (Argentina's National Commission on Disappeared People, 1986, p. XVI).

17. For a detailed account of the role of foreign investment and the process of centralisation and concentration of capital see Azpiazu *et al.* (1986) and Sourrouille *et al.* (1985). The above mentioned 'big locally-owned firms' are the so-called *Grupos Económicos Nacionales* – GEN – (National Economic Groups) which, as it is analysed below, played a crucial role in Argentina's economy during the 1970s and 1980s.

18. For more details on this period see Diaz Alejandro (1969), (1970), Mallon and Sourrouille (1975) and Fanelli and Frenkel (1989).

19. Cavarozzi quotes a Peronist trade unionist saying: 'the state must be the protecting father (of the trades union movement) as it is to industry, trade and agriculture' (1997, p. 43).

2

The 1976–83 Military Dictatorship and its Economic Legacy

In 1976 the coexistence of urban guerrillas, an organised working class and a weak government with neither political nor economic goals, was viewed by the Armed Forces and the upper bourgeoisie as sufficient reason to, once again, install their form of 'order' in Argentina. The aim of the alliance was to subordinate and control the working class, to undermine its capacity to organise itself as a class and to express itself politically. This *disciplinamiento social* was achieved by both state terrorism and a structural economic reform. The objective of this chapter is to state the political and economic legacy of the military dictatorship, and to assess to what extent the economic reform produced an overwhelming increase in the external debt, a profound concentration of capital in the hands of a small group of national corporations (GEN), and the impoverishment of the working class.

The chapter is divided into four sections. The first section analyses the early years of the military dictatorship (1976–81) when the strongest repression as well as the structural economic reform were applied. The main measures of the economic plans are examined, as well as their consequences for the agricultural sector, the industrial sector and the labour market. The section also traces the origins of the external debt. The second section covers the last years of the dictatorship (1981–83), examining the government's attempt to retain power. The third section describes the transition to democracy and the results of the 1983 general election. Finally, the conclusions turn to the legacy of the so-called *Proceso de Reorganización Nacional* (National Reorganisation Process). It analyses the consequences of the debt-led growth strategy, the concentration of capital and the impoverishment of the working class, as they constitute one of the main constraints upon Alfonsín's government.

1976–81: APOGEE OF THE DICTATORSHIP

In March 1976 a new military government was established in Argentina. The 'official' objective of the *Proceso de Reorganización Nacional* was the establishment of a new order in Argentinian society through Christian values, national security and justice. In reality, its main objectives were the removal of the guerrilla, the *disciplinamiento social* through the subordination of the working class in both the political and the economic sphere, and the recovery of the state as 'the guarantor not of the *immediate* interests of the bourgeoisie, but of the ensemble of social relations that establish the bourgeoisie as the dominant class'[1] (O'Donnell, 1988, p. 2). Its objective was the restructuring of the state and of class relations.

As a consequence of the failure of the 1966 experience, this new dictatorship tried to correct the old mistakes[2] in order to achieve its main objectives: the *disciplinamiento social* and economic 'normalisation'.[3] Therefore, the Armed Forces undertook a plan of structural reform of the Argentinian economy. Before describing this reform, it is necessary to look at the juridical and social context to which such an economic reform was applied.

'Juridical' Framework of the Dictatorship

The suspension of constitutional rights and guarantees, and a new basis of rule given by acts and statutes made up the 'juridical' framework of the dictatorship. Two acts, one statute and one law were the main legal tools of the new government: *Acta para el Proceso de Reorganización Nacional* (Act for the National Reorganisation Process); *Acta fijando el propósito y los objetivos básicos para el Proceso* (Act fixing the outline and basic objectives of the National Reorganisation Process); *Estatuto para el Proceso de Reorganización Nacional* (Statute for the National Reorganisation Process); and law 21256 concerning the functioning of the *Junta Militar*, the Executive Power and the *Comisión para el Asesoramiento*

Legislativo – CAL – (Commission for Legislative Advice) which replaced the Parliament (*Clarín*, 27.3.1976, pp. 25–6). The *Junta Militar* was the supreme body, its duties were to secure the main objectives of the government and other bodies of the state, and to appoint and to remove the President. The *Junta* was formed by the three Commanders-in-Chief who would choose the President from the highest officials from the Armed Forces. The first *Junta Militar* was formed by Lt General Jorge R. Videla, Brigadier Orlando E. Agosti and Admiral Emilio E. Massera (*Clarín*, 25.3.1976, pp. 2–3).

The *Junta* determined that the activity of political parties and trade unions was forbidden, including the ability to strike (Abós, 1984, p. 7). The principle organisation, the *Confederación General del Trabajo* (CGT), was declared illegal (Abós, 1984, p. 7).

Lt General Videla was appointed President of Argentina until March 1978[4] and named José A. Martínez de Hoz[5] as Economics Minister. While Martínez de Hoz was trying to achieve social discipline through economic structural reform, the *Junta* implemented state terrorism as another tool for achieving the *disciplinamiento*.

State Terrorism

The *Junta Militar* continued and deepened the 'dirty war' which had already begun with the *Triple A*.[6] State terrorism was imposed by kidnapping, torture and the assassination of thousands of people. Politicians, journalists, workers, trade unionists, intellectuals, students, nuns, priests and members of the *Montoneros* (the revolutionary-wing of the Peronist Party) and the Marxist *Ejército Revolucionario del Pueblo* (People's Revolutionary Army) were tortured and killed. Smith quotes General Luciano Menéndez, the head of the Third Army in Córdoba during the first years of the *Proceso*, and says that Menéndez 'observed that there existed a division of labour within the regime: "While Videla governs, I kill"'. Menéndez also acknowledged that: 'We are going to kill 50000 people: 25000 subversives, 20000 sympathisers, and we will make 5000 mistakes' (Smith, 1989, p. 232).

On 30 April 1977, a group of mothers of the *desaparecidos* went to the Plaza de Mayo to demand from the government information about the fate of their lost relatives. They formed a group called *Madres de Plaza de Mayo* (Mothers of the Plaza de Mayo). One of the founders, Azucena Villaflor de Vicenti, declared that every Thursday they would repeat the march around the square until the disappeared were accounted for (*aparición con vida*). Later, she disappeared. The Mothers of the Plaza de Mayo became a pillar of the struggle for human rights. They demonstrated that, while large sectors of the Argentinian population seemed apathetic in the face of state terrorism, a number of groups were reacting against it.[7]

State terrorism was seen as the principal political means of achieving social discipline. The Armed Forces established an organised net of terror. In the knowledge that they would not be punished, Army officials kidnapped people from their work, home or off the street. After being tortured, some were killed and some were used to lure others for kidnapping. Most of them have never been seen again. The Armed Forces argued that the situation was akin to a war and that, due to the nature of the enemy, it was a very special kind of war (Andersen, 1993). However, when the Armed Forces took control, the guerrilla movement had already been almost defeated by the *Triple A*. The guerrilla threat was essentially an excuse to justify the use of violence as a means of achieving social discipline.[8] Thus, state terrorism was another way to demobilise the working class; indeed, 30 per cent of the *desaparecidos* (the largest single group) were workers (Argentina's National Commission on Disappeared People, 1986, p. 448).

The Economic Policy of the Dictatorship

The economic policy proposed by Martínez de Hoz's team[9] implied the 'opening and reinsertion of Argentina's domestic economy into the world economy according to strict criteria of efficiency and the law of comparative advantages' (Smith, 1989, p. 234). It favoured a short-term capital market with high liquidity, increased the public and private external debt, and redistributed income through salary reductions.

Retrospectively, Martínez de Hoz, explained that the objective of his administration was to 'implement a structural reform of the economy and not only to overcome a crisis' (Di Tella and Rodríguez Braun, 1990, p. 151). Through the liberalisation and modernisation of the economy, the government wanted

to encourage individual effort and initiative, to reintroduce competitiveness into the Argentine economy, to encourage saving and investment as the launching-pad for capitalisation, to attain a more efficient resource allocation with a focus on activities with a higher productivity rate in relative terms, and thus to attain a rise in the average productivity rate and subsequently in the standard of living. (Di Tella and Rodríguez Braun, 1990, p. 153)

Martínez de Hoz describes his plan as consisting of four programmes: stabilisation, liberalisation, modernisation of the economy and streamlining of the state (Di Tella and Rodríguez Braun, 1990). The first measures were the liberalisation of prices, the opening up of domestic markets to foreign capital,[10] the liberalisation of exports and imports through the elimination of tariffs, the elimination of subsidised fuel prices, the freezing of wages and a taxation reform consisting of the generalisation of Value Added Tax (VAT).

At the very beginning Martínez de Hoz introduced two nominal exchange rates: a financial rate, applied to financial transactions and controlled to avoid sharp fluctuations until the end of 1976, and a commercial rate, applied to foreign trade and increased gradually until the end of 1976. The latter increased to achieve equality between both nominal exchange rates by the end of the year. The monthly inflation rate in April 1976 was over 50 per cent; after the application of the new exchange rates it was 7 per cent, and by the end of 1976 price growth had stabilised between 5 per cent and 9 per cent per month (Schvarzer, 1986a, p. 47).

With regard to real wages, the share of the wage earners in the national income fell dramatically, as Table 1 shows, as a result of the *Proceso*.

TABLE 1
Wage bill as a share of national income (1974–81)

Year	%
1974	50.5
1975	48.9
1976	33.6
1977	31.8
1978	33.6
1979	31.9
1980	33.9
1981	32.5

Source: Orsatti, A. (1983).

At the beginning of the dictatorship there was a substantial redistribution of income. In the first year of the dictatorship, the wage bill as a share of the national income decreased 31 per cent. The evolution of real wages between 1974 and 1976 highlights the damage done to wage earners. If in 1974 the real wage of an industrial worker was 159, in 1976 it equalled 100. During this two-year period the inflation rate went from 40 per cent in 1974 to 394 per cent in 1976. This means that as the inflation rate increased 772.5 per cent from 1974 to 1976 the real wage of an industrial worker decreased 37 per cent in the same period.

TABLE 2
Inflation rate
(1974–81)

Year	%
1974	40.0
1975	335.1
1976	349.0
1977	160.0
1978	169.0
1979	140.1
1980	87.5
1981	131.2

Source: R. Frenkel *et al.* (1992).

TABLE 3
Real wages per sector
(1974–81)
(1976 = 100)

	Industrial workers	Public administration	Services
1974	159.0	159.6	173.4
1975	149.0	166.9	139.3
1976	100.0	100.0	100.0
1977	101.0	92.9	98.5
1978	98.2	108.0	111.0
1979	112.1	113.4	125.2
1980	124.1	139.9	135.5
1981	114.2	115.5	121.2

Source: P. Gerchunoff and H. Dieguez (1984).

As a response to the reduction of real wages and despite the prohibition of trade union activities, the labour movement organised strikes, go-slows and lightning stoppages. The most persistent form of labour protest was the so-called *trabajo a desgano* (work to rule). In September 1976, there were conflicts in General Motors, Ford, Fiat, Peugeot and Chrysler. The government decided to introduce the law 21400, which determined that everyone who participated in strikes would be sentenced to six years in prison, with ten years for those instigating strike action (*New York Times*, 9.9.1976, p. 8). Nevertheless, on 5 October, a series of strikes by the electricity workers began. The cause of the strike was the sacking of 108 workers from the state electricity company of Buenos Aires, as part of the plan to rationalise state expenditure by cutting down the number of workers. The sacked workers included the entire executive committee of the unions, and a considerable number of shop floor representatives. By 11 October, in Buenos Aires city, most of the workers had returned to work; however, in Buenos Aires province the workers began a work-to-rule campaign. The day after, three union members were kidnapped from their homes by armed civilians (*Latin America Political Report*, 15.10.1976, vol. X, no. 40). The stoppages began again with power cuts in industrial areas. The light and power workers went on working 'with sadness' (*trabajo a tristeza*).[11] The confrontation ended on 29 October, following government threats to send troops to occupy the factories. In March 1977, the power workers started a work-to-rule campaign as a response to the kidnapping of their union leader Oscar Smith (*Latin America Political Report*, 1.4.1977, vol. XI, no. 13). In October 1977 there was a national rail strike (Abós, 1984, p. 11). The railway strike began on 26 October. The stoppages and go-slows among the railway and underground workers of Buenos Aires then spread to the dockers of Buenos Aires and Rosario, who also began a work-to-rule campaign. The power workers of Rosario and Santa Fé, and state oil company workers (*Yacimientos Petrolíferos Fiscales – YPF*) also began a work-to-rule campaign. At the same time, 25,000 workers in the *Alpargatas* textile industry stopped work in support of a wage claim and were joined later by the 25,000 workers of the Peugeot plant. By 11 November all the workers had gone back to work after wage increases of 40 per cent (*Latin America Political Report*, 11.11.1977, vol. XI, no. 44). These strikes show that, despite the efforts of the dictatorship to demobilise the unions – mainly through the prohibition of strikes, the 'illegality' of the CGT as the peak organisation, and state terrorism – the workers could still organise themselves and demonstrate against the military dictatorship. In this sense, they developed new forms of social demonstration such as the *trabajo a tristeza*, which were not forbidden by the dictatorship. Thus, state terrorism and economic reform could not completely demobilise the unions.

In March 1977, Martínez de Hoz applied a price freeze which was the first step in the financial reform of June 1977. The reform liberalised capital flows and deregulated the financial system. This reform, through the liberalisation of interest rates, enabled banks to recover their central position within the financial system, instead of being mere intermediaries of the Central Bank (Canitrot, 1981, p. 143).[12] The financial reform linked the banking system to short-term capital markets which made public companies look for new capital markets to satisfy their financial needs. According to Canitrot (1981, p. 123) the financial reform was a political decision connected with the long-term project of the dictatorship. As the military government sought the liberalisation of the economy, the plan required this kind of financial reform since its purpose was to make the market an instrument through which social discipline would be achieved (Cavarozzi, 1997).

The wage–price spiral of the economy (*indexación*) was the main obstacle to stabilising the economy. Therefore, in May 1978 a *desindexación*[13] plan was applied through the exchange rate and public tariffs. Damill and Frenkel (1990, p. 12) point out that, even with an accumulated devaluation of only 68 per cent in 1978, the retail price index increased 178 per cent during that year. It was clear that the plan could not stop inflation.

In December 1978 a new plan was announced, which signified that 'future exchange-rate devaluations and changes in public-sector prices would systematically be adjusted below the rate of private-sector price increases. In theory, at least, this was to force inflation downward' (Smith, 1989, p. 239). The *desindexación* was made through a *tablita* ('little table') which indicated the future rate of devaluation. This plan was applied with the liberalisation of the capital market which was to regulate the interest rate and allow the convergence of internal and international prices.

This plan had been framed using a monetarist approach to the balance-of-payments. This approach also promotes privatisation, limits government expenditure, and attempts to avoid price distortions by reducing state economic intervention. It was key to the dictatorship's *disciplinamiento social* – the elimination of any vestige of Peronism and working-class power was to be achieved by the implementation of monetarism to give to the market and money the role of regulator of the economy.

The social response to the plan of December 1978 was the first national strike during the military government on 27 April 1979 (Abós, 1984, p. 48). Although all the leaders of the trade unions who organised the strike were imprisoned, the strike occurred and enjoyed total support in the industrial sector (Abós, 1984, p. 49).

In March 1980 the winding-up of one of the biggest national banks (*Banco de Intercambio Regional* – *BIR*) caused a deep financial crisis (Schvarzer, 1986a, p. 98). The Central Bank, reversing an initial policy commitment, had to guarantee the deposits. In September 1980, the Central Bank decided to devalue the peso further. Therefore, devaluation during the last three months of 1980 was 1 per cent per month. In February 1981 the devaluation rate was 10 per cent; and 3 per cent per month until August 1981 (Schvarzer, 1986a, p. 106).

The monthly inflation rate could not be decelerated, and after five years of different plans and programmes, Lt General Videla and his Minister of Economy left the government in March 1981. At the beginning of 1981 'massive capital flight had reduced foreign-exchange reserves by more than $2 billion; interest rates had risen to annual rates of more than 200 per cent; and the public sector deficit had soared out of control' (Smith, 1989, p. 242). The fiscal deficit as a percentage of GDP went from 7.5 in 1980 to 13.5 in 1981.[14]

Before outlining the position of Lt General Roberto Viola's administration, the consequences of Martínez de Hoz's economic policy for the agricultural sector; the industrial sector; the conditions in the industrial labour market; and the origin of the external debt will be explained.

The Agricultural Sector
Argentina's main agricultural products were maize, sunflower, soya, sorghum, wheat and meat. The agricultural sector represented about 12 per cent of the GDP throughout the period 1976–81; and, according to the National Census of 1980, 12 per cent of total employment was accounted for by the agricultural sector (Di Tella and Rodríguez Braun, 1990, p. 213).

Rural sector production plays a fundamental role with regard to both short-term stability and growth: land and cattle production is the main source of foreign exchange (60 per cent of total exports originate in this sector); the goods produced by the sector represent 15 per cent of the consumer's purchases; and it contributes significantly to government revenues (Fanelli and Frenkel, 1989, p. 30).

The unification of exchange rates and the fall in export taxes were favourable to the agricultural sector. In 1976 the sown field surface of wheat increased by 40 per cent – over the average of the last five years – as a consequence of the positive measures of Martínez de Hoz's plan and of technological development.[15] Due to this increase the crop reached 11 million tons, a record quantity (Schvarzer, 1986a, p. 151). Therefore, the agricultural GDP and traditional exports rose significantly in 1976 and 1977. The growth of the production of grains for the whole period (1976–81) was about 6.8 per cent annually (Cavallo and Cottani, 1991, p. 140). Another aspect of the period was the 'increase on yields for a number of crops, especially oil seeds. This was due to technological improvements (for instance, more intensive use of chemical fertilisers and adoption of new crop varieties) which were fostered by trade liberalisation' (Cavallo and Cottani, 1991, p. 140). After 1977, because of the financial reform and the fiscal and monetary policies implemented, the situation for the agricultural sector was modified and in 1980 production and exports fell (Cavallo and Cottani, 1991, p. 142). The agricultural sector suffered due to the extreme overvaluation of the peso, and so by 1981 the situation of the farmers had deteriorated.

The main feature of the period is the technological improvements which were obtained through trade liberalisation. Because of this benefit, the agricultural sector mainly supported the economic strategy of the military dictatorship. Indeed, despite the overvaluation of the peso in 1981, in general terms the economic strategy was beneficial for the sector; most notably, the unification of the exchange rate and the fall in export taxes.

The Industrial Sector
The main branches of the Argentinian industrial sector were foodstuffs, textiles, chemicals, steel and other basic metal industries, capital goods and the automobile industry. For each of these

branches the consequences of the Martínez de Hoz administration were quite different. However, from a general point of view, scholars[16] agree that the industrial sector was the most severely affected by this economic policy. The first blow to the industrial sector was given by the financial reform of 1977 because of high interest rates which stimulated short-term transactions. Therefore, all the benefits gained by the reduction of wages – by almost 40 per cent – were lost in extra financial costs.

Smith (1989, p. 241) argues that 'protective tariffs were further reduced, thus forcing traditionally high-cost firms to face the effects of stiff competition from cheap imported goods. The magnitude of this foreign competition can be gauged by the dramatic jump in total imports: 73 per cent in 1979 and 56 per cent in 1980.' He also argues that the Martínez de Hoz team knew that this policy would severely affect the industrial sector, but they believed it was necessary to restructure the Argentinian industry (Smith, 1989, p. 241 and Cavarozzi, 1997, p. 75).

According to Kosacoff's analyses (Azpiazu and Kosacoff, 1989, p. 20) industrial production fell 20 per cent between 1975 and 1982; the share of the industrial sector in the GDP fell from 28 per cent to 22 per cent in the same period; 20 per cent of the biggest companies closed; and the share of industrial workers in national income fell from 49 per cent in 1975 to 32.5 per cent in 1982. The sectors most severely affected were textiles and metallurgical industries, while foodstuffs and chemicals were less affected than the average of the whole industrial sector (Dorfman, 1983, p. 112).

In terms of industrial branches, the paper producing branch expanded. Cavallo and Cottani (1991, p. 148) point out that 'between 1976 and 1978 officially promoted investment plans were approved for a total of over a billion dollars. Tariffs on imports were increased from 10 per cent to 15 per cent in 1976 and 20 per cent in 1977, a remarkable exception to the trade policies pursued at the same time in other branches.' Regarding the chemical branch, 'exports were promoted and increased steadily during the 1970s and both production and employment performed better than the manufacturing average' (Cavallo and Cottani, 1991, p. 148). As 'steel and aluminium were the only exceptions to the elimination of quota restrictions started in 1976' (Cavallo and Cottani, 1991, p. 149) steel production increased between 1978 and 1981, and imports fell.

The capital goods branch was discriminated against by the trade policies in two different ways: by an unscheduled acceleration in the rate of tariff reductions and by the maintenance of high levels of protection in the industries supplying basic metal inputs. The great change in the policy applied to this branch was because 'the authorities wanted to foster the incorporation of technologically advanced imported equipment to improve industrial efficiency in capital-intensive branches. Thus, in order to favour some activities, the domestic production of capital goods was hurt' (Cavallo and Cottani, 1991, p. 149). The automobile industry was also severely affected. By 1978 three plants closed (General Motors, Citroen and IME) and two others merged (Safrar-Peugeot and Fiat). Employment decreased significantly in this sector, but its productivity was less affected.

The promotion of different sectors shows a restructuring process occurring in industrial production. During the 1960s and early 1970s the promoted branches were automobiles, capital goods and metallurgy; while in the mid-1970s paper-producing, chemical, steel and aluminium branches were promoted. This process was also a response to changing international trade: as a consequence of the protectionist measures applied by the European Community and the United States, Argentina could no longer be solely an agricultural producer (Chudnovsky, 1991, p. 3).

Most importantly, the process shows that the financial sector was strengthened during this period at the expense of industrialists. Crystal (1994, p. 137) points out that 'as a reaction to "economic chaos", the regime followed a course whose essential meaning was ... in the nature of a determined drive to force all producing groups to accept the discipline of market forces'. This strategy was another way of breaking the power of the organised working class. Indeed, the promoted branches – paper production, chemical and steel and aluminium – did not have historically powerful unions, while auto-mobile, capital goods and metallurgical branches, which were discriminated against, did have historically powerful unions. The SMATA (*Sindicato de Mecánicos del Transporte Automotor*) and UOM (*Unión Obrera Metalúrgica*), which represented the workers from the automobile and metallurgical industries, respectively, are among the most historically powerful unions in Argentina.[17] Table 4 shows the industrial activity by branches.

TABLE 4
Industrial activity: main branches

Year	Foodstuffs	Capital Goods	Textiles	Paper Products	Chemicals	Basic Metals
1975	111.1	124.0	112.1	120.2	119.0	123.4
1976	114.4	121.7	106.0	105.2	121.0	115.5
1977	107.2	148.7	110.0	105.3	122.8	128.1
1978	101.5	118.5	94.4	108.7	113.1	121.1
1979	103.1	134.6	104.6	110.6	127.0	141.7
1980	102.1	130.8	92.3	101.9	128.0	128.0
Growth rate 75/80	–7.7	5.5	–17.7	–15.2	7.6	3.7

Source: A. Canitrot (1981).

Note: 1970 = 100.

According to Canitrot (1981, p. 185), between 1975 and 1980 industrial output contracted by 2.6 per cent. The growth of the capital goods branch is quite significant because as pointed out above, this branch was discriminated against. Canitrot (1981, p. 185) suggests that the growth of this branch shows that the imports of capital goods were complementary to national production. Another point of interest is the fall in paper production, despite this sector being promoted by government policies: the results of these policies would not be seen until the early 1980s.

Regarding industrial employment, Canitrot (1981, p. 185) argues that its fall was one of the most significant modifications of the period (see Table 5). Industrial employment declined 26 per cent from 1975 to 1980. It is remarkable that in all industries – whether or not their activities increased – employment fell. For instance, chemicals, which shows the highest growth rate of activity in the period, shows a fall in employment of 40.5 per cent. The economic reform was, indeed, a tool for the restructuring of class relations.

Government and Industry
Under Lt General Videla's administration, the role of the government was fundamental through the restructuring of the industrial sector,[18] its purchases in the private sector, the privatisation of some public companies, and public investment.[19]

TABLE 5
Industrial employment

Year	Foodstuffs	Capital Goods	Textiles	Paper Products	Chemicals	Basic Metals
1975	121.9	123.4	111.7	103.7	124.1	136.2
1976	122.7	116.5	107.2	94.3	125.7	130.8
1977	117.5	108.9	98.4	84.8	119.0	127.2
1978	105.6	96.9	87.4	82.8	108.9	119.0
1979	105.8	96.7	79.9	81.2	105.6	119.0
1980	108.0	88.8	64.1	81.4	73.9	114.7
Growth rate 75/80	−11.4	−28.0	−42.6	−21.5	-40.5	−15.8

Source: A. Canitrot (1981).

Note: 1970 = 100.

Daniel Azpiazu (Azpiazu and Kosacoff, 1989, p. 93), in his analysis of the promotion of the industrial sector, concludes that the beneficiaries of this policy were the national corporations, or GEN. He states that 50 projects – which represented 7.2 per cent of total projects presented in the period studied – represented 70 per cent of total investment, and were directed to highly concentrated industries. Therefore, industrial policy served, through the pattern of subsidies, to further concentrate production.

Manufacturing exports were also promoted in various ways.[20] From the manufacturing branch, the chemical industry, steel and other basic metal industries have the main share of industrial exports. These industries increased their participation in total exports as a consequence of the low demand in the internal market and also because of state promotion. On the other hand, capital goods and the automobile industry's share fell as a consequence of industrial policy. In general terms, the total volume of industrial exports increased more than 80 per cent from 1973 to 1986 (Azpiazu and Kosacoff, 1989, p. 120).

Regarding the privatisation process, Schvarzer (1986a, p. 266) emphasises that the government in many cases decided to close the company instead of selling it. This was the case with *Industrias Mecánicas del Estado*, a publicly owned steel company. There was also a process of 'peripheral privatisation', that is a subcontract between a public company and a private one through which the former delegated some of its activities.

The restructuring of the industrial sector meant increasing the concentration of capital in the biggest national corporations, destroying the small and medium-sized companies. As said before, the latter had constituted the so-called 'domestic bourgeoisie' which, allied with the working class, had been Peronism's support base. The GEN were strengthened at the expense of the 'domestic bourgeoisie'.

The Industrial Sector after Martínez de Hoz
After Lt General Videla's government the problems of the industrial sector were de-industrialisation, the limited internal market, high costs and the 'denationalisation' of important sectors of the industry. This policy led to the closure of a large number of small and medium-sized companies, most of them related to the metallurgical industries, producing significant 'idle capacity' of capital goods (50 per cent) and considerable dependency on industrial exports (Dorfman, 1983, p. 583). In addition, there was a process of external disinvestment and capital repatriation. In 1973 the share of the transnational corporations in the value of the industrial production was 30.8 per cent; in 1981 their share fell to 28.6 per cent, rising slightly to 29.4 per cent in 1983 (Azpiazu and Kosacoff, 1989, p. 194). Most of the transnational corporations were automobile and capital goods industries; these industries slumped during the early 1980s, and some transnational corporations left Argentina.[21]

A comparison between the National Economic Census of 1974 and 1985 shows that in 1974 there were 129,678 companies in the manufacturing industry with 1,555,538 employees; in 1985 there were 111,767 companies with 1,359,489 employees, which means that in 11 years the number of firms had decreased by 17,911 (Minsburg, 1987, p. 99).

An analysis of the situation of the 100 biggest companies (according to their sales) in 1975 and 1981 concludes that from the group of 1975, 33 do not appear in the group of 1981. From this 33, 20 go down in the ranking and 13 disappear. The number of companies with a negative balance in their sales increased from 14 in 1975 to 39 in 1981. The analysis of the changes shows that six companies were absorbed by others and 15 companies changed ownership (Schvarzer, 1986a, p. 202). Therefore one of the consequences of the Martínez de Hoz plan was the trend towards the concentration of big 'economic groups' which diversified their activities to minimise risk. Most of them were organised around one holding company whose success was a consequence of the protectionist activities of the state. These groups grew up during a period of economic stagnation.

Another indicator of crisis in the industrial sector is the increasing level of unemployment. From a base index of 100 in 1975, the level of employment in the second six months of 1980 fell to 84.5; in the same period of 1981, to 74.4; and in the same period of 1982, to 72 points (Dorfman, 1983, p. 113). According to the *Unión Industrial Argentina* in 1980 the number of unemployed and underemployed was 1,500,000 which represented 14 per cent of the population of working age (Caputo, 1982, p. 124).

Martínez de Hoz himself explains:

> our policy was not meant to wipe out our industry but, on the contrary, to strengthen it through competitiveness. A slogan proclaims that we are to blame for the 'destruction' of the productive apparatus, but the word 'modernisation' would be more to the point. While it is true that many industries disappeared – due perhaps to their own obsolescence – they were replaced by more modern newcomers. (Di Tella and Rodríguez Braun, 1990, p. 159)

The national corporations, or *Grupos Económicos Nacionales* (GEN), are these 'modern newcomers'. However, Martínez de Hoz does not explain that their development was not directly connected to the economic development of the country. On the contrary, while these 'modern newcomers' appeared, Argentina was undergoing a profound economic crisis. Their economic growth was based on the closure of companies and the absorption of some activities which were previously assumed by the state. The success of these groups was a consequence of the redistribution of ownership and of a new distribution of activities between the public and the private sector. Most of the GEN owed their success to government sponsorship. The GEN controlled big industrial companies which were connected to the agricultural, financial and construction sectors (Basualdo and Azpiazu, 1990, p. 15). Another significant result of

Martínez de Hoz's economic strategy was the diversification of the transnational companies, which adopted the same characteristics of the GEN (Basualdo and Azpiazu, 1990, p. 15). Generally, both, the GEN and the transnational companies, were oligopolies. For instance, Celulosa Argentina and Massuh controlled paper production. Garovaglio y Zorraquín and Perez Companc controlled the most important national banks. The latter also controlled petrochemical and metallurgical production. Bunge y Born controlled the biggest companies in the foodstuff sector, an important textile company and a paint company (Basualdo and Azpiazu, 1990, p. 156). The industrial promotion applied by the military dictatorship further accelerated this centralisation and concentration of capital in the GEN and transnational companies.[22]

The development of the GEN and the transnational companies can be analysed through the evolution of the number of subsidiaries they held. There were 30 GEN in 1973 which had 277 companies, 33 in 1983 with 586 companies, and 31 in 1986 with 665 companies. For the same years, there were 31 transnational companies with 327 companies, 31 with 434 companies and 29 with 426 companies, respectively (Acevedo *et al.*, 1990, p. 52). Therefore, although the years of the military dictatorship can be characterised as a period of economic stagnation, the GEN as well as the diversified transnational companies achieved a quite significant expansion. Another factor which helped the development of the GEN was their international connections which allowed them to obtain foreign credits.[23] The private external debt, 68 per cent of which was accounted for by the GEN and the transnational companies (Basualdo, 1987, p. 74), was transferred to the state in 1982, a decision of the president of the Central Bank, Domingo Cavallo.[24]

The emergence of the GEN was, therefore, a consequence of the absorption by the biggest companies of small and medium-sized companies which went bankrupt, and of the creation of new companies through government financing.[25] In this sense, Martínez de Hoz's modernisation produced significant changes in the industrial structure.

Others beneficiaries of Martínez de Hoz's policy were the financial mediators and the most concentrated sector of the *Pampeana* bourgeoisie. The latter began to transfer its profit to the financial market, instead of investing it in the agricultural sector, without losing productivity. The biggest companies gained benefits from the transfer of both their funds and activities to the financial arena. Thus, the state was losing control of the system, which started to depend on the decisions of a growing private financial sector (Schvarzer, 1986a, p. 35). Therefore, as a consequence of Martínez de Hoz's 'modernisation', there was a crucial transformation in social relations and in the role of the state.

Martínez de Hoz's economy policy promoted the modernisation of a small group of large firms which achieved considerable economic growth in a context of stagnation. What the former Minister does not explain is the other side of the coin, that is, the impoverishment of the working class. An analysis of the industrial labour market shows this to be the other side of Martínez de Hoz's 'modernisation'.

Conditions of the Industrial Labour Market
After the dictatorship, the two main results for the industrial labour market were its *desasalarización* and its *terciarización*. The former derives from the reduction of the number of wage-earners because of the transfer of workers from the industrial sector to the 'black market'. The latter refers to the transfer of workers from the industrial sector to the service sector. A brief description of the conditions of the labour market will help to understand these two processes.

There were two moments which severely affected the labour market. The first was in 1975 with the so-called *Rodrigazo* and its redistribution of income; the second was at the beginning of the dictatorship, with another redistribution of income through the freezing of wages (Gerchunoff and Dieguez, 1984, p. 4).

Workers' real wages decreased between 1974 and 1978 by 49 per cent.[26] Real wages in the manufacturing sector, in 1977, were 66.3 per cent of those prevailing in 1975 (Azpiazu and Kosacoff, 1989, p. 176). As Table 1 shows, the percentages of income going to wage earners decreased 31 per cent from 1975 to 1976. During the military government this percentage was around 33 per cent of national income while in the early 1970s it had been 45 per cent. The real wage of an industrial worker had decreased 37 per cent in the same period. The decline in the purchasing power as well as the saving power of an industrial worker can be shown through the increase of poverty in Greater Buenos Aires (the most industrialised area of Argentina).

TABLE 6
Percentage of poor population of Greater Buenos Aires[27]

Year	Poor population	Poverty groups	
		Structurally poor*	Pauperizados**
1974	34.30	31.10	3.20
1980	31.30	21.20	10.10
1982	51.10	23.10	28.00

Source: A. Boron (1992).

Notes:
* Structurally poor are those with severe problems of housing, social infrastructure, and incomes inadequate to cover basic needs.
**Pauperizados* means working-class families that had, in the past, a reasonable standard of living but had been pushed into conditions of poverty no different from that of the 'structurally poor'. As Minujin (1991) points out, 'they did not inherit poverty; they acquired it' as a consequence of economic crises.

In eight years the *pauperizados* group increased 775 per cent, while the structurally poor group decreased 25 per cent and the total poor population rose by 49 per cent. The *pauperizados* are the most relevant group since their position is a clear consequence of Martínez de Hoz's political economy and 'modernisation'. The *pauperizados* are the consequence of the dismantling of the industrial sector, the closure of small and medium-sized companies, and the fall in real wages. After Martínez de Hoz's 'modernisation', the 'structurally poor' were still living in *villas miserias* (shanty towns) without sanitary services, with four or more people sharing a single room. Although their situation followed the general economic recession, it did not change dramatically. However, as it is defined, the *pauperizados* were working-class families pushed into, and beyond, the conditions of the 'structurally poor'.

The increase in poverty was caused by the decreasing number of industrial workers which went from 1,165,000 in 1975 to 740,000 in 1982, representing a fall of 36 per cent in seven years (CEPAL, 1990, p. 23).

On the other hand, from the employer's point of view, labour costs decreased from 43 per cent in 1974 to 35.7 per cent in 1976 (Azpiazu *et al.*, 1986, p. 113). In addition, productivity was increasing 37.6 per cent from 1974 to 1983. These two factors meant that the absolute profit level and profit rate increased. As wages decreased, it was calculated that the funds appropriated by the industrial employers increased 69 per cent from 1974 to 1983 (Azpiazu *et al.*, 1986, p. 115).

Therefore, the conditions of the industrial labour market were severely affected by Martínez de Hoz's political economy. Moreover, these new conditions also affected the power of the trade unions and the power of the working class, because the fall in the number of wage-earners implied that the trade unions were losing members as well as power. For instance, in 1978 the *Unión Obrera Metalúrgica* (Metallurgical Union) had 287,000 members, whereas in 1988 it had 267,000. The SMATA (*Sindicato de Mecánicos del Transporte Automotor*) had 87,000 members in 1976, and in 1986, 54,000. The union of textile workers decreased from 87,000 in 1976 to 73,500 members in 1986. Conversely, the *Confederación de Empleados de Comercio* (Commerce Employees Confederation) increased its membership from 279,000 in 1978 to 407,000 in 1988 (Morales Solá, 1990, p. 290). It is important to highlight the fact that the union in which membership did increase belongs to the tertiary sector.

The main conclusion is that the changing structure of the Argentinian economy created new conditions for the industrial labour market which were its *desasalarización, terciarización* and the *pauperización* (impoverishment) of the workers. These processes modified the social structure of the country by deepening its inequalities. The industrial working class became both economically worse off, and politically weaker. Those who could, moved into the tertiary or the 'black market', but this was not sufficient to absorb all the movement away from the industrial sector.

External Debt
In the mid-1970s the international context contributed to the accumulation of external debt. The quadrupling of the oil price in 1973 weakened the situation of the non-oil-producing developing countries. Together with an increase in their import expenditure, there was a decrease in their export earnings as a consequence of the recession in developed countries. By contrast, the OPEC countries (Oil Producing and Exporting Countries) experienced a massive increase in their current account surplus. They placed many of the so-called 'petrodollars' in US and British banks. The rise in inflation

resulting from the oil shocks meant that real interest rates were very low or negative in the developed countries. The governments of developing countries were 'keen to avoid having to adopt deflationary measures to control their current account deficits. Instead they sought to borrow funds to finance the deficits' (Pilbeam, 1992, p. 408). This led to a 'recycling' of the 'petrodollars' in the form of massive lending to the developing countries. Most of the loans were made with floating rates of interest based upon a margin over LIBOR (the London Inter-Bank Offered Rate). While the banks were protecting themselves, this left developing countries such as Argentina exposed to the risk of a rise in world interest rates.

The external debt was one of the most serious consequences of the dictatorship in the sense that it would continue severely to constrain the future of the Argentinian economy. The accumulation of external debt can be divided in three periods of time: (1) that of the initial expansion, 1976–78 (16.6 per cent per year); (2) a period of explosive growth, 1979–81 (41.9 per cent per year); and (3) that of the compulsory accumulation of debt, 1982–89 (7.6 per cent per year) (Bouzas and Keifman, 1990, p. 3).

The main feature of Argentinian external debt is that in the first two periods the accumulation of debt was a result of commercial deficits caused by the overvaluation of the peso, commercial openness and capital flight (Bouzas and Keifman, 1990, p. 5). The mismanagement of the exchange rate combined with an opening of the capital account are key explanations for the massive debt accumulation (Dornbusch and De Pablo, 1988, p. 20). These were the consequences of the Martínez de Hoz's political economy, especially his financial reform and the opening up of commercial and capital markets.

From 1976 to 1982, public debt increased 407.5 per cent, private debt by 364.5 per cent, and net debt by 479.5 per cent (Frenkel *et al.*, 1988). However, as it was shown above, the time of the dictatorship was a period of economic stagnation, and the increase in the external debt does not mean an increase of investment funds for developing the Argentinian economy.

Despite the fact that in 1978 the balance of trade surplus was over $2,500 million dollars and the foreign currency reserves were over $6,000 million, one year later an explosive growth of the debt commenced, mainly as a result of the anti-inflationary policy of December 1978. The so-called *tablita* was the prior announcement

TABLE 7
External debt (million current dollars)

Year	Public debt	Private debt	Gross debt	Net Debt*
1976	5,189	3,090	8,279	6,467
1977	6,044	3,634	9,678	5,639
1978	8,357	4,139	12,496	6,459
1979	9,960	9,074	19,034	8,554
1980	14,459	12,703	27,162	19,478
1981	20,024	15,647	35,671	31,794
1982	26,341	14,362	40,703	37,477

Source: R. Frenkel *et al.* (1988).

Note: *Net debt = gross debt – foreign currency reserves.

of a series of gradually declining mini-devaluations. By decreasing the rate of depreciation, the government tried to decrease inflation 'by exposing domestic producers to international competition and thus reducing the *peso* price of tradables' (Crystal, 1994, p. 137). The policy failed – partly due to the large budget deficit – and the result was an increasingly overvalued real exchange rate. The result was substantial capital flight 'estimated at around US$25 billion between 1978 and 1982' (Crystal, 1994, p. 137). This explained the overwhelming increase of the private debt.

From 1978 to 1979, public debt increased 19 per cent while private debt increased 119 per cent; from 1979 to 1980, public debt rose by 45 per cent and private debt by 40 per cent; and from 1980 to 1981, public debt rose by 38 per cent and private debt by 23 per cent. In 1978–79, the private sector was the origin of the accumulation of debt while, afterwards, both private- and public-sector increases were around 30 and 40 per cent. On the other hand, the foreign currency reserves decreased 26 per cent from 1979 to 1980, and 49.5 per cent from 1980 to 1981 (Frenkel *et al.*, 1988, Figure 5).

The growth of private debt between 1978 and 1979 was not the result of new external credits, but rather the product of transactions made by Argentinians who had deposits abroad (Basualdo, 1987, p. 65). They brought their money back to Argentina and this transaction appeared as a new credit. Capital flight during 1979–81 – which amounted to US$16.2 billion – was around 23 per cent of Argentina's GDP (Fanelli and Frenkel, 1989, p. 11).

It is also important to look at the composition of the private sector, which got into debt with foreign banks. Thirty GEN got into debt with foreign banks for a total of $7,349 million dollars – 34.5 per cent of total private debt – and 106 transnational corporations amassed a debt of 7,238 million dollars – 34 per cent of the total (Basualdo, 1987, p. 74). Therefore, the share of the economic corporations and the transnational corporations represented 68 per cent of total private debt, the rest belonged to public and medium-sized companies.

The government promoted, until 1980, the accumulation of private external debt through the maintenance of a domestic interest rate higher than the international one. Due to the financial crisis of 1980, the private sector started to substitute domestic assets for foreign assets, and in order to maintain the devaluation rate fixed by the *tablita*, the government compensated for the capital flight with an expansion of public debt. According to Frenkel *et al.* (1988, p. 12), this mechanism was the first step towards the nationalisation of the private debt: the government ran up debt acquiring foreign currency to sell it to the private sector at an undervalued dollar rate. Therefore, the private sector could cancel its external liabilities with a subsidised price.

The second step towards the nationalisation of the private debt was the guarantee of *seguros de cambio* (swaps) through which the government guaranteed a future exchange rate below the market value.[28] By November 1982, the Central Bank decided to take charge of the private debt due to the inability of the private sector to repay it. The Central Bank would replace the private debtor after the cancellation of the debt in pesos. In other words, the private debtor paid the Central Banks in pesos and the Bank had to pay it to the external creditor in dollars (Graziano, 1986, p. 46). The main official objective in nationalising the debt was to prevent a crisis not only in some national companies but also in the domestic financial system.

In 1980 public debt grew significantly because the government had started to increase the foreign currency reserves which were required by the private sector. The increase in the international interest rate as a cause of the growth of public debt must also be taken into account (Schvarzer, 1986a, p. 419). It also seems probable – although difficult to confirm – that the expansion of public debt was linked to the purchase of arms. The military dictatorship was on the verge of a war against Chile in 1978, and finally was at war against the United Kingdom in 1982. Scholars[29] agree that a large amount of public debt was created by the purchase of arms.

The consequences of external debt became a crucial issue for Argentina's future. First of all, the 'owners' of the private debt transferred to society, by nationalisation of the debt, their losses but not their profits. Because of this, as the debt became mainly public, the external crisis produced a fiscal one. Fanelli and Frenkel (1989, p. 19) explain that

> the core of this issue is that while the government has to pay the interest of the foreign debt, the private sector 'owns' the surplus of the trade account which provides the foreign exchange necessary for the payment on the interest due. In other words, the public sector must buy the external surplus from the private sector and the government must obtain the funds to do so by either reducing its expenditure or raising taxes. Both of these measures tend to depress the activity level and to restrain growth.

Therefore, the government became dependent upon the activity of the private sector to repay external credits. Secondly, private external debt and its nationalisation implied a redistribution of income, in the sense of the 'socialisation' of losses, while profits remained private. Finally, external debt, combining redistribution of income with concentration of capital, rendered national governments unable to control the domestic economy (Basualdo, 1987, p. 117). Henceforth, international creditors – commercial banks, international organisations of credit and foreign governments – played a crucial role in the decision making process of the Argentinian economy.

External debt was another tool for the restructuring of the state. Through debt the international creditors increased their leverage over debtor countries. The IMF became the international regulator of debt and the World Bank became more concerned with long-term structural adjustment. Both promoted monetarism as the means to achieve internal price stability and a balance on the external account. Debt repayment was the 'cost' paid to tie Argentina's economy into the international system. Its consequence was that the restructuring of the state and of class relations begun by the 1976 military dictatorship could not be reversed by the incoming democratic government.

THE COLLAPSE OF THE DICTATORSHIP: FROM VIOLA TO MALVINAS

The results of Martínez de Hoz's economic policy were that between 1980 and 1981 the rate of the GDP went from 0.7 to –6.2, per capita GDP from –0.9 to –7.7, and gross national income from 1.8 to –7.0. External debt increased from US$27,162 million in 1980 to US$35,671 in 1981 (United Nations, 1985, p. 76). These modifications were concentrated in one year as a result of the economic policy applied in the previous four years. The implementation of Martínez de Hoz's economic policy weakened the already vulnerable Argentinian economy.

As had been planned, Lt General Videla and his ministers left the government in March 1981 when Lt General Roberto Viola, Commander-in-Chief of the Army, took office. The new military administration abandoned the trade-liberalisation programme. The new programme consisted of stabilising the peso, achieving a surplus in foreign trade, promoting a larger market for national products, changing internal relative prices in favour of producers of tradable goods, favouring employment over real wages, keeping the financial system open with state, foreign and private national banks appropriately balanced, encouraging private participation in the public investment programmes, and making both fiscal expenditure and the public deficit, as well as Central Bank credit, consistent with monetary policy, in order to fight inflation effectively (Di Tella and Rodríguez Braun, 1990, p. 188).

As soon as the new Minister of the Economy, Lorenzo Sigaut, took office, the demand for dollars increased. In just one day the Central Bank lost US$300 million (Schvarzer, 1986a, p. 120). On 2 June the economic team devaluated the peso by 30 per cent. On 22 June a double exchange market was created: the financial, or free, market and the commercial one (Di Tella and Dornbusch, 1989, p. 298). The former exchange rate was 30 per cent higher than the latter, representing another 30 per cent devaluation. The 'discrepancy between the commercial and financial rate widened over time from 30 per cent to 60 per cent, reflecting a growing imbalance between the attempt to avoid the inflationary impact of depreciation and the need to check capital flight by a rapid depreciation of the financial rate' (Di Tella and Dornbusch, 1989, p. 298).

Another measure was a new export tax of 12 per cent in agricultural products. On the other hand, the industrial sector could maintain its benefit which was a subsidy for manufactured goods of 25 per cent. Dornbusch (Di Tella and Dornbusch, 1989, p. 298) describes this short period as follows: 'inflation had been artificially lowered by the exchange rate policy, but this had been achieved at the cost of building up an external lack of competitiveness as well as a large external debt. Sigaut therefore had to restore competitiveness and could not avoid some increase in inflation.'

Under Viola's government, in July of 1981, there was a second national strike called by the banned CGT – once again the leaders were imprisoned – against the military dictatorship. This enjoyed total adherence in both the industrial and the tertiary sectors. In November 1981, there was a protest march against the dictatorship with the slogan 'Bread, Peace and Jobs' (Smith, 1989, p. 240).

In December 1981 a palace coup against Lt General Roberto Viola showed the internal problems of the Armed Forces and 'represented a regrouping of various right-wing military sectors in a new complex realignment with the economic and financial interests associated with the Martínez de Hoz group' (Smith, 1989, p. 244). Many reasons have been put forward to explain this *coup d'état* within the military dictatorship. On the one hand, Lt General Viola radically changed the economic policy. While Martínez de Hoz's team had represented the objectives of the economic establishment, Lt General Viola's Minister of the Economy did not. On the contrary, his economic plan changed radically the rules of the economy. Although there were some groups against Martínez de Hoz's economic policies,[30] the liberals, supporters of Martínez de Hoz, became more powerful within the Army through the promotion, by the end of 1981, of old generals. When Lt General Viola was removed, the new President chose as his Minister of the Economy a man of the economic 'establishment', Roberto Alemann.

Another cause of Lt General Viola's forced retirement was that he started a political dialogue with the main political parties and appointed seven civilian ministers in a Cabinet of thirteen ministers (Smith, 1989, p. 242). Moreover, during his short presidential period the *Multipartidaria* (an organisation joined by the main political parties) was created by the Peronist party, the Radical party, the *Movimiento para la Integración y Desarrollo* (Movement for

Integration and Development), the Christian Democrats and the *Partido Intransigente* (Intransigent party). By this time, the *Junta* publicly warned Lt General Viola that political dialogue was premature (Fontana and Llenderrozas, 1992, p. 167). While Lt General Viola believed that the democratic transition had to be started, this was not an opinion shared by the Armed Forces.

The change of men in the House of Government was not just a change of names. After the coup against Lt General Viola, Lt General Galtieri – Commander-in-Chief of the Army – attempted as the new President to return to the origins of the *Proceso*, both economically and politically. By the end of 1981 GNP fell a record 11.4 per cent; 'industrial production declined by nearly 23 per cent and real wages declined almost 20 per cent' (Smith, 1989, p. 244). Therefore, Lt General Galtieri's Economics Minister, Roberto Alemann, had to cope with a serious crisis. He emphasised deflation, deregulation and denationalisation. Alemann's plan was based on 'freezing state employees' wages (responsible for approximately 50 per cent of government expenditure), raising taxes, and hiking public sector prices' (Smith, 1989, p. 245). The objectives of the plan were a 'drastic compression of domestic demand and radical cuts in public spending to reduce inflation and further open the economy to the international market' (Smith, 1989, p. 245). Another wage freeze, this time only for state employees, suggested that the new military government wanted to deepen the restructuring of the state which had been begun by Videla and Martínez de Hoz.

A second protest march was held on 30 March 1982, again under the slogan 'Peace, Bread and Jobs'. Three days later the Malvinas adventure started as the last attempt of the dictatorship to maintain control of the government. The military defeat in the Malvinas signalled the beginning of the end of the dictatorship. Because of the war the economic situation radically changed. For instance, Smith (1989, p. 246) points out that 'in April 1982 alone, the equivalent of more than $500 million was withdrawn, generally to buy dollars in neighbouring Montevideo'.

The defeat in the Malvinas was also a defeat for the Armed Forces as a government. Lt General Galtieri resigned and Lt General Reynaldo Bignone was the President of the last period of the dictatorship. The transition to democracy began as a result of the Malvinas defeat.

THE TRANSITION TO DEMOCRACY: A CONSEQUENCE OF THE MALVINAS DEFEAT

The defeat in the Malvinas[31] was the beginning of the end for the military dictatorship. The transition to democracy was the result of the collapse of the *Proceso*. Unable to overcome the economic crisis, to quash the guerrilla groups through the power of the state apparatus or to win an external war, the government of the Armed Forces collapsed. The breakdown of the authoritarian regime was a consequence of its own contradictions and failures.

The Malvinas represented the final blow to the authoritarian regime and marked the beginning of the transition to democracy. However, the disintegration of the *Proceso* began with the failure of Martínez de Hoz's plan to bring down inflation, reduce the fiscal deficit and overcome economic stagnation. Viola's attempt to change the economic strategy and start a process of political 'liberalisation' revealed the absence of consensus within the regime. Viola's effort was in turn interrupted by the Armed Forces' 'coup within a coup'. Galtieri's presidency tried to reimpose a freezing of political activity and to ally the government once again with the 'economic establishment', appointing Roberto Alemann as Minister of the Economy. It was in the midst of these efforts that Lt General Galtieri began the Malvinas campaign.

During the *Proceso*, the Armed Forces' alliance with the upper bourgeoisie was undermined. It was weakened initially during Viola's presidency because of the shifts in economic policy and the evident failure of the Martínez de Hoz plan. The Malvinas campaign served to undermine the alliance even further. Rouquié (1983b, p. 582) argues that the foreign policy of the military dictatorship became incoherent and that 'one can understand that the Argentine conservatives should be disoriented, even alarmed, by the statements of Sr. Costa Méndez at the non-aligned meeting of 9th June 1982 according to which "the struggle for the Falklands is similar to the liberation struggles of Algeria, India, Cuba, Vietnam and the Palestinian people"'. The Malvinas war provoked the economic and political isolation of Argentina which was not welcomed by the upper bourgeoisie. It also highlighted that a military dictatorship is much more unpredictable than any democratic government. The same government which was helping the United States' struggle against 'communism' in Central America, sought support for its

Malvinas campaign from the non-aligned movement. Therefore, another cause of the *Proceso*'s collapse was the breakdown of the social alliance which had supported it.

In conclusion, a combination of four factors provoked the collapse of the authoritarian regime: first, the failure of the efforts to overcome the economic crisis; second, the contradictions within the Armed Forces; third, these two factors provoked the weakening of the alliance with the upper bourgeoisie; fourth, the defeat in the Malvinas war. By the time the transition to democracy had begun, the Armed Forces were in danger of internal fragmentation.[32] The collapse of the authoritarian regime and the internal crisis of the Armed Forces made the transition to democracy quite distinctive.

The Transition Process
After the military defeat, Lt General Galtieri resigned (*Clarín*, 18.6.1982, p. 3) and the Commander-in-Chief of the Army, Lt General Nicolaides appointed Lt General Bignone as President (*Clarín*, 23.6.1982, p. 3). This provoked the Navy and Air Force to leave the *Junta Militar* since Nicolaides had not respected the *de facto* provision of the *Proceso* referring to the *Junta*'s responsibility to appoint the President. Therefore, the Army assumed total responsibility for government. On 1 July 1982, Lt General Bignone took office and lifted the ban on political activity (*Clarín*, 1.7.1982, p. 2). Bignone's main objective was to conduct the transition to democracy.

Despite the lifting of the ban on political activity, the *Multipartidaria* was quite cautious at the very beginning of the transition process and did not seek to provoke social mobilisation. In fact the role of the *Multipartidaria* as the opposition against the military dictatorship was undermined by its support for the Malvinas war. Indeed, the war had provoked a split within the *Multipartidaria*, some politicians enthusiastically supporting the campaign, others – most notably Raúl Alfonsín – withholding such support.

Nevertheless, the last few months of 1982 can be considered as a turning-point in the transition process. First, human rights organisations[33] organised a public demonstration, to exert pressure for investigations into human rights violations committed under the military government (*Clarín*, 6.10.1982, p. 2). Second, after changes in the highest positions of the Navy and Air Force, their

Commanders-in-Chief decided to reconstitute the *Junta Militar* (*Clarín*, 11.9.1982, p. 3 and Romero, 1995, p. 323).

In October the *Junta* and the President tried to negotiate some conditions to achieve an 'agreed transition' (*transición concertada*). A list of issues, from human rights violations to the role of the Armed Forces in the democratic government, was published before being discussed with the political parties. As a consequence of this, the *Multipartidaria* rejected the possibility of a *concertación* or agreement (*Clarín*, 6.12.1982, p. 2). The breakdown of the *concertación* unleashed a general strike and a popular demonstration for a quick return to democracy, called for by the *Multipartidaria* (*Clarín*, 16.12.1982, p. 2).

It was, by then, clear that the military government could no longer control the transition process. In February 1983, President Lt General Bignone announced that elections would be held on 30 October and a civilian government would take office on January 1984 (*Clarín*, 10.2.1983, p. 2). The political parties became preoccupied with establishing their leadership teams. The Armed Forces became worried about the past.

Indeed, in April 1983, the Armed Forces published a 'final' document on the struggle against the guerrillas. The document emphasised that the struggle against guerrillas had been ordered by the constitutional government of María Estela Martínez de Perón. The document was followed by an 'Institutional Act' (*Acta Institucional*) 'declaring that all military actions during the campaign were carried out "in the line of duty" on orders from the military high command' (*Latin America Weekly Report*, 6.5.1983, p. 10). The document and the act were rejected by all the political parties. Nevertheless, the Armed Forces attempted a final defensive move: a legal framework to avoid the investigation of the human rights violations. On 23 September, a law was passed establishing an amnesty for the perpetrators of subversive activities and 'excesses' of repression from 25 May 1973 to 17 June 1982 (*Clarín*, 24.9.1983, p. 2). The law was rejected by all the political parties, although Italo Luder,[34] leader of the Peronist party, was somewhat ambiguous regarding whether or not he would reverse the law (*Clarín*, 24.9.1983, pp. 2–3).

From July 1982 to December 1983, the most important decision, in the economic sphere, was Domingo Cavallo's policy. As president of the Central Bank, he applied 'a drastic financial reform that in only six months resulted in the liquidation of about 40 per cent of the private sector's debt' (Smith, 1989, p. 257). In July 1982 for the first time Argentina had difficulties with its international obligations and the economic authorities admitted the need to renegotiate the external debt with the IMF.

Economically, the last years of the dictatorship can be summarised as follows: 1981 was the year of the devaluation and *seguros de cambio* (swaps) – as the first step of the nationalisation of the private debt – to cope with the commercial and current account deficits as well as with capital flight. 1982 was the year of the liquidation of private liabilities. Finally, 1983 was the year of wage increases due to pressures from trade unions which took advantage of the weakness of the dictatorship (Frenkel *et al.*, 1988, p. 7). Stagnation, high inflation, impoverishment and external debt were the legacy of the *Proceso*.

The transition to democracy was an unstable period. Neither the Armed Forces nor the political parties could control or lead the process of transition. For 18 months the transition to democracy was precarious. A new military coup could not be discounted. The competitive electoral campaign revealed an absence of a consensual approach amongst the political parties towards democracy. And, lastly, a growing number of accusations, both from inside and outside the country, of human rights violations against the government of the Armed Forces also increased tensions.

The long transition showed that, in 1982, the main political parties were not yet ready to govern. The Peronist party was still in disarray after its 1973–76 administration and Juan Perón's death. The Radical party's leader, Ricardo Balbín, died in September 1981. While Perón's death cost the Peronist party dearly, Balbín's death seemed to be beneficial to the Radical party since it allowed the latter to renovate itself. The main political parties were, therefore, undergoing a transition process themselves. This explains why they could neither control nor lead the transition process. Thus, although Argentina's transition to democracy emerged due to the collapse of the dictatorship, it lasted more than a year.

Some of the features of the transition process would be present during the first democratic government: the lack of consensus or co-operation between the main political parties and the mobilisation of civil society by human rights organisations.

THE 1983 ELECTIONS

The 1983 elections were held on 30 October. The Radical party won 51.75 per cent of the total vote cast and the Peronist party, 40.16 per cent. The remainder of the vote was divided between an assortment of small parties (*Clarín*, 1.11.1983, pp. 2-3).[35] In the provinces, Peronism won 12 of the 22 governorships representing 21 of the 56 senators' seats at the National Congress. The Radical party obtained a majority in the Chamber of Deputies, 129 compared with 111 for Peronism (*Clarín*, 1.11.1983, pp. 2-10).

Since 1946 the Peronist party – whenever there were genuinely free elections – had obtained a majority, while the Radicals had obtained between 25 and 30 per cent of the total vote. In 1983 there were many factors which militated against a Peronist victory. First, the absence of a leader able to replace Perón. Second, the degree of influence and power of the trade unionists in the decision making of the Peronist party invoked memories of Perón's widow's government, which ended in a military coup. Third, the aggressive electoral campaign which ended in the burning of a coffin bearing an effigy of Raúl Alfonsín. Finally, the ambiguity of Dr Italo Luder's attitude towards human rights violations.

The strong presence of the trade unions brought back memories of Isabel's presidency and its chaos and violence.[36] The aggressive electoral campaign terrified a society which wanted to end a violent period in its history. Dr Luder was unable to convince the electorate that he would be able to control either the factions within the Party or the trade unions. Nor could he convince the electorate that he genuinely sought to bring human rights violators to trial.

Alfonsín's campaign emphasised democratic and pacifist values. He stated categorically that a Radical party government would convict the perpetrators of human rights violations. Eight months before the elections Alfonsín denounced a pact between some officials from the Armed Forces and a number of trade unionists. The denounced pact apparently stated that a Peronist government would not investigate the violations of human rights under state terrorism, would maintain the hierarchy of the Armed Forces, would not impose a reorganisation of the Armed Forces or reduce their budget, and would not pursue charges of corruption which had occurred under the military government. In return, control of the trade unions and *Obras Sociales* (Health Service Funds) would pass directly to their existing leaders without the need for either a new law or internal elections (Gaudio and Thompson, 1990, p. 17). Although the existence of the pact was never substantiated, Alfonsín's announcement was nevertheless a key factor in his electoral victory. Indeed, although Alfonsín was accused of 'socialist' tendencies by some politicians from the Peronist party, the moderate-right electorate voted overwhelmingly for him. In the last days of the electoral campaign individuals supporting centre-right parties shifted their vote to Alfonsín (Mora y Araujo, 1986). Alfonsín's denouncement of the pact, together with the high profile of trade unionists in the Peronist camp and the violent campaign tactics of some Peronist politicians, contributed to Alfonsín's victory. The Radical leader emphasised the democratic values of the Radical Party and showed himself as Argentina's most democratic politician. In contrast, Peronism was presented as promoting exactly the things Argentinian society had had enough of – that is, violence and disorganisation.

On 10 December 1983, Alfonsín took office and a new democratic process began. Before turning to analyse the democratic period, the conclusions below suggest the ways in which the main consequences of the 1976 military dictatorship would constrain the democratic government.

CONCLUSION

As the main threat to the maintenance of the capitalist order came from the armed urban guerrillas, the primary objective of the Armed Forces was to banish guerrilla activity. Through the implementation of state terrorism the armed urban guerrillas literally 'disappeared'.

The subordination of the working class in both the economic and the political spheres was achieved through applied economic structural reform. In addition, owing to the dismantling of the industrial sector and the transfer of workers to the tertiary sector and the 'black market', the trade unions lost members and power. Historically, the tertiary sector has not had strong trade unions. Likewise, the redistribution of income meant a defeat for the working class in the conflict over wealth distribution. Tables 2 and 3 (see p. 28) show that while the price of a commodity was 100 pesos in 1976, by 1981 it was 7,276 pesos, whereas the real wage of an industrial worker was 100 in 1976 and 114.2 in 1981. The process of impoverishment was overwhelming.

The dictatorship failed to stabilise the economy. However, despite the stagnation of the economy, the national agro-industrial corporations connected to the international financial circles increased their profits. They found the path to growth through the financial market and speculation, the purchase of small and medium-sized companies which had gone bankrupt, the increase of their external debt, the diversification of their activity – from industry to finance, and even within the industrial sector from petrol to fisheries – and peripheral privatisation. They grew under the protection of the state. The analysis of the policy of industrial promotion shows that the GEN were the beneficiaries of this process (Azpiazu and Kosacoff, 1989). The nationalisation of the private debt also provided important assistance from the government to the GEN. Most directly the government was the main purchaser of the production of some of the GEN.[37] While economic liberalisation was praised as *the* solution to Argentina's problems, the dictatorship did, in fact, mix economic liberalisation with government intervention. This has been called 'liberalism from above' and 'liberalism with import substitution industrialisation' (Cavarozzi, 1997, p. 77, and Palermo and Novaro, 1996, p. 56, respectively).

The growth of the GEN was the result of the promotion of some factions of the industrial bourgeoisie at the expense of other factions – mainly the small and medium-sized companies. The high concentration of capital in these GEN was a new feature of Argentinian social relations. Another feature was the *desasalarización, terciarización* and the *pauperización* of the workers.

Argentina's 'new economy' could not easily be changed after the dictatorship because, despite the process of democratisation, in practice Argentina's international creditors and the trans-nationalised faction of the national bourgeoisie remained influential. In this sense, the military dictatorship had achieved a limited objective. To what extent the military dictatorship achieved its substantive objectives will be analysed in the following chapters because the achievement of these aims meant that the *disciplinamiento social* would last longer than the dictatorship itself. Nevertheless, some arguments can be considered here based on constraints created by the military government.

The first factor which would restrict the action of the next government was the external debt. As explained above, the external debt became a fiscal problem since the government had to service increasing interest payments. As Fanelli and Frenkel (1989, p. 19) point out, the essential part of this issue is that the private sector socialised its losses but still '"owned" the surplus of trade account which provides the foreign exchange necessary for the payments on the interest due'. Therefore, the public sector had to buy the external surplus from the private sector and the government had to obtain the funds to do so either by reducing its expenditures or raising taxes. Both of these measures tended to depress the activity level and to restrain growth (Fanelli and Frenkel, 1989, p. 19).

The second factor which would limit the room for manoeuvre of the democratic government was the concentration of capital. The GEN expanded in a regime of high inflation and a context of economic stagnation. The growth of the GEN was connected with relative prices because they operate in oligopolistic markets with high inflation which gives them the capacity to set prices above the average for the economy (Basualdo, 1987, p. 50). Likewise, due to the financial overvaluation of the surplus and their insertion in international and national financial markets, the GEN obtained more benefits than other companies. Therefore, they were both influential, through the determination of prices, and independent, through their powerful place in financial markets. Likewise, their power of speculation constrained the decision making power of the incoming government.

An impoverished working class would also be a constraint on the margin of manoeuvre of the democratic government. After seven years of dictatorship with social and political repression, the working class expected social, economic and political compensation. Nevertheless, because of the constraints and the economic legacy of the dictatorship, the democratic government had to heed the requirements of the IMF adjustment plan, and balance them with the demands of the working class.

Alfonsín's new government thus found itself severely constrained by the legacy of the *Proceso*. Juan Alemann, a member of the Martínez de Hoz team, said that the changes in the economic situation would restrain the action of the new democratic government and that the latter would therefore fail (Schvarzer, 1986a, p. 227). As Smith (1985, p. 74) points out 'the project's architects hoped to make it impossible for any future civilian or military regime to embark on dangerous *"retorno al pasado"* (return to the past) in terms of social and economic policies'. The method to achieve that objective was the redistribution of social power in Argentine society 'particularly the destruction of the economic bases which in the past had made possible the cyclical re-emergence of defensive alliances between organised labour and the subordinate factions of capital' (Smith, 1985, p. 74).[38]

The democratic government found itself trapped between the conflicting pressures of its international creditors demanding repayment of the debt, of the bourgeoisie demanding the protection of its interests, and of the working class, demanding economic compensation after seven years of impotence. Likewise, the democratic government had to deal with the social demand that human rights violators be brought to trial – which obliged it to confront the Armed Forces.

The military dictatorship did not resolve the crisis of the Argentinian state. It did, however, lay the foundations for the restructuring of the state and of class relations. The incoming democratic government had to work from these 'foundations'.

NOTES

1. My italics.
2. One of the measures to avoid old mistakes was to divide the government between the three Forces, this was to avoid the emergence of a strong leadership as had happened with Onganía in 1966 (Palermo and Novaro, 1996, p. 52).
3. As O'Donnell (1988, p. 90) points out, economic normalisation has two dimensions: 'the first involves the restitution of the economic supremacy of the oligopolised and transnationalised units in such a way that they regain heavy influence over the performance of the economy's main variables. The second dimension of normalisation consists of the restoration of close links between the local economy and the world capitalist system, in ways that involve, in contrast to the pre-Bureaucratic Authoritarian period, capital movements away from as well as toward the capitalist centres.'
4. Later the *Junta* renewed his designation until March 1981.
5. Martínez de Hoz is a man from the 'economic establishment' who had occupied crucial places such as the presidency of the *Consejo Empresario Argentino* (Argentinian Business Board) and of *Acindar*, a steel company.
6. As explained above, the Argentinian Anti-Communist Alliance – *Triple A* – was a paramilitary group formed by José López Rega, Isabel Perón's Minister of Social Welfare.

7. For a detailed account of the actions of human rights organisations during the military dictatorship see Brysk (1994), Bousquet (1983) and Fisher (1989).

8. For a detailed account of the dirty war and its consequences see Bonasso (1984), Argentina's National Commission on Disappeared People (1986), and Andersen (1993).

9. Regarding the international economic support to the new military government and to its economic policy, after one week of the *coup d'état*, the IMF approved a credit of US$110 million of Special Drawing Rights (SDR). In August 1976, the IMF approved another credit of US$ 260 millions of SDR (Schvarzer, 1986a, p. 46).

10. Law 21382 of August 1976 concerning foreign investment stated that all areas of economic activity were open to foreign investment, and guaranteed the settlement of profits and the repatriation of capital even in case of the implementation of an exchange-rate control (Minsburg, 1987, p. 85). This law also established equality between foreign and national investment and accepted the juridical independence of the transnational companies with respect to their head offices. Between 1976 and 1983 foreign investment was guided to petrol and financial sectors. Basic references are Minsburg (1987), Azpiazu and Kosacoff (1989), and Sourrouille *et al.* (1985).

11. This was a variety of work to rule developed to circumvent anti-strike legislation (Abós, 1984, p. 10).

12. Canitrot (1981, p. 143) explains that, as a consequence of the financial reform, the nationalised deposits system ended; therefore, the banks recovered a main role in the financial system. For more details see also Frenkel (1980).

13. *Desindexación* means a restriction to the mechanism of increasing prices due to the past inflation rate.

14. Argentinian Central Bank (*Banco Central de la República Argentina)*, unpublished data.

15. See Obschatko (1988).

16. See Azpiazu and Kosacoff (1989), Schvarzer (1986a) and (1983), Canitrot (1981) and Katz and Kosacoff (1989).

17. See Torre (1988) (1989) and Godio (1989).

18. Law 21608 concerning promotion of the industrial sector gave the right of promotion to national as well as international companies (Schvarzer, 1986a, p. 189).

19. Public investment during the 1960s and the beginning of the 1970s was between 7.5 per cent and 8.5 per cent of the GDP; between 1976 and 1980 it was 11.7 per cent of the GDP. The energy sector was the most relevant with a share of 50 per cent of the total of public investment between 1976 and 1980 (Comisión Económica para América Latina y el Caribe (CEPAL), 1990, p. 29).

20. This promotion started in the 1960s with the proposal of increasing industrial exports. This policy tried to take advantage of the development that the industry had achieved through Import Substitution Industrialisation – ISI – Due to this promotion, while in the beginning of

the 1960s the manufacturing sector did not export, in the 1970s its exports were over US$1000 million which represented 25 per cent of total exports (Azpiazu and Kosacoff, 1989, p. 101).

21. Most notably General Motors, Citroen and Chrysler which was bought out by Volkswagenwerk A.K. (Sourrouille *et al.*, 1985, p. 159).

22. Basualdo and Azpiazu (1990) made an excellent analysis of the impact of industrial promotion as applied by the military dictatorship in the process of concentration and centralisation of capital.

23. For more details on the development of the GEN and the 'diversified' transnational companies under military dictatorship see Basualdo (1987), Azpiazu *et al.* (1986), Acevedo *et al.* (1990) and Basualdo and Azpiazu (1990).

24. This policy is explained below.

25. For more details see Ostiguy (1990).

26. Measured at 1976 levels, average wages in 1974 were US$217, falling to US$109 in 1978 (Villareal, 1985, p. 249).

27. Although the author does not explain how poverty is defined, it could be assumed from his comments that poverty is defined as the impossibility of satisfying basic needs such as housing, drinking water, electricity, education and health service.

28. For more details on the nationalisation of the private external debt, see Graziano (1986) and Basualdo (1987).

29. See Basualdo (1987), Frenkel *et al.* (1988) and Bouzas and Keifman (1990).

30. Particularly the Navy whose Commander-in-Chief, Admiral E. Massera, was publicly against it.

31. For basic references on the Malvinas conflict, see Boron and Faúndez (1989), Cardoso *et al.* (1987), Gamba (1987), and Freedman and Gamba-Stonehouse (1990).

32. Fontana (1984, 1986) points out that the crisis of the Armed Forces was within themselves as well as within each of the Forces, especially the Army which was viewed as the most compromised in the implementation of state terrorism and the most responsible for the defeat in Malvinas.

33. These were specially: *Madres de Plaza de Mayo* (Mothers of May Square), *Asamblea Permanente por los Derechos Humanos* (Permanent Assembly for Human Rights), and *Centro de Estudios Legales y Sociales* (Centre of Legal and Social Studies).

34. Dr Luder had been stand-in President (*Presidente Provisional*) when María Estela Martínez de Perón was ill in 1975.

35. These were mainly: the Intransigent party (left-wing) (*Partido Intransigente*), the Movement of Integration and Development (moderate-right) (*Movimiento de Integración y Desarrollo*), Federal Alliance (right-wing) (*Alianza Federal*), Democratic Centre Union (right-wing) (*Unión del Centro Democrático*), Christian Democrats (moderate-right) (*Demócratas Cristianos*), Democratic Socialism Alliance (moderate-left) (*Alianza Demócrata Socialista*) and Movement towards Socialism (left-wing) (*Movimiento al Socialismo*).

36. An excellent study of the role of trade unionists in the last Peronist government is Torre (1989).
37. Fanelli and Frenkel (1989, p. 27) state that 'the state is the most important client of 20 of the 100 leading firms of the economy (ranked by sales)'.
38. For more details on this alliance see O'Donnell (1978).

3

A Failed Attempt to Resolve the Crisis, 1983–85

The main political objective of Alfonsín's government was the consolidation of democracy (Alfonsín, 1992, p. 49). In this sense, the Radical government was, at the very beginning, much more aware of the political aspects of the Argentinian crisis than of the economic ones. Alfonsín believed that, in order to consolidate democracy, his government had to 'democratise' the unions and the Armed Forces. By 'democratise' Alfonsín meant the incorporation of both these actors into the democratic system (Alfonsín, 1992, p. 19). He believed that both the unions and the Armed Forces were deeply authoritarian. While, in the case of the Armed Forces, this assumption was correct, in respect of the unions it was very simplistic. Behind Alfonsín's objective of 'democratising' the unions, there was the objective to '*desperonizar*' the unions, that is, to break down the traditionally powerful role of Peronist trade unionists within the union movement. There was, also, the objective of controlling the disruptive power of the unions. The unions were viewed as a vehicle of social unrest which could provoke a military coup. The Radical government, by 'democratising' the unions, wanted to restrain and ultimately defuse their political power.

Alfonsín tried also to restrain the political influence of the Armed Forces. Throughout his period in office, he tried to prevent an alliance between the Armed Forces and the unions which might threaten democracy. The assumption that such an alliance could threaten social stability was based on the history of military coups in Argentina. Most notably, Alfonsín tried to avoid a new breakdown of democracy like that which occurred in Illia's presidency, which was perceived as having been provoked by the social unrest unleashed by the unions (Alfonsín, 1992, p. 16). The analysis of the first two years of Alfonsín's mandate shows a failed attempt to control the unions and to implement Alfonsín's human rights violations policies.

Economically, the 1983–85 period is important for the negotiations regarding the external debt. During this period the government initially resisted, but then agreed to sign, the first 'letter of intent' with the IMF. In February 1984, the Economics Minister, Bernardo Grinspun, declared that 'we are not negotiating a stand-by (with the IMF) and we will not accept any recessive formula' (*Latin America Weekly Report*, 17.2.1984, p. 8). Seven months later Grinspun affirmed that an agreement with the IMF would be necessary (*Clarín*, 3.9.1984, p. 1). This chapter seeks to explain this U-turn.

The chapter is divided into four sections. The first section analyses Alfonsín's policies towards human rights violations. It highlights the reasons why Alfonsín's objectives failed, and the consequences of this failure for the rest of his presidency. The second section analyses Alfonsín's first attempts to control and to politically demobilise the trade unions. It shows the power of the trade unions in blocking and modifying state policies. This indicates that the political demobilisation achieved by the military dictatorship was only temporary. The third section analyses the domestic economic strategy and the negotiations surrounding the external debt. It begins by analysing the consequences of the external debt crisis for Latin American countries and, specifically, for Argentina. As one of the main economic problems was high inflation, the political side of this phenomenon is briefly analysed. This section also studies the gradual change of Alfonsín's policies as a result of the failure of the first economic strategy to prevent high inflation, and of the negotiations for the payment of the external debt to avoid an IMF plan. Due to these failures the Radical government was unable to resolve the crisis of the Argentinian state. The last section concludes by suggesting reasons why the government's strategies failed to resolve the crisis.

COPING WITH THE CONSEQUENCES OF
STATE TERRORISM

The Radical Government's Objectives

One of the worst consequences of the military dictatorship was the
desaparecidos ('disappeareds'). Human rights organisations calculated
that 30,000 people disappeared due to the implementation of state
terrorism. These organisations, most notably the *Madres de Plaza de
Mayo*, demanded *Aparición con Vida y Castigo a los Culpables*
(literally, Appearance Alive and Punishment of the Guilty). While
the first demand was, obviously, impossible to satisfy; the second
was almost unavoidable. Indeed, nationally, the pressure for the
punishment of human rights violators was very great (Fontana and
Llenderrozas, 1992 and Brysk, 1994).

During the first two years of his government Alfonsín attempted
to undermine the political power of the Armed Forces, to
democratise their internal structures, and to set in motion the
process for bringing the military to trial for human rights violations.

To weaken the political power of the Armed Forces, the
government applied budget cuts, reduced the number of conscripts,[1]
proposed the transfer of some institutes and corps from Buenos
Aires to the provinces, and modified the role of the Armed Forces
in internal matters of state. Military spending was cut back from
5.98 per cent of GDP in 1983 to 3.71 per cent in 1984 (*Latin America
Weekly Report*, 17.8.1984, p. 10). 'Defence expenditures plummeted
by 40 per cent between 1983 and 1986 ... Although the deepest cuts
were made in operations (42 per cent) and equipment (50 per cent)
army salaries fell 25 per cent between December 1983 and October
1984 alone' (Pion-Berlin, 1991, p. 552).[2] Alfonsín's Defence Minister,
Raúl Borras, announced that no funds would be made available for
development projects in the military sphere with the exception of
those linked to the production of arms for export (*Latin America
Weekly Report*, 17.8.1984, p. 10). The *Prefectura Naval Argentina*
(Coast Guard Agency) and the *Gendarmería Nacional* (Frontier
Police Corps), which were dependent on the Navy and the Army
respectively, were transferred to the jurisdiction of the Ministry of
Defence. Finally, around 100 military officials were released from
the Intelligence Service (*Latin America Regional Reports Southern
Cone*, 16.11.1984, p. 5). For his second objective, the

democratisation of the Armed Forces, Alfonsín tried to apply a different syllabus of studies at their main institutes introducing courses taught by civilians on the role of the Armed Forces in a democracy (Fontana, 1989, p. 17 and Huntington, 1993, p. 245).[3]

Alfonsín's policy of bringing the military to trial for human rights violations was the focus of his relationship with the Armed Forces. During the electoral campaign, Alfonsín had explained his proposal to deal with the human rights violations. He emphasised the concept of 'due obedience' based on three different levels of responsibility in the commission of human rights violations (Alfonsín, 1992, p. 108). He had defined that the degree of punishment was to vary between those who had been responsible for the planning and supervision of the repression, those who had committed 'excesses' during the repression, and those who had simply obeyed orders from their superiors (Alfonsín, 1992, p. 108). This was the main framework for Alfonsín's policies towards the Armed Forces. This framework was known as the 'due obedience' proposal.

According to the 'due obedience' proposal, Alfonsín's main objectives were to prosecute and to punish the highest members of the Armed Forces, specifically the three *Juntas Militares* which governed the country between 1976 and 1983, and to forgive those members of the Armed Forces who had obeyed orders from their superiors. In order to achieve these objectives, Alfonsín reformed the Military Justice Code. He attempted to give the Armed Forces the opportunity for 'self-cleansing', assuring them that a 'political decision' – the 'due obedience' proposal – would forgive the thousands of officials who had committed aberrant acts (Fontana, 1987, p. 387). Alfonsín did not attempt to punish all those who had participated in the implementation of state terrorism, rather he intended to prevent the repetition of such state terrorism by showing that anyone, including the holders of the highest office, can be judged (Alfonsín, 1992, p. 69). However, his objectives would be obstructed by pressure from human rights organisations, public opinion, and the Judiciary for the punishment of all members of the Armed Forces who were involved in the implementation of state terrorism.

From the Opportunity of 'Self-cleansing' to the Public Judgement of the Juntas

Three days after taking office, Alfonsín sent to Congress his proposal to abolish the self-amnesty law sanctioned by the military dictatorship (*Clarín*, 14.12.1983, p. 1).[4] Alfonsín's proposal to abolish this law meant that human rights violations and subversive activities carried out under the 1976 military dictatorship could be investigated by the Judiciary. In addition to this, he ordered judgements to be made on Mario Firmenich, Fernando Vaca Narvaja, Ricardo Obregón Cano, Rodolfo Galimberti, Roberto Perdía, Hector Pardo and Enrique Gorriarán Merlo – all members of the armed urban guerrilla – and of Lt General Jorge Videla, Admiral Emilio Massera, Brigadier Orlando E. Agosti, Lt General Roberto Viola, Admiral Armando Lambruschini, Brigadier Omar Graffigna, Lt General Leopoldo Galtieri, Admiral Jorge Anaya and Brigadier Basilio Lami Dozo – all members of the *Juntas Militares* (*Clarín*, 14.12.1983, pp. 2–3).

Alfonsín also set up the *Comisión Nacional sobre Desaparición de Personas* – CONADEP – (National Commission on Disappeared People) made up of well-known figures such as the Catholic Bishop Jaime de Nevares, the Protestant Bishop Carlos Gattioni, the Rabbi Marshall Meyer, Professor of Epistemology Gregorio Klimovsky, jurist Ricardo Colombres, Doctor Rene Favaloro, the former Chancellor of the University of Buenos Aires Hilario Fernández Long, the philosopher Eduardo Rabossi, the writer Ernesto Sábato and the journalist Magdalena Ruiz Guiñazú. There were also six places for MPs and senators. The Commission was to accept denunciations and evidence of human rights violations and send them to the Judiciary. It was also charged to discover the whereabouts of the *desaparecidos* and of the abducted children, and to present, within six months, a report to the President with a detailed account of its findings (Fontana, 1987, p. 386).[5]

In addition, Alfonsín sent his proposal for the reform of the Military Justice Code to the Congress (*Clarín*, 14.12.1983, pp. 2–3). His proposal decreed that the *Consejo Supremo de las Fuerzas Armadas* (Supreme Council of the Armed Forces) had to deal with the offences attributable to members of the Armed Forces, and those members of the security forces, the police and the penitentiary service, operating under the orders of the Armed Forces. The

Consejo was to examine those offences committed between 24 March 1976 and 26 September 1983 (*Clarín*, 14.12.1983, pp. 2–3). In case of delay in the judicial procedures, the *Consejo* had to inform the Federal Chamber of Justice on the causes of this delay. If the Federal Chamber considered that the delay was unjustified, it would take over responsibility for the judgements. Finally, the reform laid down that in the cases of individuals who had acted under orders of the highest officials of the Armed Forces and the *Junta Militar*, it could be presumed that these individuals acted under a mistaken belief in the legitimacy of these orders (Fontana, 1987, p. 384).

In February 1984 the Congress passed the law for the modification of the Military Justice Code, but Senator Elías Sapag of the provincial *Movimiento Popular Neuquino*, invoked modifications to the legislation. Sapag's amendments laid down that those individuals who had acted under orders could not be excused from punishment when they had committed aberrant and atrocious acts (*Clarín*, 2.2.1984, p. 8).[6] One of the objectives of Alfonsín's reform was to enshrine the three levels of responsibility distinguished by him – the so-called 'due obedience' proposal. Senator Sapag's modification undermined the juridical applicability of these distinctions. Alfonsín did not reject it, however, and sanctioned the law. He believed that the sentence of the *Consejo Supremo* would enable him to apply his 'due obedience' proposal since the sentence would clarify the hierarchy of the Armed Forces for the implementation of state terrorism (Fontana, 1987, p. 388).

The first military crisis under the democratic government was unleashed in September 1984 when the report of the National Commission on Disappeared People was published (*La Nación*, 20.9.1984, p. 1). This report revealed the extent of state terrorism. It gave details of concentration camp locations, tortures, the fate of some of the *desaparecidos* and the whereabouts of their bodies. The Army Chief-of-Staff, General Jorge Arguindegui, publicly alleged the existence of a campaign within the Army against his authority; therefore the Minister of Defence decided to replace him with General Pianta (Fontana, 1987, p. 389).

By this time, after two delays, the *Consejo Supremo* sent, to the Federal Chamber of Justice, a report supporting the Armed Forces' procedures in their struggle against the guerrilla (*La Nación*, 26.9.1984, p. 1). This report was condemned by the Federal Chamber, which decided to take over, due to the unjustified delay of the *Consejo* (*La Nación*, 5.10.1984, p. 1). This was the first defeat of Alfonsín's policies towards the Armed Forces, since the *Consejo* did not condemn the struggle against the guerrilla movement, undermining the possibility of the 'self-cleansing' process.

On 22 April 1985 the Federal Chamber of Justice began the public judgement against the *Juntas Militares* (*La Nación*, 23.4.1985, p. 1). This was a historic event. Never before had the Argentinian military dictatorships been judged for their 'excesses'. From Alfonsín's point of view the public judgement established the foundations for the consolidation of democracy, since it would prevent future generations of generals, admirals and brigadiers overthrowing democratic governments (Alfonsín, 1992, p. 69).

Failure of the 'Self-cleansing' of the Armed Forces

Alfonsín's policies towards human rights violations failed on two issues which would influence his subsequent years in office. First, the government misunderstood the perception of the Armed Forces over the accusations of human rights violations. The attempt to bring about a 'self-cleansing' of the Armed Forces required that they should recognise the struggle against the guerrilla as illegitimate. Alfonsín expected them to condemn state terrorism through the judgement of the members who applied it, but in fact the *Consejo Supremo* did not condemn state terrorism. On the contrary, the Armed Forces, time and again, supported their struggle against the guerrillas and proudly recognised it as a complete success.

In fact, the defence of state terrorism unified the Armed Forces. During the military government the tension between them had been evident – especially between Massera's Navy and Videla's Army leadership. Horizontal divides had appeared. These divisions, based on ideological and professional differences, cut across hierarchical lines of authority. Ideological differences had emerged in reference to Martínez de Hoz's economic strategy, which was resisted not only by former President Viola but also by a considerable number of low-ranking officials. The professional differences concerned the management of the Malvinas war. Those low-ranking officials who did not approve Martínez de Hoz's plan were the same ones who went to the Malvinas war and later criticised the management by generals in their Buenos Aires offices. Despite these differences, the Armed Forces were united in their defence of state terrorism.

Alfonsín misunderstood the importance that the Armed Forces attached to their struggle against the guerrillas.

The second failure was Alfonsín's attempt to set in motion the juridical applicability of the three levels of responsibility. Senator Sapag modified Alfonsín's proposals. Sapag's modification undermined the concept of 'due obedience' since, in fact, most of the actions under the implementation of state terrorism had been aberrant and atrocious acts.

Alfonsín's main objective was that once the *Consejo Supremo* had 'cleansed' the Armed Forces, the government would apply the concept of 'due obedience' to the rest of the officials. However, the *Consejo Supremo* and Senator Sapag's modification aborted Alfonsín's plan.

As noted earlier, these two failures were to have an influence in subsequent years. At the very beginning of the democratic government the Armed Forces were discredited. Information on concentration camps, torture, assassinations and abduction of children swamped the first period of the democratic government. Also, the defeat in the Malvinas campaign had discredited the Armed Forces as a military force. Eighteen-year-old soldiers had died in the war while the military hierarchy sat in its Buenos Aires offices. These two consequences of the military dictatorship would exacerbate the anger felt towards the Armed Forces. Indeed, under the democratic government, public opinion required not only the acknowledgement and disclosure of the truth about the 'dirty war' but also the punishment of those who both ordered and committed the acts.

Alfonsín could no longer control his policies towards the Armed Forces. Pion-Berlin (1997, p. 102) explains Alfonsín's situation:

Judicial autonomy cut both ways. On the one hand, the judiciary's unwavering resistance to any form of intimidation, most especially from the military itself, made possible the completion of the trials against the ex-commanders and handed Alfonsín a major political victory. The judicial branch had done its work, unfettered by forces outside of it. The human rights organisations helped, providing some of the most critically damaging evidence needed to build a case against the nine defendants. On the other hand, a similar spirit of judicial independence expressed toward the executive branch later meant a loss of presidential control once Alfonsín began to search for legal closure. The judges would not be moved. Once having unearthed evidence of

criminality at lower levels of the military hierarchy, they were prepared
to let justice run its course. Alfonsín left the courts alone and yet always
retained an undiminished faith that they would interpret the law to his
liking. When they did not, he resorted to subterfuge (i.e. the
instructions to military courts) to spare himself the ordeal of
confronting the justices head-on.

The combination of the Judiciary's attitude with the pressure from
human rights organisations put Alfonsín in a very difficult situation
which dramatically influenced the following years.

COEXISTENCE WITH THE *SINDICALISMO PERONISTA*

The Radical Government's Objectives

From 1983 to 1985, Alfonsín's government applied two different
strategies towards the trade unions. At the beginning Alfonsín's
administration adopted a policy of confrontation. This failed, due to
a number of factors. First, within the government there were two
different approaches towards trade unionism. On the one hand, a
combative line with the objective of undermining the power of the
trade unions, taking advantage of Peronism's recent electoral defeat
(Beliz, 1988, p. 169). This sector wanted to *desperonizar* the trade
unions, breaking down their historical alliance with Peronism. The
desperonización, therefore, involved the political restructuring of the
trade unions. However, it was also understood as the way through
which Radicalism could find a powerful place in the trades union
movement (Gaudio and Thompson, 1990, p. 38). If this was the
long-term objective, in the short term to *desperonizar* meant to
break down the historical alliance between the trades union
movement and Peronism, which gave the former a powerful place in
the Argentinian political process.

On the other hand, there was a moderate line, within the Radical
party, which argued that the government should consolidate
alliances with the trade unions and business organisations in order to
secure future achievements (Beliz, 1988, p. 169). A consequence of
the struggle between these two approaches was that the government
policy itself was not unified and its decision making process lacked
coherence. Alfonsín, himself, on many occasions changed his

position. At the beginning of his term in office, he supported the combative line. Arguing that unionists in charge of the main trade unions were those who had confronted Illia's government, Alfonsín believed that they no longer represented the workers (Gaudio and Thompson, 1990, p. 17). He argued that the trades union movement was totalitarian (Abós, 1984, p. 101). In this sense, he attempted to 'democratise' the trades union movement. By 'democratise', the government was trying to modify a historical tendency of the trade union elections, namely the predominance of presenting only one candidate for the elections. In other words, there was only one candidate for each union and therefore no opposition (Gaudio and Thompson, 1990, p. 36). Based on this assessment, Alfonsín argued that the trade unionists did not represent the workers (Gaudio and Thompson, 1990, p. 17). Alfonsín wanted to end this practice, giving full participation to minorities.

Alfonsín favoured the establishment of a social agreement among the government, the trade unions and the business organisations (Gaudio and Thompson, 1990, p. 20). However, before achieving it, the trades union movement, it was argued, should be 'democratised'. Alfonsín explained his objectives towards the 'democratisation' of the trade unions, arguing that 'the new trade union must be organised from the bottom to the top ... It has to be organised by the genuine expression of the workers without any influence from the state, the political parties or the business organisations; its electoral procedures must be controlled by the Judiciary, assuring the participation of minorities ...' (*Discursos Presidenciales*, 1983, p. 17). In this sense, the Radical government promoted the abolition of the legislation of the last military dictatorship on the trades union movement and its replacement by new legislation to guarantee the participation of minorities and secure independence from any one political party. It also proposed that the *Obras Sociales* (Health Service Funds) would be independent from the trade unions and would be incorporated into a National Health Plan (*Plataforma Electoral Nacional de la Unión Cívica Radical*, 1983, p. 24).

Regarding the new legislation for electoral procedures, the Radical government's proposal was based on the non-recognition of the unionists who had been elected under the military dictatorship. Therefore, the first elections would be controlled by the government. The Radical government argued that, as the current unionists did not represent the workers, they could not be relied upon to control the elections (Gaudio and Thompson, 1990, p. 52). The objective of this strategy was essentially to control the trade union elections and to undermine the power of the unionists by connecting them with the military dictatorship. It was a tool for weakening the role of Peronism within the trades union movement, and, therefore, politically to demobilise the workers. However, the Radical government failed in this attempt.

Regarding wage policy, Alfonsín's administration maintained the decree-law of the last dictatorship which empowered the government to determine the level of wages. In order to match changes in the inflation rate the Radical administration decided to increase wage rates every three months (Gaudio and Thompson, 1990, p. 46). The trade unions were demanding the establishment of free collective bargaining; the government argued that the economic situation was too unstable to establish this demand since this would undermine government control of wage and price increases (Gaudio and Thompson, 1990, p. 133). After the attempt to 'democratise' the trade unions failed, the discussion between the government and the trade unions focused on the level of wages and the establishment of free collective bargaining.

The analysis of Alfonsín's government shows that, despite the modifications undergone by the labour movement under the military dictatorship, the trade unions proved to be still quite powerful. Indeed, the democratic government could not control the more combative sections of the trades union movement.

The Trade Unions' Position

Under the military dictatorship, the trades union movement had been modified. As explained above, the economic structural reform which led to the dismantling of the industrial sector and the *desasalarización*, *terciarización* and *pauperización* of the working class, directly hit the power of the trades union movement. Moreover, the implementation of state terrorism provoked the disappearance of the most combative sector of unionists (Gaudio and Thompson, 1990, p. 26). Finally, the peak organisation, the CGT, was divided into two sectors the *CGT–Brasil* which confronted the military dictatorship and the *CGT–Azopardo* which negotiated with the military government. One of the main objectives of both CGTs was the unification of the organisation.

Under the democratic government the trades union movement position was represented by 'unified' CGT policies. The CGT's priorities were to improve real wages, to reactivate the economy, and to modify the labour legislation enacted by the military dictatorship, specifically to establish free collective bargaining (*La Voz*, 26.1.1984, p. 5). The CGT argued that democracy would be established only after an improvement in real wages and the achievement of full employment (*Clarín*, 3.2.1984, p. 3).

The first confrontation with the Radical government was focused on the new legislation for trade union elections. The CGT argued that the legislation was a tool to institutionalise state intervention in the internal matters of the trade unions. The CGT proved to be still able to block the government strategy through its connections with Senators from the Peronist party and other provincial parties. After this confrontation, the main discussion focused on wage increases and the legislation for free collective bargaining.

The confrontation policy of the trades union movement was mainly based on the deterioration of the workers' economic situation. It pushed for the establishment of free collective bargaining, and the abolition of the military dictatorship laws. Beyond these objectives, the CGT was trying to regain the historical power of the trades union movement. Thirteen general strikes and thousands of official labour conflicts were the means through which the union movement confronted the democratic government. However, the most significant event was the support given to the Radical government by the unions at the first military rebellion. Indeed, this was the first time that the trades union movement supported a non-Peronist democratic government threatened by the Armed Forces.

Although the trade unions proved to be powerful, achieving their most important objectives, they could not modify the government's overall economic strategy, and thus, they could not achieve an improvement in the workers' situation. An analysis of the first two years of confrontation between the trade unions and the Radical government follows.

From Confrontation to Concertación

In order to deal with the *sindicalismo Peronista*, Alfonsín appointed Antonio Mucci of the graphic workers as Minister of Labour. Mucci belonged to the combative wing of the Radical party whose objective was to *desperonizar* the trades union movement (Beliz, 1988, p. 169). One week after taking office Alfonsín sent his proposals for trade union elections to the Congress (*Clarín*, 21.12.1983, p. 2). The main objective was to 'democratise' the trade unions through a call for elections under a special regime; this applied to trade unions that were still subject to government intervention or under the direction of a 'normalising delegate' (*delegado normalizador*). Under the proposal, the Labour Minister would appoint a delegate who would form a *Junta Fiscalizadora* (Regulation Board) with representatives from all the different leadership teams. The *Junta* would control the delegate who, in order to call for elections, would assume the attributes of the General Secretary of each of the trade unions. The proposal also provided for the presence in the commissions of electoral minorities, the reduction of the term of office, the control of Electoral Justice and the implementation of secret, direct and compulsory voting (*Clarín*, 19.12.1983, p. 2).

Trade unionists were unified in defending their role against Alfonsín's proposal: in January 1984, the leaders of both *CGT–Brasil* and *CGT–Azopardo* agreed on the reunification of the CGT and the appointment of four co-secretaries: Saúl Ubaldini of the beer workers and Osvaldo Borda representing the rubber industry from *CGT–Brasil*, and Jorge Triaca of the plastic workers and Antonio Baldassini the post-office workers from *CGT–Azopardo* (*Clarín*, 11.1.1984, p. 9). They rejected the role of the government in designating a delegate to conduct the electoral process. Ubaldini argued that Alfonsín's proposal was an attempt to legalise government intervention in the trades union movement (*Clarín* 3.2.1984, p. 12).

Indeed, the democratic government, owing to its non-recognition of the trade unions authorities, attempted to intervene in the electoral procedures by appointing a delegate to control the elections. Although the government stated that this intervention was only for the first round of elections, its main objective was to *desperonizar* the trades union movement. In this sense, the unionists, arguing for the independence of the movement, were also trying to block the *desperonización*. The Radical government, behind the slogan of 'democratising' the unions, was attempting to break down union connections with Peronism, which was seen as a tool to achieve the political demobilisation of the workers. In this regard, the Radical government intended to restructure social relations by modifying the historically powerful role of the unions in the political scenario and their connections with Peronism.

However, the government's proposal was rejected by the Senate. Senator Elías Sapag argued that only the workers had the right to decide on the internal organisation of the trade unions (*Clarín*, 15.3.1984, p. 3).[7] The opposition of Sapag's party determined that the law was rejected.

After the failure of this first attempt to increase influence over the trade unions, the government attempted to achieve a *concertación social* (social agreement), the first step towards which was the appointment of Juan Manuel Casella as Minister of Labour (Gaudio and Thompson, 1990, p. 58).[8] The *concertación social* attempted a three-sided accord among labour organisations, business organisations and the government to attack inflation and change the economic situation. In addition, a new post was created, a presidential delegate responsible for 'normalising' the trades union movement. Hugo Barrionuevo, a trade unionist, was appointed to the new position. His main task was to begin a new round of negotiations with the trade unionists to organise elections. (Gaudio and Thompson, 1990, p. 55). Alfonsín had moved towards the more pro-unionist sector of the Radical party. He was now trying to achieve an agreement with the trade unions after being unable to undermine their political power. As said, the appointment of Juan Manuel Casella was the first sign of Alfonsín's new approach to the trade unions.

As the CGT had won the first confrontation with the government, now it began to demand the establishment of free collective bargaining as one of its most important objectives. The government was first arguing that free collective bargaining would be established after the trade union elections (Gaudio and Thompson, 1990, p. 53). After the elections, the democratic government argued that the economic situation made free collective bargaining very risky, in the sense that the government would lose its control over wage and price increases, which could provoke increases in the inflation rate (Gaudio and Thompson, 1990, p. 133). In this sense, the government implied that inflation derived only from wage increases. Later, however, the government would argue that the main cause of inflation was the high fiscal deficit.

Nevertheless, the economic situation was always employed as an excuse to postpone the sanctioning of free collective bargaining legislation.

The main discussion in the *concertación* framework focused on wage increases and, as shown below, the government took the final decision on the size of increases without taking into account the CGT's demands. But, by trying to agree with the CGT within the framework of the *concertación*, the government attempted to prevent labour conflict. While the CGT was joining the *concertación*, it could not oppose the government's economic strategy outside this framework. Indeed, the CGT left the *concertación* during the two general strikes, only to rejoin the process at a later date. The *concertación* was, in this sense, a means of controlling the opposition of the trades union movement.

In the beginning the *concertación* attempt focused on the electoral system for the trades union movement. One of its first outcomes was a proposal for electoral procedures, agreed between the trade unions and the government. This differed from Alfonsín's proposal in that the existing authorities – precisely those that Alfonsín did not consider representative of the workers – would call for elections. In July, the new proposal was passed by the Congress (*Clarín*, 5.7.1983, p. 7).

In August, the first meeting of the *concertación* attempt was held at the Home Affairs Ministry. Representatives of the CGT, other workers' organisations,[9] and employers' organisations discussed the agenda with the Ministers of Economy, Health, Labour and Home Affairs. The objective of the government move was to avoid a struggle in the distribution of wealth, to prevent inflation, to increase wages, and to attain economic growth (*Clarín*, 3.8.1984, p. 3).

The government, despite the *concertación*, decided to increase the statutory minimum wage (*salario mínimo vital*),[10] the conventional base wage for collective bargaining which would include a bonus (for attendance, seniority, productivity), and general wage levels by 18 per cent. The CGT accepted the increase but demanded that the bonus should be over and above the minimum wage arguing that it was an incentive for the workers and a supplement to the basic wage (Gaudio and Thompson, 1990, p. 97). As the government refused to grant this demand, the CGT decided to call a general strike for 3 September and to leave the *concertación* process (*Clarín*, 30.8.1984,

p. 2). By this time, the government had signed its first 'letter of intent' with the IMF. In this, the government committed itself to 'continue to decree wage adjustments for the public and private sector on a monthly basis, with catch-up increases from time to time' (Stiles, 1987, p. 70). This clause was crucial since it represented Alfonsín's commitment to maintain the buying power of the workers (*Clarín*, 26.9.1984, p. 2). However, despite Alfonsín's commitment, purchasing power fell between 1984 and 1985: from a base index of 100 in 1986 for the private sector, purchasing power went from 101.62 in 1984 to 98.50 in 1985, while for the public sector it went from 105.29 to 100.17, over the same period (Banco Central de la República Argentina, 1992, Fig. II.8).

According to CGT calculations, adherence to the first general strike was 87 per cent, 60–65 per cent according to the government (*La Nación*, 4.9.1984, p. 1). After the September general strike the CGT returned to negotiate with the government within the framework of the *concertación* process (*La Nación*, 6.9.1984, p. 1). As a condition for its return, the CGT demanded that it be the only workers' organisation involved in the *concertación* attempt (Gaudio and Thompson, 1990, p. 105). The government accepted this condition, and thus the *Grupo de los 20* left the *concertación* attempt.

In October, Casella resigned his position as Labour Minister[11] and Hugo Barrionuevo was named by Alfonsín as his successor (Gaudio and Thompson, 1990, p. 107). Barrionuevo, a militant of the *Grupo de los 20*, had previously been appointed as the presidential delegate to agree with the trade unions the organisation of the electoral process.

Owing to its failure to come to an agreement with the government, in January 1985 the CGT once again left the *concertación* process. It demanded the establishment of free collective bargaining, the reactivation of the economy, the restitution of the *Obras Sociales* to the trade unions, and *concertación* without the 'interference of international capital' (referring to the negotiations with the IMF) (*Clarín* 7.1.1985, p. 3). After a meeting with Alfonsín who then took the compromise decision to reduce the fiscal deficit and to clamp down on tax evasion, the CGT rejoined the *concertación* process (Gaudio and Thompson, 1990, p. 109). The government presented a report announcing its economic strategy for the next five years, the main objectives being to improve investment in order to increase exports, and to transform the productive basis of the country focusing efforts on investment and exports (*La Nación*, 14.1.1985, p. 8).

In February, the so-called *Grupo de los Once* (Group of 11),[12] presented to the government its proposal for a social agreement and an economic development programme. The main difference from the government report was that the *Grupo de los Once* referred to the necessity of an economic adjustment. The report proposed an economic adjustment in order to attain growth, to prevent inflation, to maintain real wages, to reduce public expenditure and to achieve full employment (*Clarín*, 9.2.1985, p. 2). The organisations demanded the reduction of the fiscal deficit, the control of tax evasion, the promotion of public and private investment, the reduced participation of the state in the economy and the promotion of exports. They also demanded steady economic growth as the guarantee to maintain real wages. Regarding the external debt, they stated that the effort to service the debt should be balanced by negotiations to postpone interest payments (*Clarín*, 9.2.1985, p. 2). Another difference between this plan and the government's economic policy was that the latter was promoting exports without increasing domestic demand while the *Grupo* emphasised the need to expand domestic demand. These elements were designed to mainly benefit the working class, and the industrial and agricultural sectors. However, the government argued that such a plan, in a context of high inflation, would simply increase the inflation rate even more (*Clarín*, 10.2.1985, p. 15).

The temporary coalition of the *Grupo de los Once* was a quite significant effort from the CGT and the employers' organisations to achieve an agreement on economic policy. However, by this time the government had short-term troubles: in January, because of an inflation rate of 25 per cent, the IMF considered that the September 1984 agreement had been broken (Machinea, 1990, Table II.2). The government was confronting both an increasing inflation rate and a new round of negotiations with the Fund. Moreover, because of his inability to prevent rising inflation, Bernardo Grinspun, Alfonsín's first Economics Minister, resigned (*Clarín*, 19.2.1985, p. 14). Juan Vital Sourrouille, the new Economics Minister, began to prepare the ground for the *Austral* plan.

Under Grinspun's strategy, from a base index of 100 in 1980, the median wage index was 100.5 in 1983 and 127.1 in 1984 (Economic Commission for Latin America and the Caribbean, 1987, p. 17).

However, the Consumer Price Index (CPI) was 343.8 in 1983 and 626.7 in 1984 (IMF, 1988, p. 119). Therefore, purchasing power in 1984 was only 68 per cent of the 1983 level. As Grinspun's economic policy could not prevent the rise of inflation, the periodic wage increases it sanctioned did not improve the workers' situation.

In April 1985, the Labour Minister announced his decision to increase wages by 90 per cent of the previous month's inflation starting from May.[13] This measure represented a further decrease in workers' purchasing power and as a response to it, the CGT approved a 'plan of action' (*Plan de Lucha*), comprising social demonstrations between 30 April and 17 May in Rosario, Tucumán, Córdoba, Neuquén and Mendoza, to be followed by a general strike on 23 May with a social demonstration at *Plaza de Mayo* (*Latin America Weekly Report*, 3.5.1985, p. 10).

On 23 May the general strike, together with the social mobilisation at *Plaza de Mayo*, ended the first stage of the CGT's *Plan de Lucha*. This strike had total adherence in the industrial and tertiary sectors (Fraga, 1991, p. 25). It also had the support of the Argentinian Industrial Union (UIA), the Argentinian Rural Society (SRA), the Construction Chamber, and human rights organisations (Gaudio and Thompson, 1990, p. 118). In his speech, Ubaldini argued that if the government was unable to modify its economic policy, it must go (*La Nación*, 24.5.1985, p. 1). After the *Plaza de Mayo* demonstration, the CGT rejoined the negotiations with the government to press for a change of economic strategy and to discuss the *Grupo de los Once* proposal (*Clarín*, 3.6.1985, p. 2). However, only a few weeks later, the CGT demanded a 50 per cent wage increase, and once again left the *concertación* (*Clarín*, 3.6.1985, p. 2).

With the launching of the *Austral* plan, the government destroyed its own *concertación* strategy.

Failure of the Concertación *Strategy*

The Radical government's objective to politically demobilise the trades union movement failed. The trade unions proved to be powerful enough to continue blocking the *desperonización* process which forced the government into *concertación*. The *concertación* attempt was defeated not only by the inability of the government to control the trade unions but also by the aggravation of the economic situation.

When the *Grupo de los Once* presented its economic proposal, the government did not even discuss it because, by this time, Grinspun had been replaced by Juan Sourrouille who was planning a *heterodox* economic programme. This signified the government's abandonment of *concertación*. Discussing the *Grupo de los Once* proposal could have achieved an agreement between the government and *los Once*, which could have given the necessary domestic support for the 1985 economic reform. However, the government rejected such agreement because it had already decided on a solution to the 'external debt dilemma'. The improvement of investment in order to increase exports, one of the objectives of the government's proposal, was necessary to pay the interest on the debt (the proceeds from exports being the main source of revenue). Thus, in the dilemma – to pay or not to pay the debt – the government had already decided to service the debt. For the Radical government non-payment was the greater evil, since it would have put the whole democratisation process at risk. This meant that the *disciplinamiento social* started by the military dictatorship was not going to be reversed.

Regarding the rejection of the *Grupo de los Once* proposal, the economic team emphasised the significance of the 'surprise element' in the launching of the *Plan Austral*.[14] However, the 'surprise element' was no more essential than winning domestic support for the reform. The government would, later, be widely criticised for its authoritarian way of applying the economic reform (*Clarín*, 16.6.1985, pp. 4–5). At least some pillars of the 1985 economic reform and the *Grupo de los Once* proposal could have been discussed in order to try to obtain domestic support. The government, however, preferred to keep the economic reform secret, arguing that a price and wage 'freeze' could not be announced since it would, of course, be pre-empted by large price rises before the imminent 'freeze'. Thus, instead of being a means to reach a social agreement for the launching of the 1985 economic reform, the *concertación* was merely the framework within which the government and the trade unions fought over the level of wage increases.

In order to understand the government's attitude towards both the *concertación* attempt and the *Grupo de los Once* proposal, one must look at the government's decision regarding the 'external debt dilemma'. When Grinspun's economic strategy failed, the government found itself under pressure from international creditors and Argentinian public opinion. While the former demanded the payment of the external debt, the latter required economic growth. Indeed, by this time, the international creditors were threatening a *cesación de pagos* – suspension of payments – while Argentinian public opinion was unhappy with an annual inflation rate of 626.7 per cent for the first year of the democratic government (Fanelli *et al.*, 1990, Table 20) and a modest 2.2 per cent growth rate, GDP was still below its 1980 level (Fanelli *et al.*, 1990, Table 1). Payment of the debt and the achievement of economic growth were clearly incompatible. The government took a decision which was an ambiguous path between the two extremes of the 'external debt dilemma'. The *Austral* plan was a *heterodox* strategy – as opposed to orthodox IMF plans – through which the debt would be partially repaid without implementing harsh economic adjustment. But, the government did not clearly communicate the 'external debt constraint' – that is, the incompatibility between paying the debt and achieving economic growth. Hence, while the CGT was demanding economic growth, the government was trying to negotiate the *degree* of adjustment with its international creditors. The government was happy with what it had achieved: the *Austral* plan was an alternative programme to orthodox IMF plans. The CGT was unhappy with the government's strategy: the *Austral* plan was not an economic growth strategy. The *concertación* attempt failed due to the government's unilateral decision over the 'external debt dilemma'. The government's decision, in not according growth full priority, served to deepen the effects of the dictatorship *disciplinamiento social.*

Thus, the Radical government could neither control the political power of the trade unions nor avoid implementing an economic adjustment. The adjustment required by the IMF exacerbated the confrontation with the trade unions but could not ultimately be resisted by the Radical government. The section that follows analyses why this was so.

THE ECONOMY: RESISTING THE INTERNATIONAL MONETARY FUND

External Debt: the Power of International Creditors over a New Democracy

Latin America, in the 1980s, has seen the development of two contradictory processes. On the one hand, the military dictatorships began to fall. On the other, from 1982, the external debt crisis emerged. Much has been said and written about these two processes.[15] With the benefit of hindsight, it can be stated that while external debt clearly limited economic policy choices, it did not reverse the process of democratisation. The international creditors – namely the IMF, the commercial banks,[16] the World Bank – and the US government became crucial actors in the economic policy making process. In Dornbusch's (1990, p. 322) words 'today no Latin American government undertakes significant economic change without checking first in Washington'. Alfonsín's *Austral* plan was mooted in IMF circles before it was discussed even by the Radical Party itself.[17]

The 1980s were labelled the 'lost decade', since Latin American countries had to deal with both a deep internal economic crisis and the external debt. In 1989 the Economic Commission for Latin America and the Caribbean (CEPAL, 1989, Table 9.1) estimated that per capita output in the 1980s in the region as a whole declined by almost 10 per cent, following increases of almost 40 per cent in the 1970s and 30 per cent throughout the 1960s.

Despite their internal crisis and the differences between them, Latin American countries were compelled to apply IMF adjustment plans in order to deal with the internal crisis in such a way as to allow them to pay the external debt. The dilemma was either to pay the debt or to be 'let out' of the international financial system. It was not debt repayment *or* democracy – as most democratic politicians believed, most notably Alan García and Raúl Alfonsín – but rather debt repayment *and* democracy (Drake, 1989, p. 53). Indeed, while foreign governments (mainly that of the US) (Canitrot, 1991, p. 129) supported democracy they also demanded debt repayment. There was no other choice for a liberal democratic state than to negotiate with the IMF. Although the new democracies made efforts to avoid the IMF's plans, eventually all of them were obliged to accept IMF conditions.[18]

The so-called 'Washington consensus' was the set of policies that was 'suggested' as a uniform solution for all Latin American countries, despite the considerable differences between them. The 'Washington consensus' has been defined as macroeconomic prudence, outward orientation and domestic liberalisation (Williamson, 1990, p. 1). 'Washington' was understood as the IMF, World Bank, US executive branch, the Inter-American Development ment Bank, those members of the US Congress interested in Latin American politics and the think tanks concerned with economic policy (Williamson, 1990, p. 1). The main policy instruments of the 'consensus' were defined as fiscal discipline and the reduction of some public expenditures such as subsidies, tax reform, market-determined interest rates, competitive exchange rate, import liberalisation, promotion of foreign direct investment, privatisation, deregulation and new laws on property rights.[19] However, the so-called 'Washington consensus' did not take into account either the differences among Latin American economies or the domestic consequences of the external debt services.

The main criticism of this 'consensus' was that, in the face of spiralling interest payments on the debt, public expenditure could not easily be cut. This forced the new democratic governments to look for reductions in social expenditure, cutting back their already minimal 'welfare states' (Meller, 1990, p. 33).

Moreover, Latin American countries transferred to the developed countries a net flow of resources amounting to US$203 billion between 1982 and 1989 (Iglesias, 1990, p. 346). This amount was nearly half of the region's total debt. The 'consensus' did not take into account these transfers and how they constrained the possibilities for Latin American economies to grow. On the contrary, while the 'Washington consensus' was being suggested as the solution for Latin America, periodical increases in interest rates raised interest payments on the debt. Latin American countries could do nothing to prevent the spiral.

Likewise, a decline by 20 per cent in the terms of trade during the 1980s was, by 1989, costing Latin America an additional US$30 billion per year (Iglesias, 1990, p. 346). Once again, Latin America failed to control this situation.

The philosophy behind the 'Washington consensus' was that internal structural reforms were necessary to stabilise Latin American economies and enable them to gradually pay off the external debt. However, what this strategy ignored was the detrimental effect such programmes would have on economic growth in Latin America. In the process of implementing the measures, which would permit a reduction in the external debt liability, the new democratic governments of Latin America provoked deep economic crisis.

The experiences of adjustment showed that the 'Washington consensus', in promoting stabilisation, restricted rather than fostered economic growth. This was notably the case in Bolivia where the New Political Economy[20] (considered as an orthodox adjustment programme), applied in 1985 by Paz Estenssoro, stabilised the economy but also produced a deep economic recession.[21] Argentina is the best example of a government which, recognising the negative effects of the IMF plan, tried to avoid full implementation of the latter.

Indeed, as explained in more detail below, in the first years of the democratic government, Argentina tried to treat the external debt as a 'political issue' and to negotiate with the creditor governments and the commercial banks without committing itself to an agreement with the IMF. The debt was a 'political issue' in two respects. First, Argentina argued, at the Quito Conference in January 1984, that the debt had a 'legitimate' and an 'illegitimate' component. It stated that '40 to 50 per cent of the private debt is fictitious, yet the state assumed responsibility for it, indiscriminately, in late 1982' (*Latin America Weekly Report*, 13.1.1984, p. 2). Alfonsín's government explained the 'illegitimate' side of the debt, arguing that between mid-1980 and March 1981

> local takers covered their positions by purchasing cheap foreign exchange on the free market while keeping their commitment registered (with the Central Bank), which enabled them to repatriate capital ... Through this undeclared outflow of foreign exchange they cancelled 40 per cent to 50 per cent of the private external debt-commitments which the state later assumed as its own. (*Latin America Weekly Report*, 13.1.1984, p. 2)

This was the 'illegitimate'[22] side of the external debt, which Argentina felt it was not obliged to pay. Second, the debt was viewed as a 'political issue' since the debt crisis emerged simultaneously with the democratisation process. Alfonsín wrongly believed that the international creditors would be more lenient with a democratic government. He thought that the creditor governments would show their support for democracy by not pressing for repayment of the debt. This would allow Argentina to avoid an IMF negotiation which would impose an economic adjustment. However, after one year in office, the government signed its first letter of intent with the IMF. The debt was not regarded by the IMF as a 'political issue'. Neither the 'illegitimate' side nor the significance of democracy were considered by international creditors.

For the incoming democratic government, the burden of a US$45.069 million[23] external debt became the most serious legacy of the military dictatorship. The interest payments created a vicious circle. In order to service the interest payments, the government had to take away from the economy some resources, while asking Argentinian society to adjust according to the IMF plan. However, after seven years of military dictatorship, most of the population were expecting concrete and short-term benefits from democracy. This was notably the case with the working class, which had suffered most under the dictatorship, with a 17 per cent decline in real industrial wages from 1971 to 1981 (Gerchunoff and Dieguez, 1984, p. 25). Therefore, in such a context, the democratic government had to deal with both the interest payments of external debt and the social demands of the working class. If it did not pay and did not apply the economic adjustment, it had to confront the international creditors. If it did pay and did apply the adjustment, it would have to confront the opposition of the trade unions.

Of course, the money which would be reused to service the debt would use up resources which could otherwise be invested in improving the productive capacity of the Argentinian economy. Such investment was essential since the original debt taken out by the military dictatorship had not been used to undertake structural improvements in the Argentinian economy. Rather it had been used for speculation on the financial market or had been transferred abroad through the process of capital flight (Crystal, 1994). Moreover, the private debt, which represented approximately 30 per cent of the total debt (see Table 7), had been 'nationalised' during the last period of the dictatorship, transferring liability to Argentinian citizens. With the 'nationalisation', the debt became a fiscal problem by way of an increase in the fiscal deficit. Taken together, these problems rendered the incoming democratic government incapable of servicing the debt. However, a moratorium would worsen the situation, since it would provoke the closure of any financial aid to Argentina. It was a vicious circle.

Facing this dilemma, the democratic government decided that servicing the debt would be more beneficial than declaring a unilateral moratorium. The attempts to organise a debtors' club among the Latin American countries failed and each country started a negotiation process with the IMF. Alfonsín was influenced by the example of Peru, where Alan García's plan for paying only 10 per cent of export revenues provoked the international creditors and the US government to withdraw financial aid even though Peru's poverty together with the threat of *Sendero Luminoso* ('Shining Path' guerillas) and of the drugs dealers put the democratisation process at risk.[24]

Despite the 1982 Malvinas war, Argentina was still reliant on its commercial relations with European countries. Although Alfonsín's electoral victory was welcomed by France and Spain, this did not lead to an improvement in economic relations.[25] The protectionist measures applied by the European Community to its agricultural products damaged trade between Europe and Argentina. Owing to the protectionist measures and the attitude of the European countries towards Argentina after the war, Alfonsín's administration tried to improve relations with Europe instead of further harming the already damaged relationship (Russell, 1988). To service the debt became crucial in order to maintain Europe's support.

The relationship with the US government was also damaged because of the war and, once again, in order to improve this relationship, Alfonsín felt obliged to pay the external debt. Moreover, the US Reagan administration, despite having welcomed the return to democracy, was quite clear that it regarded negotiation with the IMF as a prerequisite to starting negotiations with the commercial banks and the debtor countries.[26]

In order to rebuild Argentina's international relations, Alfonsín's government decided not only to pay the debt but also to accept the IMF conditions. The external debt constrained the democratic government since the decision whether or not to pay determined the fate of the government. Both decisions restricted its margin of manoeuvre. Whether it paid or not, its resources were going to be scarce. Argentina possessed few resources to continue servicing its debt. However, this very situation rendered non-payment, and the isolation which this would lead to, hard to contemplate. Either way, non-payment would have put the democratisation process at risk.

As indicated earlier, debt was viewed as a threat to democratisation, however, with the benefit of hindsight, the threat was not to the consolidation process but to the power of the government. Not denying the broader importance of democracy for countries which have suffered military dictatorship for years, it seems that the legacy of the dictatorship had left Alfonsín's government with limited economic policy choices. Thus, the two choices – to pay or not to pay the external debt – both promised serious difficulties.

Furthermore, Alfonsín was not merely faced with the contradictory demands of the IMF for economic stabilisation and domestic pressures for immediate improvements in living standards. He also had to contend with the concerns of Argentina's main economic groups over debt repayment. Owing to the dictatorship's nationalisation of the private debt, resources for the interest payments now had to be found through an adjustment of fiscal policy. This obliged Alfonsín to raise export taxes, a move which would be sharply opposed by Argentina's agricultural conglomerates. These economic groups, being internationally oriented, were of course concerned that Argentina not be isolated from the international economic system. However, when Alfonsín shifted the debt liability to fiscal policy, directly hitting these economic groups, with the prospect of higher taxes, the latter became more ambivalent towards government efforts to service the debt.

The Political Side of Inflation

Economically, inflation is understood as a distortion of economic variables. The 'monetarist' approach always assumes the cause of inflation to be excessive monetarist expansion (Goldthorpe, 1978, p. 186). Other schools of monetarism (mainly followers of von Hayek's theories) understood inflation as caused by wage increases due to the pressure from organised labour. However, Goldthorpe's sociological analysis of inflation correctly states that inflation is the 'particular manifestation, within a given historical context, of the social divisions and conflicts which such an economy tends always to generate' (1978, p. 197). Thus, inflation is the monetary expression of the distributional conflict of the society and of the 'on-going changes in social structures and processes' (Goldthorpe, 1978, p. 195). In this sense, Argentina's high inflation was the economic expression of the crisis of the state and its social relations. Peralta-Ramos (1987, p. 40) argues that inflation and the speculative prac-tices associated with it was, historically, the result of 'a particular relation of forces between the main factions of the bourgeoisie, that is, the most powerful sector of industrial, financial and agrarian capital. The systematic confrontation between these sectors for the redistribution of income, and their recurrence to the exercise of speculative practices as a form of making their specific demands known ... gave rise to the uncontrolled development of inflation.'

As the following analyses show, the Radical government explained high inflation in terms of the high fiscal deficit and wage increases. The high fiscal deficit was mainly caused by interest payments on the external debt, tax evasion and state subsidies to the private industrial sector. Therefore, behind the fiscal deficit were Argentina's wealthiest sector and the international creditors. The wage increases themselves – the other economic cause of inflation – represented one aspect of the fight by workers to maintain their purchasing power. In this sense, the workers rather than producing inflation were reacting to it.

Thus, if Goldthorpe's analysis is followed, it can be argued that Argentina's inflation was an expression of its class conflict. As analysed below, the government had greater difficulties reducing the fiscal deficit than preventing high inflation rates. Indeed, the government was able to temporarily control the inflation rate, which was finally unleashed by the expansion of the fiscal deficit.

The political side of inflation shows that in order to prevent high inflation the government should reduce the fiscal deficit by non-payment of the external debt, a tax reform to avoid tax evasion and the suspension of state subsidies to the private sector. That is, to reverse the *disciplinamiento social* of the military dictatorship. As the Radical government did not reverse it, the last years of the democracy saw an exacerbation of the class conflict expressed by a hyper-inflation process. The first government's attempt to stabilise the economy and to resist the IMF is now analysed.

The Radicals' Attempt to Stabilise the Economy and Resist the IMF

When the Radical government took office, the external debt and the concentration of capital were the main features of an economy out of control with an inflation rate of 600 per cent for the last quarter of 1983, a fiscal deficit of 14 per cent of GDP, an external debt of 67 per cent of GDP, and international reserves of US$1 billion while arrears with external creditors amounted to US$3.2 billion (Machinea, 1990, p. 12). The external debt was US$44 billion while capital flight was estimated at US$22.4 billion; hence, the latter accounted for no less than half of the debt (Dornbusch, 1989, p. 8).

Bernardo Grinspun[27] was appointed Minister of Economy and Raúl Prebisch economic adviser. The government defined its economic objectives as the reactivation of the economy, the increase of real wages and the elimination of inflation (*Ambito Financiero*, 2.1.1984, p. 9). Prebisch stated that there were two main problems: inflation, caused by the high fiscal deficit which had to fall from 14 per cent of the GDP to 4 per cent by the end of 1984, and the debt, which he defined as a political problem (*Clarín*, 17.12.1983, p. 8). Regarding the latter, in his first week in office, Grinspun announced that he had requested from Argentina's international creditors a period of six months in which to investigate the total amount of the external debt and to prepare a payment proposal (*Clarín*, 16.12.1983, p. 3).[28] Enrique García Vázquez, President of the Central Bank, stated that this measure was a unilateral moratorium and that the government would distinguish between 'legitimate' and 'illegitimate' debt to decide its payment proposal (Schvarzer, 1986b, p. 39). This 'illegitimate' side of the debt was the capital flight favoured by the exchange rate mechanisms of the military dictatorship. As explained above, the Radical government argued that Argentina did not have to pay this 'illegitimate' external debt.

Turning to the domestic economy, Grinspun presented his plan – *Lineamientos de un programa inmediato de reactivación de la economía, mejora del empleo y los salarios reales y ataque al obstáculo de la inflación* (Outline of an immediate programme for the reactivation of the economy, an improvement of employment and real salaries, and an attack on the obstacle of inflation) – whose main objectives were to achieve, in 1984, an increase in the level of real wages of 6–8 per cent, a reduction in inflation of 50 per cent, an increase in economic growth of 5 per cent, a reduction in the public sector deficit of 10 per cent of GDP, and a reduction in public expenditure and interest rates (*Clarín*, 25.1.1984, p. 12). With respect to the external debt, this report argued that the main problems were the high cost of debt servicing which necessitated a renegotiation of terms. It also stated that Argentina had decided to meet its obligations and, in order to do this, the country 'needed the co-operation' of the creditor country governments since the debt, in its origins and nature, was a political problem (*Clarín*, 25.1.1984, p. 12). As said above, the debt was viewed as a political problem since a significant part of the debt was 'capital flight', and the debt, increased by a military dictatorship, had to be paid by a new democratic government. Therefore, the Radical government demanded the 'co-operation' of the creditor country governments to distinguish the 'illegitimate' side of the debt, and to avoid a deepening of the economic crisis which could put the democratisation process at risk.

As early as January 1984, Alfonsín's policy towards the external debt negotiations became clear. The policy constituted three concurrent strategies. First, the Radical government suspended all payments on the principal of the debt and, consistently, delayed interest payments. Second, the government tried to negotiate the interest payments with the banks and the Paris Club although it had not achieved a prior agreement on the interest payments with the IMF. This was the 'co-operation' demanded from foreign governments; namely, their support for an alternative to the IMF plan. Third, Argentina participated at the Quito Conference held in January 1984 which was an effort to achieve a common front of Latin American debtors. At this conference, Argentina insisted on the distinction between 'legitimate' and 'illegitimate' obligations, and that the negotiations should cover only the former (*Latin America Weekly Report*, 13.1.1984, p. 2).

The Cartagena Consensus of May 1984 – signed by Argentina, Brazil, Colombia and Mexico – was another effort to emphasise the political aspect of the external debt. The Consensus declared that external circumstances had exacerbated the Latin American situation. Of these circumstances, the increase in the US prime rate – the third increase in two months – and the protectionist measures of the US and the European Community were particularly debilitating to the economic situation of the debtor countries (*Clarín*, 27.5.1984, p. 2). The former increased the interest payments while the latter decreased the possibility of export earnings. Regarding the prime rate increase, Alfonsín underlined that the rise over the last two months added over US$600 million to the country's external indebtedness. Thus, Argentina's ability to meet its international obligations were under severe strain. Alfonsín said 'it is as if the (financial) centres had gone mad, but we will not pay usury. It would seem as if the developing countries were being attacked with a neutron bomb in reverse, which would leave men, women and other creatures alive, while destroying the nation's productive apparatus. This madness must be ended once and for all' (*Latin America Weekly Report*, 18.5.1984, p. 2).

The main decisions of the Cartagena Consensus were to pay the external debt and for this payment to proceed on a country-by-country basis (O'Connell, 1988, p. 373). Therefore, Latin America could not establish a unified 'debtor front' to press the international creditors for concessions, at least in the rescheduling of interest payments. The Latin American governments decided to negotiate bilaterally which meant that henceforth they would be competing among themselves. Therefore, the Cartagena Consensus, despite having organised periodical meetings between governments, was not able to co-ordinate the negotiations between the governments and their international creditors. The Latin American governments believed that a negotiation on a country-by-country basis would give them more benefits. This was mainly the position of Mexico and Brazil, which as the largest debtors had a better level of bargaining than Argentina or Uruguay (O'Connell, 1988, p. 373). Thus, the strategy of converting the external debt into a political issue and achieving a common front of Latin American debtors failed.

Alfonsín's second strategy towards the external debt also failed. The main cause of his failure was the refusal of international creditors – the banks, creditor governments and the Paris Club – to begin negotiations without an agreement between Argentina and the IMF having been achieved. The agreement with the IMF meant, principally, that the Fund would control Argentina's economic strategy, imposing an economic adjustment programme which would enable Argentina to service its debt. As explained above, the so-called 'Washington consensus' was an economic strategy to enable the debtor countries to pay the debt. A negotiation without such IMF agreement gave Argentina the opportunity to apply any type of economic strategy, which could risk future interest payments. Control by the IMF assured payment of the debt, and thus, the banks, the creditor governments and the Paris Club refused to begin negotiations with Argentina before it reached an agreement with the Fund.

The Argentinian government's strategy of delaying interest payments and negotiations with the IMF achieved limited objectives. Although in the first eight months the democratic government did not obtain money with which to pay its creditors, it did gain more time to pay its debt. Nevertheless, the main goal of Alfonsín's strategy was that, by delaying interest payments, Argentina could increase its low level of international reserves which went from US$1 billion at the end of 1983 to US$3.5 billion by mid-1984 (*Latin America Weekly Report*, 27.7.1984, p. 5). This gave Argentina a stronger negotiating position with its international creditors since it did not need fresh money in the short term. The government believed that if Argentina did not strengthen its position as far as possible, the attitude of the international creditors would become more implacable (*Clarín*, 26.2.1984, p. 11). In this sense, Alfonsín argued that Argentina would pay the debt 'without accepting recessive recipes, because we (the Radical government) are committed to raising the workers' real wages' (*Latin America Weekly Report*, 13.1.1984, p. 3). This was the main element of the strategy: a tough initial position, realising the need to compromise later. The first negotiations with the banks show the tough early bargaining stance and the subsequent change in Argentina's negotiating stance.

Negotiating with the Banks and the Fund

Argentina had to meet interest payments to the commercial banks every three months. In March and June 1984, last-minute plans were arranged between the government and the banks. These arrangements were made due to financial aid from the governments of Brazil, Colombia, Mexico, Venezuela and the United States; therefore, Argentina did not use its international reserves for these payments.[29] For the fast-approaching deadline of September, the Argentinian government changed its strategy. A round of negotiations with the IMF began in order to avoid the declaration of a *cesación de pagos* (suspension of payments) by the commercial banks, and to reach an agreement with them before September (*Latin America Weekly Report*, 17.8.1984, p. 10). In August 1984, an IMF report announced that Argentina had agreed with the Fund on some objectives to be implemented in a future economic plan (*Clarín*, 12.8.1984, p. 2). This communiqué was intended to introduce more flexibility into the negotiations with the commercial banks regarding the September-deadline interest payments. These interest payments had been refinanced since 1982, however, as a way to press Argentina to accede to an IMF agreement which would oblige it to service its debt, the commercial banks did not refinance them in September, rather they decided to renew these credits daily (Schvarzer, 1986b, p. 45). Argentina, then, paid US$125 million to the banks (*Clarín*, 16.8.1984, p. 2). The banks decided to renew the credits daily since they distrusted Argentina's sudden decision to reach an agreement with the IMF. By this time, it was clear that if Argentina did not begin to service its interest payments, a *cesación de pagos* (suspension of payments) would be declared by the banks. As *The Economist* (4.8.1984, p. 13) put it: 'an agreement (between Argentina and the IMF) now seems possible some time next month, because the alternative for President Alfonsín is economic, followed by political, bankruptcy'. Indeed, an exacerbation of the economic crisis was viewed as a threat to the consolidation of democracy since the crisis would provoke social unrest which had been, historically, the first step towards a military coup. Alfonsín tried to prevent the economic crisis becoming a political crisis. An agreement with the IMF seemed to be the only solution to the economic crisis which would not undermine democracy.

Thus, Alfonsín's initial strategies towards the external debt failed: the Latin American countries did not organise a 'debtor front', the European and the US governments together with the commercial banks imposed an IMF plan to start negotiations with Argentina, and thus, Argentina could no longer maintain its strategy of delaying interest payments. It was then clear that, like Mexico in 1982, Argentina had to start negotiating with the IMF. Alfonsín's government tried to avoid the full implementation of an IMF adjustment programme since, as he stated, the government wanted to improve the workers' real wages. Moreover, as explained above, an IMF orthodox plan gives to the market the role of regulator of the economy. This was contrary to Radical party ideology, which gives this role to the government (Alfonsín, 1992). However, as the attempt to resist the IMF failed, the government had no way out other than to negotiate with the Fund. Despite this, the Radical government did not implement an orthodox IMF plan.

The day of the first general strike, Grinspun affirmed that an agreement with the IMF would be necessary (*Clarín*, 3.9.1984, p. 1). After nine months, the Economics Minister had gone from rejecting the implementation of an IMF plan to reaching an agreement with the Fund. In September 1984, Alfonsín announced in New York that an agreement with the IMF had been reached (*Clarín*, 26.9.1984, p. 1). He also affirmed that the agreement facilitated negotiations with the commercial banks and the Paris Club (*Clarín*, 26.9.1984, p. 1). Alfonsín and his Economics Minister, after nine months in office, had changed their strategy towards the external debt negotiations.

The agreement with the IMF was based on a plan to reduce the rate of inflation – from its 1984 annual level of 1200 per cent to 300 per cent and eventually to 150 per cent – a gradual elimination of price controls, a reduction of the public deficit from 8.1 per cent of GDP to 5.4 per cent by the end of 1985, and an increase in exports (Stiles, 1987, p. 70). However, as early as January 1985, the IMF considered that the agreement had been broken because of the existence of a monthly inflation rate of 25 per cent (Machinea, 1990, Table II.2).

Domestically, Grinspun's economic strategy to prevent inflation had failed. He had assumed a Keynesian strategy, similar to that applied by the Radical government 20 years earlier. His strategy attempted to stimulate demand through an increase in real wages. He tried to prevent inflation through a gradualist approach by setting at 10 per cent the monthly rate of prices and wages adjustment, together with a larger adjustment for public utility rates and the exchange rate (Machinea, 1990, p. 13). As a consequence of these measures, there was an increase in prices, which, together with the indexation of wages on a monthly basis to preserve purchasing power, pushed the inflation rate to a still higher level (Machinea, 1990, p. 13). As Machinea concludes (1990, p. 13) 'within the context of an easy monetary policy and a large fiscal deficit, full indexation resulted in a continuous acceleration of the inflation rate up to September 1984 (27.5 per cent)'. The economic team believed that wage increases and 'cheap' credit would induce a rise in supply through the reactivation of 'idle capacity', and thus, stability and growth would be achieved (Canitrot, 1991, p. 131). However, the strategy failed since it did not take into account the profound modifications of the economy, namely, the concentration of capital, the burden of the external debt, the high levels of inflation, the high fiscal deficit and the powerful role of the financial sector (the so-called *patria financiera* – financial fatherland). Moreover, in the context of global capital, 'Keynesianism in one country' proved not to be a viable solution. Grinspun's plan of implementing 'a tougher monetary policy, together with the attempt to increase public utility rates and to devalue the exchange rate in real terms did not lead to a significant slowdown in the inflation rate and caused instead a sharp drop in economic activity' (Machinea, 1990, p. 14). Under Grinspun's strategy, the annual Consumer Price Index (CPI) was 688 per cent, and the Wholesale Price Index (WPI), 585.0 per cent (CEPAL, 1991). While the annual rate of price increase was 625 per cent in the last quarter of 1983, it reached 1,080 per cent in the third quarter of 1984 (Torre, 1990b, p. 10). Thus, because of his incapacity to prevent increasing inflation rates, in February 1985, Grinspun resigned (*Clarín*, 19.2.1985, p. 14).

New Economics Minister, New Economic Strategy

The new Economics Minister, Juan V. Sourrouille was more an *Alfonsinista* (a follower of Alfonsín) than a Radical member. He was the author of a number of books on Argentina's economy.[30] He was considered by the Radical Party as an outsider and a technocrat. Likewise, most of the men of the economic team were *Alfonsinistas*, notably Adolfo Canitrot, Under-Secretary of Economic Co-ordination, José Luis Machinea, Under-Secretary of Economic Policy, and from August 1986 President of the Central Bank, and Mario Brodershon, President of the *Banco Nacional de Desarrollo – BANADE –* (National Bank of Development). This would, later, cause some disagreements between the Radical party and the economic team. However, initially, due to Alfonsín's powerful leadership and the success of the *Austral* plan, the Radical party, in general terms, supported the economic team.

As Planning Secretary, Sourrouille had presented a report, *Lineamientos de una estrategia de crecimiento económico 1985–1989* (Guides for an economic strategy for growth 1985–1989), whose main objectives were to improve investment in order to increase exports, and to transform the productive basis of the country focusing efforts on investment and exports (*La Nación*, 14.1.1985, p. 8). Sourrouille had recognised the external debt as a *condicionante* (constraint) on Argentina's development (*La Nación*, 14.2.1985, p. 8). According to him, because of this *condicionante*, Argentina had to increase its exports to service its debt. As this would transfer crucial resources, investment was needed to increase exports and bring in foreign currency reserves (*La Nación*, 14.2.1985, p. 8).

As Economics Minister, Sourrouille defined his objectives as the recovery of economic growth and the 'fight against inflation' (*Ambito Financiero*, 1.3.1985, p. 12). He confirmed that wages would be increased monthly by 90 per cent of the past inflation rate, the fiscal deficit would be reduced by controlling public expenditure, and Argentina would pay its external debt obligations (*Ambito Financiero*, 1.3.1985, p. 13). He stated the necessity to reform the tax system and the financial sector. Finally, he pointed out that the domestic market would expand because of the effect on demand from the increase in exports and private investment; if this did not occur, he argued, the domestic market would be hit by inflation and stagnation (*Ambito Financiero*, 1.3.1985, p. 18).[31]

From now on, some measures were taken to prepare the ground for the launching of the *Austral* plan: controls on industrial prices were made more flexible, public utility rates were increased, from April to June the peso was devalued against the dollar at a monthly rate of 34 per cent, and export taxes were increased (Machinea and Fanelli, 1988, p. 124). Nevertheless, the new economic team could not prevent increases in the CPI and the WPI. The former increased to 29 per cent in April before dropping to 25.1 per cent in May, and the WPI increased significantly, reaching 31.5 per cent in April and 31.2 per cent in May (*Ambito Financiero*, 8.1.1987, p. 6).

On 26 April, Alfonsín called for a popular demonstration to support democracy against threats of a new military coup. In his speech, he stated that there was a demand from the working class for wage increases, a demand for organising the economy by an adjustment policy, and a demand for economic growth. He defined this context as one of 'war economy' (*La Nación*, 27.4.1985, p. 12). He focused the economic problem on the high inflation rate and argued that the government would concentrate its efforts on bringing it down. What Alfonsín called 'war economy' would be later defined as the economic reform of 1985: the *Austral* plan.

Despite these 'introductions' to the *Austral* plan, the essential element in 'preparing the ground' for the *heterodox*[32] shock was the negotiations with the IMF and the US government to obtain their support. In April, Sourrouille and Machinea went to the US to present the economic reforms to the IMF.[33] In May, an IMF staff member, Ted Dessa, went to Buenos Aires to meet Alfonsín to find out his decision regarding the implementation of the reforms. Alfonsín confirmed his decision to apply the plan. Sourrouille also explained the reforms to the IMF member who finally confirmed the acceptance of the plan by the Fund (*Clarín*, 16.6.1985, p. 14). This marked a 'U-turn' in the Radical government strategy. Before analysing the new strategy, some conclusions on the first two years and the cause of the economic 'U-turn' are drawn below.

A Changing Perspective: the Relationship with the IMF

After nine months in office, Alfonsín understood the constraints imposed by the international creditors upon his economic policy making process. As his Home Affairs Minister, Antonio Tróccoli, put it: 'Argentina is condemned to twenty five years of constraints' (Schvarzer, 1986b, p. 45).

Although by delaying interest payments Argentina had achieved some goals, it was finally forced to reach an agreement with the Fund owing to pressure from the commercial banks, the Paris Club and the US government. Alfonsín's strategy to avoid an IMF plan had collided with the attitude of foreign governments and commercial banks. Indeed, they denied the possibility of achieving an agreement with Argentina if the country did not have a previous agreement with the Fund. As Victor Ferreyra Aldunate, leader of *Partido Blanco* of Uruguay, put it, 'all European countries have said to us *we will help you as soon as you achieve an agreement with the IMF*. This is true for all the European countries ... there is no alternative to the IMF. However, it is also true that this path *has no way out*'[34] (Schvarzer, 1986b, p. 42). This attitude, together with the pressure from the commercial banks for the interest payments of March, June and September 1984, put Alfonsín's government in crisis. By September, it was clear that Argentina had to pay in order to avoid the declaration of a *cesación de pagos* (suspension of payments) from the banks. Some 'threats' made this risk clearer: Robert McNamara, Secretary of the Treasury of the United States, wondered 'could you imagine what can happen to a President if his government was suddenly unable to import insulin for diabetics?' (Schvarzer, 1986b, p. 48). This was the kind of veiled 'threat' used to persuade

Argentina's government of the 'benefits' of reaching an agreement with the IMF. Indeed, after nine months, Argentina understood its domestic 'benefits': the first agreement with the IMF coincided with the first general strike.

The September 1984 agreement marked the end of the government's strategy of resisting the IMF. Indeed, it was the starting point of the government's decision on the 'external debt dilemma'. The agreement signified that Alfonsín had finally accepted the rules of the IMF. Pressure from international creditors, mainly the commercial banks, showed that Argentina's new democracy had no solution other than to service its external debt. Alfonsín's strategy of resisting the IMF was condemned by the US government, European governments, and – of course – the commercial banks. By September 1984 Argentina was threatened by the commercial banks with the declaration of *cesación de pagos* (suspension of payments). The democratic government could not pursue its strategy of delaying interest payments. The 'external debt constraint' became evident: from now on Grinspun's gradualist approach to the economic crisis and economic growth had to be abandoned.

CONCLUSION

During its first two years in office, the Radical government was unable to resolve the crisis of the Argentinian state. The government could not control the power of the trades union movement. It could not implement its own policies towards human rights violations. And finally, it could not resist an agreement with the IMF which defeated its initial economic strategy.

Grinspun's strategy was an attempt to avoid a 'monetarist' restructuring of the state and its class relations. However, it did not attempt to modify the *disciplinamiento social*, and, in this sense, it could not prevent high inflation rates. As a result, the economic crisis was exacerbated. From now on the government began to be more worried about the economic situation than the political situation. While the first two years were dominated mainly by the 'democratisation' of trade unions, and human rights policies, subsequent years would be dominated by the 1985 economic reform and its failure.

However, regarding the main political objective of the government, that is, the consolidation of democracy, the public judgement of the *Juntas Militares* was the basis for undermining the political power of the Armed Forces. Nevertheless, owing to the exacerbation of the economic crisis, human rights violations would become a secondary issue and therefore the government lost the necessary domestic support to confront the Armed Forces. In this sense, the government would be forced to make concessions in its policy towards human rights.

The economic crisis also strained the relationship with the trades union movement. The government attempted to control the trade unions by different strategies, all of which the trade unions were able to block. This was one of the factors which complicated the 1985 reform which the next chapter analyses.

NOTES

1. In Argentina military service was compulsory at the age of 18. It lasted between 12 and 16 months. Military service consisted of three months of military training and later of any kind of service such as working as a waiter, driver, or secretary.
2. See Table A18 on military expenditure in the Appendix.
3. For more details see Fontana (1984) and (1987), López and Pion-Berlin (1996) and Pion-Berlin (1997).
4. As explained above, this law established an amnesty for the perpetrators of subversive activities and 'excesses' of repression from 25 May 1973 to 17 June 1982 (*Clarín*, 24.9.1983, p. 2).
5. For more details on the Commission's work see its report CONADEP (1986).
6. According to Pion-Berlin (1997, p. 79) 'Sapag had lost two children in the dirty war and wanted to ensure that the due obedience defence [did] not serve as a giant loophole through which offenders could go free'.
7. In the Senate House there were 56 seats, 21 from the Peronist party and the rest divided among the Radical party and provincial parties such as the *Movimiento Popular Neuquino,* the *Pacto Autonomista-Liberal* from Corrientes province, and the *Partido Bloquista de San Juan.* There were 24 votes against Alfonsín's proposal corresponding to the Peronist Senators and three Senators from the *Movimiento Popular Neuquino* led by Senator Elías Sapag (*Clarín*, 15.3.1984, p. 2).
8. The appointment of Juan Manuel Casella, then a Radical Deputy, was viewed by Peronism as a triumph because the new minister belonged to the conciliatory line of the Radical party (Beliz, 1988, p. 169).
9. Mainly the *Grupo de los 20.* The third Minister of Labour of the Radical

government, Hugo Barrionuevo, belonged to this group which could be characterised as close to the *CGT–Azopardo* line. The inclusion of the *Grupo* in the *concertación* was due to the government's argument that the CGT was not representative of the workers.

10. It was the lowest wage a worker could earn and was fixed according to the cost of a basket of goods considered necessary to the monthly consumption of a four-member family. Both, the basket and the wage, were calculated by the National Institute of Statistics and Census (INDEC).

11. Casella resigned in order to return to party politics (Acuña, 1995).

12. The constitution of the *Grupo de los Once* was mainly a consequence of the government's call for the *concertación*. The group became a coalition between employer organisations and trade unions against the political economy of the Radical government. It was formed by the CGT, the *Sociedad Rural Argentina* (Argentinian Rural Society), the *Confederaciones Rurales Argentinas* (Argentinian Rural Confederations), *Confederación Intercooperativa Agropecuaria* (Agrarian Confederation of Co-operatives), the *Unión Industrial Argentina* (Argentinian Industrial Union), the *Cámara de la Construcción* (Construction Chamber), the *Cámara de Comercio* (Chamber of Commerce), *Asociación de Bancos Argentinos* (Argentinian Banks Association), *Cámara de Actividades Mercantiles* (Chamber of Trading Activities), *Unión de Empresas Comerciales Argentinas* (Union of Commercial Organisations) and the *Confederación del Comercio, la Industria y la Producción* (Confederation of Trade, Industry and Production).

13. This meant to exclude the first three months of 1985 when the inflation rate was 25.1 per cent, 20.7 per cent, and 26.5 per cent respectively (Machinea, 1990, Table II.2)

14. Interviews with senior officials from Alfonsín's government, 19.10.1993 and 25.10.1993, Buenos Aires.

15. There is an extensive bibliography on this issue, for instance, Stallings, B. and Kaufman, R. (1989), Bianchi *et al.* (1985), Thorp, R. and Whitehead, L. (1987), Roett, R. (1984), Lessard, D. and Williamson, J. (1987), Williamson (1990) and (1993), Ffrench-Davis *et al.* (1986), Nelson *et al.* (1989), Nelson (1990), Sachs (1989a) and (1989b), Balassa (1986), Remmer (1991), Fanelli *et al.* (1990) Solimano and Serven (1993), Hilt and Pastor Jr. (1993), Haggard and Webb (1993), Linz and Stepan (1996), Morales and McMahon (1996) Edwards (1997), and Haggard and Kaufman (1995) .

16. Argentina's main creditor banks were Manufacturers Hanover, Citicorp, Morgan Guaranty, Chase Manhattan, Continental Illinois, Midland and National Westminster (Branford and Kucinski, 1990, p. 118).

17. Interview with senior official from Alfonsín's government, 19.10.1993, Buenos Aires.

18. For more details see Williamson (1990).

19. This is the set of policies also named as the 'orthodox approach'. Orthodoxy is well defined by Stallings and Kaufman (1989, p. 2) as 'market-oriented approaches ... that emphasise fiscal and monetary restraint, reductions in the size of the state sector, liberalisation of trade restrictions,

and collaboration with creditors'. A heterodox approach is defined as a policy where the state plays a more active role in regulation and investment decisions and more emphasis is placed on distribution and employment (Stallings and Kaufman, 1989, p. 2). For a detailed account of the differences see Nelson *et al.* (1989) and (1990), Kahler (1990) and Haggard and Kaufman (1989).

20. It has to be highlighted here that the New Political Economy implied a substantial debt relief. Paz Estenssoro argued that the economic situation was so severe that a period of complete moratorium on interest payments was required. For more details see Sachs (1988) and (1989a).

21. For more details on the Bolivian case see Williamson (1990), Sánchez de Losada (1985), Stallings and Kaufman (1989), Bianchi *et al.* (1985), Thorp and Whitehead (1987), Roett (1984), Palermo (1990) and Sachs (1988) and (1989a).

22. This 'illegitimate' side of the debt was the capital flight favoured by the exchange rate mechanisms of the military dictatorship. See Crystal (1994), Lessard and Williamson (1987), Pastor (1990), and Dornbusch and De Pablo (1988).

23. Argentinian Central Bank, unpublished data.

24. For the Peruvian case see Schydowlsky (1986), Stepan (1978), Lowenthal (1983), Carbonetto (1987) and Sachs (1990).

25. For an account of Alfonsín's foreign policy at the beginning of his presidential period see Russell (1987), (1988) and (1990), Escudé (1989) and Escudé and González de Oleaga (1996).

26. For more details on the relationship with Reagan's administration see Russell (1987) and Canitrot (1991).

27. Bernardo Grinspun was Trade Secretary under Illia's presidency (*Clarín*, 10.12.1983, p. 3).

28. Lázara (1997, p. 349) states that, at the beginning of its term, the Radical government was unaware of the significance of the external debt problem.

29. For more details on these negotiations see Schvarzer (1985) and (1986b), Stiles (1987), Smith (1989) and (1990), and *Latin America Weekly Report* (9.3.1984) and (6.7.1984).

30. For instance, Mallon and Sourrouille (1975) and Sourrouille, Kosacoff, and Lucángeli (1985).

31. He was proved right, as this did not happen the domestic market was hit by inflation and stagnation.

32. As said above, a heterodox plan relies more on government controls and guidance and less on the market mechanism which is the central characteristic of IMF orthodox plans. For a detailed account of the differences see Nelson *et al.* (1989) and (1990).

33. Interview with senior official from Alfonsín's government, 19.10.1993, Buenos Aires.

34. Italics in original.

4

The Deepening Crisis, 1985–87

From 1983 to 1985, the Radical government saw all its attempts to resolve the crisis fail. The launching of the *Austral* plan marked the beginning of a new strategy. From now on, the economic aspect of the crisis became more important, intensifying as inflation could not be contained. The *Austral* plan was an attempt to resolve the economic aspect of the crisis which would allow the government to resolve its political elements. However, the early failure of the plan frustrated this attempt.

The first military rebellion showed that the crisis would not be resolved, this time, with the seizure of state power by the Armed Forces. Nevertheless, the rebellion showed the constraints of Alfonsín's policies towards human rights violations. He could no longer afford a serious confrontation with the Armed Forces in a context of deepening economic crisis.

Finally, the government attempted to control the trades union movement by dividing it. However, it also failed in this attempt. The trade unions proved to be still powerful enough to block or modify state strategies.

This chapter is divided into four sections. The first section analyses the *Austral* plan and the causes of its failure. It analyses to what extent the Radical government attempted to modify the dictatorship's *disciplinamiento social*. The second section describes the opposition of the trade unions to the *Austral* and the government's attempt to, once more, control the labour movement. This time the Radical government attempted to control the trade unions by dividing them and by including a Peronist unionist in the

Cabinet. The third section deals with the first military rebellion, analysing its causes and consequences. The reasons why the rebellion did not end in a military coup are analysed. Finally, the fourth section concludes by highlighting the reasons why the Radical government, despite having changed its strategy, was unable to resolve the crisis of the state.

THE *AUSTRAL* PLAN

With the IMF's blessing, on 14 June 1985 the President announced the implementation of the *Austral* plan. He stated that the main objective of the economic reform was the 'fight against inflation'. Due to high inflation rates, gradualism was now ineffectual. He presented the plan as a profound reform of Argentina's economy (*Clarín*, 15.6.1985, p. 3). His Economics Minister explained that it rested upon three main pillars. First, a general wage and price freeze was decreed (with the exception of prices in flexible price markets such as meat, fruits and vegetables for which only maximum profit margins were fixed). Wages were increased by 23 per cent before the freeze in order to compensate for the price rises during the first half of the month. The exchange rate parity was set at 0.80 *austral* to 1 US dollar. Interest rates on deposits and loans were reduced from 28 per cent and 30 per cent per month, respectively, to 4 per cent and 6 per cent per month (*Clarín*, 15.6.1985, p. 4).

Second, the plan aimed to reduce the fiscal deficit. The target was to decrease the fiscal deficit from its 1984 level of 12.8 per cent of GDP to 2.5 per cent of GDP by the second half of 1985. This would be attained through increases in the prices of public services, increases in export taxes, improvements in the collection of direct taxes, the implementation of a 'compulsory savings tax' paid by taxpayers in proportion to their income and wealth taxes paid in 1984, and a reduction in the Central Bank deficit due to the fall in nominal interest rates. Likewise, as a result of the fall in the inflation rate, the real value of collected taxes would increase. The fiscal deficit would be financed by external credit; no extra money would be issued to finance it (*Clarín*, 15.6.1985, p. 34).

Third, a new currency and the de-indexation of the economy were applied in order to prevent 'inertial' inflation[1] and the redistribution of wealth as a result of the sudden decrease of the inflation rate. The *austral* was the new currency (1 *austral* = 1000 pesos) and it would be revalued daily against the peso according to a conversion scale (*Clarín*, 15.6.1985, pp. 34–5).

As the *Austral* plan had been previously approved by the IMF and the US government, the reaction of Argentina's international debtors was quite positive. On 22 July the government signed a new letter of intent with the IMF.[2] Argentina would respect the targets of the *Austral* plan and the IMF would issue a US$1.2 billion loan together with one of US$470 million from the Treasury of the United States (*Clarín*, 25.7.1985, p. 3). These two loans were a sign of approval of the plan by the IMF and the US government.

An agreement was also reached with creditor banks concerning the 1984–85 Financial Plan which had started to be negotiated under Grinspun's administration (*Ambito Financiero*, 28.8.1985, p. 1). Argentina would receive a credit of US$2.2 billion in fresh funds, and would pay the arrears on interest payments which had been accumulated from February 1985 (*Ambito Financiero*, 28.8.1985, p. 1). A timetable was agreed for the gradual repayment of matured debts from 1982 to the end of 1985. For the first time since the beginning of the debt crisis, Argentina would be up to date in its interest payments by the end of November 1985 (Stiles, 1987, p. 76). These commitments ensured the necessary external financing and the essential political support from the IMF, the commercial banks, the European governments and the US government to enable the successful launching of the *Austral* plan.

The initial effects of the *Austral* plan were much better than the government expected.[3] The inflation rate for consumer prices fell from 30.5 per cent in June to 6 per cent in July and again to 3 per cent in August; and for wholesale prices from 42 per cent to –0.9 per cent, and to 1.5 per cent, respectively (*Ambito Financiero*, 8.1.1987, p. 6). The fiscal deficit decreased from 8.3 per cent of GDP in the first half of 1985 to 2 per cent in the second half (Machinea, 1990, p. 27). The fiscal revenue rose from 23 per cent of GDP to 28 per cent as a result of the automatic increase in the real value of tax revenues, the heavier taxes on exports and fuel, and the 'forced saving' system mentioned above (Machinea, 1990, Table II.7).

A significant improvement in the balance of payments was another result of the plan. The current account and balance of payments deficits fell from US$2,390 million and US$1,744 million to US$953 million and US$556 million, respectively. International reserves increased by US$2 billion between June 1985 and the end of the year (Machinea, 1990, p. 41).

A slight upturn in the economy took place during the last quarter of 1985 and gathered pace in 1986. The amount of idle capacity in the industrial sector fell from 32 per cent in the second quarter of 1985 to 23 per cent by the second quarter of 1986 (Machinea, 1990, p. 28). In the last quarter of 1985 overall seasonally adjusted GDP increased over 4 per cent and industrial output rose by 13 per cent (Machinea and Fanelli, 1988, p. 136). In 1986 the increase in GDP was 5.7 per cent. Likewise, in 1986 fixed gross investment increased by 11 per cent, this rise being led by purchases of productive equipment which rose over the previous year by 16.7 per cent (Machinea and Fanelli, 1988, p. 138).

Political measures, however, undermined the economic reform. In October pressures for wage increases from the Armed Forces distorted the economic strategy. As said above, from April the three *Juntas Militares* of the last dictatorship were on trial for human rights violations. In order to avoid another confrontation with the Armed Forces, Alfonsín suggested to his economic team a wage increase for the military.[4] The Radical government decided to increase pensions by 15 per cent and wages of Armed Forces personnel by 25 per cent (Machinea, 1990, p. 33). To avoid presenting these measures as a special concession to the Armed Forces a general wage increase of 5 per cent was established together with an increase of 25 per cent for teachers (Machinea, 1990, p. 33). These increases were, undoubtedly, political measures ahead of the legislative elections to be held in November 1985. Moreover, from January 1986 wages increased by 5 per cent and private companies were authorised to grant up to a further 5 per cent against increases in productivity (Machinea, 1990, p. 33).

As explained above, one of the main pillars of the *Austral* plan was a general wage freeze. This, together with the de-indexation of the economy, was applied in order to prevent 'inertial inflation'. These wage increases contradicted the basis of the plan. The increases would fuel 'inertial inflation'. However, Alfonsín, aware of the unrest within the Armed Forces due to the public judgement of the *Juntas Militares*, preferred to sacrifice economic stability to political concerns.[5] The wage increases also pushed up government expenditure and the fiscal deficit. Thus, in November 1985, the IMF stopped the disbursement of a US$213 million instalment because

Argentina had not met the agreed fiscal target: the public-sector deficit was over 4.5 per cent of GDP instead of the agreed 3.6 per cent. Argentina had to start new negotiations with the IMF (Machinea, 1990, p. 42).

These wage increases transgressed the monetarist approach, since the Radical government was unable to control monetary expansion. Because of this, the IMF withdrew its support of the *Austral* plan. The Radical government had different objectives from the Fund. Alfonsín's priority was to preserve political – rather than economic – stability. Thus, the government needed to regulate the economy, contradicting the Fund's monetarist preferences.

As stated, the main causes of these wage increases were the public judgement of the *Juntas Militares* and the approaching legislative elections. The November legislative elections were viewed by the government as a test of support for its economic policy.[6] The ruling party, *Unión Cívica Radical,* won in 20 of the 24 electoral districts. It obtained 43 per cent of the total vote cast while the Peronist party obtained 34 per cent. The Radical party gained 1 parliamentary seat, the Peronist party lost 8, the Intransigent party (moderate left wing) won 3, and the *Unión del Centro Democrático* (right wing) won 1 (*Clarín*, 6.11.1985, p. 40).

At the beginning of 1986, some indicators were suggesting that the economic stabilisation achieved due to the implementation of the *Austral* plan was beginning to weaken. From December to March, the CPI rose by 3.2 per cent in December, 3 per cent in January, 1.7 per cent in February and 4.6 per cent in March; the WPI went from 1 per cent in December, 0 per cent in January, 0.8 per cent in February, to 1.4 per cent in March (*Ambito Financiero*, 8.1.1987, p. 6). Likewise, nominal wage increases granted by the private sector were generally higher than the official guidelines. In addition, by March 1986, the real exchange rate had appreciated against the dollar by more than 20 per cent (Canavese and Di Tella, 1988, p. 175), reducing, therefore, the competitiveness of the Argentinian economy. The October wage increases were viewed as the main cause of the acceleration of the inflation rate, mainly because they provoked a rise in the fiscal deficit and thus the government had to print more money.[7]

To prevent further increases in the monthly inflation rate, in February 1986, a second phase of the *Austral* plan was announced. Alfonsín described it as a phase of growth with stability (*Clarín*,

7.2.1986, p. 4). In his speech, he referred to the trade unions' requirement of a unilateral moratorium on the external debt. For him, it was wrong to believe that resources from foreign trade could be redirected to domestic development instead of being used to pay debt interest. With a moratorium these resources would disappear, since they came from Argentina's foreign trade with those who were also its creditors. If Argentina transgressed the rules of the international system, its foreign trade would decline, and thus, no resources could be invested for domestic growth (*Clarín*, 7.2.1986, p. 5). Alfonsín argued that the Latin American situation was the consequence of an unjust international economic order. The decline in the terms of trade, and the increase in interest rates worsened the situation of Latin American countries. He explained that this was due to the industrialised countries 'egoism', condemning the underdeveloped countries to poverty and stagnation. He demanded from the industrialised countries the reduction of interest rates and the elimination of trade discrimination (*Clarín*, 7.2.1986, p. 38).

In his speech, Alfonsín was justifying his economic strategy and his acceptance of the IMF plan and arguing that most of the reasons for Argentina's economic crisis were to be found in the effect of the international economic system. Alfonsín emphasised the constraints imposed by the external debt. He pointed to the choice between servicing the debt or declaring a moratorium, and declared the intention of his government to pursue the former. To justify this view, he asserted that no government had declared a moratorium without incurring substantial costs. By explaining the restrictions on Argentina's foreign trade, Alfonsín was indicating Argentina's low bargaining leverage with international creditors. He also recognised the negative impact of some measures over which his government had no control. Alfonsín had communicated to the population his concern about the constraints upon Argentina's economic growth.

Sourrouille subsequently explained that the objective of the new stage was to ratify and deepen the *Austral* plan through the 'rationalisation' of the state apparatus (mainly by privatising public enterprises), industrial regeneration and the reduction of export taxes (*Clarín*, 7.2.1986, p. 2, 38–9). The Economics Minister recognised the decline in real wages over the last year and awarded a compensatory 5 per cent increase (*Clarín*, 7.2.1986, p. 2). He stated that the interest payments on the debt amounted to 5 per cent of GDP, and that the tax reform and the 'compulsory saving' scheme were implemented to finance the interest payments. These measures were based on the nationalisation of the private debt. The minister explained that as the government had to service the private debt, these measures, directed against the wealthiest sector of the population, were a trade-off for the nationalisation of the debt of 1982 (*Clarín*, 7.2.1986, p. 38). Sourrouille argued that 1986 would be a year of growth with stability. In order to overcome the stagnation of the economy and the constraint of the debt, the solution was to expand exports and investment. Export taxes were reduced to promote exports. He also announced a privatisation plan which included *Somisa*, *Petroquímica General Mosconi*, *Petroquímica Bahía Blanca* and *Petroquímica Río Tercero* (steel and petrochemical industries). These measures had to be approved by the Congress. Finally, he agreed with Alfonsín over the diagnosis of the crisis: the extraordinarily high interest rates together with the decline in terms of trade (*Clarín*, 7.2.1986, p. 39).

The tax reform and the 'compulsory saving' scheme were partially implemented since the government never really fought against tax evasion which was one of the main causes, together with interest payments on the external debt, of the high fiscal deficit (Dornbusch and De Pablo, 1988, p. 156). Therefore, these measures did not have a significant impact. Moreover, the government decided to reduce export taxes benefiting the exporters, who, in Argentina, constituted a large part of the wealthiest sector. Therefore, while the government was taking resources from the wealthiest sector of the population, it was also assisting them through the reduction of export taxes. Thus, ultimately the tax reform (and the 'compulsory saving' scheme), a trade-off for the nationalisation of the private debt, was a 'dead letter'.

The February 1986 measures, like the *Austral* plan, did not attempt to change the restructuring of social relations which had been achieved by the military dictatorship. In fact, privatisation had been an objective of the dictatorship itself. The objective of privatisation, as Sourrouille expressed, was to reduce government expenditure and to improve productivity levels (*Clarín*, 7.2.1986, p. 38). However, these enterprises were not loss-making. The petrochemical and steel industries, both private and public (but especially the former) were one of the most dynamic sectors (Ostiguy, 1990). Therefore, in privatising them the government would have lost resources. It would also have provoked an even higher concentration of capital, since the most likely buyers were the GEN (Ostiguy, 1990). In fact, the privatisation plan was not implemented, owing, in large part, to the opposition of the Peronist party in Congress.

Failure of the Austral *plan*

In April 1986, nine months after the launching of the *Austral* plan, Sourrouille announced several modifications to the strategy. The main change was the suspension of the wage and price freeze ('defreezing'). Rigid price controls were replaced by a new scheme of administered prices, wherein realignments would be accompanied by changes in costs. Nominal wages in the private sector could be adjusted within a band determined by the government. Public utility rates would shift in accordance with predetermined increases. In order to maintain the exchange rate value in real terms, exchange rate variations would be set in terms of a crawling peg; the exchange rate was, therefore, semi-fixed between two limits determined by the government (*Clarín*, 5.4.1986, p. 4). The *austral* was devalued 3.6 per cent against the dollar; there was an increase of 6 per cent in public services tariffs, and a general increase in wages by 5 per cent (*Ambito Financiero*, 7.4.1986, p. 1).

Administered prices supposed a degree of negotiation with trade unions and employers organisations. However, the Radical government had, of course, been unable to negotiate with these sectors during its first years in office. There had been an endless confrontation, mainly with trade unions, against the government's economic strategy. Therefore, the policy of administered prices assumed a level of co-operation between the government, trade unions and employers organisations, which was overambitious (Torre, 1990b, p. 16). Moreover, the administered prices policy and the gradual public price increases implied the end of the original philosophy of the *Austral* plan since these measures re-established indexation mechanisms which would fuel 'inertial inflation' (Canavese and Di Tella, 1988, p. 163). The Radical government gradually began another 'U-turn' to resolve the economic crisis. However, its new 'U-turn' could not prevent the rise of the inflation rate.

Nominal wages in the industrial sector increased 18 per cent in the second quarter of 1986 and 16.5 per cent between July and August. In public enterprises the real wage increased 8.7 per cent between the third quarter of 1985 and the third quarter of 1986, and in the banking sector by 20 per cent in the same period (Canavese and Di Tella, 1988, p. 175). These increases, and an increase in aggregate demand, were understood as the cause of the acceleration of inflation (Canavese and Di Tella, 1988, p. 175). The CPI growth was 4.7 per cent in April, 4 per cent in May, 4.5 per cent in June, 6.8 per cent in July and 8.8 per cent in August. The WPI growth was 3 per cent in April, 2.7 per cent in May, 4.6 per cent in June, 5.1 per cent in July and 9.4 per cent in August (*Ambito Financiero*, 8.1.1987, p. 6).

A new set of measures was announced in late August which included an increase of 3 per cent per month in public utility rates and the exchange rate in order to meet the inflation target. The exchange rate was indexed and public service prices were 'over-indexed'[8] to help public enterprises and the Treasury solve the fiscal problem. Real interest rates began to increase steadily from 0 per cent in September to 5 per cent per month in December. Another devaluation of the *austral* was implemented, 3.1 per cent against the dollar. In August the *austral* had been devalued six times by a total of 12 per cent. By the end of the month the official exchange rate was US$1 = 1.13 *australes*, and for the black-market dollar, 1.20 *australes* (*Clarín*, 30.8.1986, p. 2).

As a result of the August economic measures the inflation rate fell between October and December. The CPI growth in September was 7.2 per cent; in October, 6.1 per cent; in November, 5.3 per cent; and in December, 4.7 per cent. In these months the WPI growth was 6.8 per cent, 5.3 per cent, 4.9 per cent and 3 per cent, respectively (*Ambito Financiero*, 8.1.1987, p. 6).

Industrial activity declined in December 1986 to August 1985 levels reducing tax revenues. Likewise, the terms of trade deteriorated by almost 22 per cent during 1985 and 1986. As a result, there was a fall in the 1986 trade surplus which became a US$2.5 billion current account deficit (*Ambito Financiero*, 13.1.1987, p. 18). All this contributed to an increase in the fiscal deficit which went up to 9 per cent of GDP by the last quarter of 1986 (Machinea, 1990, p. 60). Despite all these negative effects, from September 1985 to September 1986 GDP rose by 11 per cent, industrial output by 26 per cent, and investment in machinery and equipment by 35 per cent. In the same period the inflation rate ran at 50.1 per cent (Smith, 1990, p. 14).

At the beginning of 1987, new agreements with the IMF were

reached. The Fund granted Argentina a US$1.35 billion standby until March 1988. Because of Argentina's losses from the fall of international prices for agricultural products a compensatory financing facility of US$480 million was granted. Argentina's target was to reduce the fiscal deficit to 3 per cent of GDP and inflation to 40 per cent. The World Bank also decided to lend Argentina US$2 billion for the period 1987–88 for a programme of growth and structural changes such as privatisations, the final works of the hydroelectric central *Yaciretá*, and a power distribution project. Likewise, Argentina presented its proposal for a 1987 financial plan, which was approved by the Committee of Banks. The plan determined the refinancing of US$29,500 million. A new agreement was also reached with the Paris Club which rescheduled US$1,462 million (*Ambito Financiero*, 13.1.1987, pp.1–2).

In its letter to the Fund, the government recognised that the April measures had been inflationary. The report stated that the deficit of the balance of trade had increased from US$950 million in 1985 to US$2,650 million in 1986. This was due to the decline in the terms of trade and the surge in imports because of the reactivation of domestic activity. According to the government's estimations, the arrears of US$500 million with the Paris Club would be paid by 15 June 1987. The external debt would increase by US$2.7 billion in 1987, amounting to US$51.5 billion. Finally, the government declared that the steady growth of the GDP and investment were essential elements of its economic strategy and that *this growth was necessary to facilitate the external debt payments*[9] (*Ambito Financiero*, 13.1.1987, p. 18).

The government aimed to achieve economic growth to service the external debt. The Radical government had now made a full 'U-turn' from its initial objectives. Alfonsín had argued, in 1984, that Argentina would pay the debt 'without accepting recessive recipes, because we (the Radical government) are committed to raising the workers' real wages' (*Latin America Weekly Report*, 13.1.1984, p. 3). However, in reality three years later, real wages had fallen. From a base index 1986 = 100, real wages in the private sector went from 115.83 in 1984 to 92.06 in 1987, and in the public sector, from 119.51 to 92.96 (Banco de la República Argentina, 1992, Table 8.A). In order to avoid a recessive programme, the Radical government did not implement an IMF plan. Neither, however, did it change the economic structure implemented by the military dictatorship, and thus it did not improve the workers' situation. Because of the failure of Grinspun's strategy to prevent high inflation, and of the pressure from international creditors to apply a set of policies which enabled interest payments, the Radical government could not change the economic structure formed by the dictatorship.

The Australito

In its attempt to control the economic situation, in February 1987, the government introduced, once again, a price and wage freeze (*Ambito Financiero*, 26.2.1987, pp. 1–2). The new plan – the *Australito* – contained three main objectives: to improve the position of the Argentinian economy in the international system, to reform capital markets, and to restructure and privatise public companies. The price and wage freeze of the *Australito* lasted until the end of June. Before the freeze, as a partial compensation for past inflation, a wage increase of 3 per cent was granted, on top of the 13 per cent for the private sector and the 9 per cent for the public sector already agreed for the first quarter of the year. Likewise, before the freeze, public tariffs rose by 2 per cent and the *austral* was devalued by 6.6 per cent against the dollar. The *Australito* plan determined that the exchange rate would be frozen during March and April, while in May and June the *austral* would be devalued by 2 per cent per month against the dollar (*Ambito Financiero*, 26.2.1987, pp. 1–2).

In the first half of 1987 the inflation rate was above its annual projection. In June the *Australito* was abandoned, mainly because of its unpopular wage and monetary policies. In this month the devaluation of the *austral* was greater than expected, the value of the dollar rose by 10.2 per cent overtaking the envisaged rate (*Latin America Weekly Report*, 9.7.1987, p. 9).

Sourrouille announced some new measures, such as the elimination of export taxes on wheat and other crops, the privatisation of most public companies, the assumption of public companies' debts by the Treasury and an increase of 10 per cent in transport fares and petrol prices (*Clarín*, 21.7.1987, pp. 2–3). By July the inflation rate reached double figures, 11.9 per cent (Smith, 1990, p. 22). The gap between the official and the parallel dollar exchange rate was increasing; in August it reached 43.36 per cent. There were mini-devaluations of 9.72 per cent in July and 14.95 per cent in August (Manzetti and Dell'Aquila, 1988, p. 21).

In July the government signed a new standby agreement with the IMF which imposed the correction of relative prices through increases in public utility rates and the exchange rate. In return, the IMF agreed to disburse US$1.04 billion, including the first payment of the US$1.5 billion credit approved the previous February (*Clarín*, 11.7.1987, p. 2). In the agreement, the government recognised that it did not reach the targets of the last agreement of January 1987 since the inflation rate was greater than estimated, the balance of payments was deeply in deficit and the fiscal deficit was higher than expected. The objectives of the new agreement were to implement a fiscal adjustment, a restrictive monetary policy and to limit to 5 per cent wage increases for the third quarter of the year. The report also stated that the government would further open up the economy. The control of the IMF over Argentina's economy was increased, as now, the Fund would control the development of strategies every two months (*Clarín*, 11.7.1987, p. 2). These new measures constituted a deepening of the 1976–81 economic structural reform. They were also an attempt to reduce the role of the state as regulator of the economy. The Radical government, with IMF supervision, was preparing the ground for the full implementation of a monetarist restructuring of the state and its social relations.

In September 1987 elections were held to renew half of the Chamber of Deputies, all the provincial governorships, provincial Congresses and municipal authorities. As with all the elections in a democratic system, the September elections were a test of support for Alfonsín's policies. The Radical party obtained 37.4 per cent of the total vote cast while the Peronist party reached 41.4 per cent (*Clarín*, 9.9.1987, p. 12). The Radical party lost its majority in the Chamber of Deputies. It also lost all but two (Córdoba and Río Negro) of its seven governorships (*Clarín*, 8.9.1987, pp. 8–9). The biggest loss was in Buenos Aires province (one of the largest districts in Argentina). The Peronist party won 16 out of 22 governorships (*Clarín*, 8-9-1987, pp. 8–9). The September elections showed that Alfonsín had lost political credibility and support.

Reasons for the Austral Failure

Analysing the failure of the *Austral* plan, one conclusion to be drawn is that the plan was insufficient to achieve a durable stabilisation. The *Austral* plan, after having prevented the hyper-inflation process, did not have a well-defined second stage.[10] The plan gave Alfonsín's administration a significant opportunity to bring down inflation but this period was not used to consolidate the disinflationary process. The lack of fiscal discipline was one important cause of the failure of the *Austral* plan, and was one of the reasons why inflation accelerated.

The measures taken by Sourrouille's economic team did not go to the core of the fiscal question. One of the main factors here was the tax system and tax evasion. In 1985, corporation taxes represented 1 per cent of GDP. Only one and a half million inhabitants were registered as taxpayers. Less than one-third presented the declaration of their obligation to pay tax and less than one per cent of the registered taxpayers declared their obligation to pay some kind of tax. Moreover, 84 per cent of the total income of VAT and corporation tax was paid by just 6 per cent of the registered taxpayers (Dornbusch and De Pablo, 1988, p. 156). Likewise, there was a huge variety of authorised exemptions especially established through industrial subsidies.[11] The *Austral* plan neither implemented any significant change in the tax system nor did it improve the system of tax collection.

The main problem of the *Austral* plan was that its objectives were limited. Its concern was to prevent hyper-inflation, and it did not propose a plan of action once this had been achieved. Likewise, the main cause for the failure of the *Austral* was its policy ambiguity. It neither restructured the main features of Argentina's economy, nor attempted to deepen them. As an example, the plan attempted to reduce the fiscal deficit without changing the main causes of it: the interest payments of the external debt, tax evasion and a high variety of government subsidies to the industry – most notably tax exemptions. This was one of the causes of the existence of high inflation rates.

The plan also collapsed because of a negative external shock. The decline in the terms of trade was regarded as having been particularly detrimental.[12] From an index of 100 for 1980, the terms of trade were 98.8 in 1984, 91.4 in 1985 and 79.9 in 1986 (World Bank, 1988). Despite a record 43 million tons of grain exports in 1985[13] (*Clarín*, 7.2.1986, p. 39), the fall in the terms of trade led to a deficit in the trade account. Due to an increase in productivity as a result of the positive effects of the plan, there was an increase in imports which provoked a decline in the surplus on the trade account. Both the decline in the terms of trade and the increase of imports provoked a fall in the surplus on the balance of trade. In 1985, the surplus on the balance of trade was US$4,315 million; in 1986, US$1,555 million; and in 1987, just US$257 million (Fanelli and Frenkel, 1990, p. 196). The international prices of agricultural products were 20 per cent lower in 1987 than in 1985. The effect of the deterioration in terms of trade from 1985 to 1987 amounted to 3.4 per cent of the GDP, accounting for almost 50 per cent (U$S1,900 million) of the reduction in the balance of trade surplus for this period (US$4,500 million) (Machinea, 1990, p. 64). In addition, the fall in international agricultural prices was the main factor behind the reduction of export taxes, which contributed to an increase of the fiscal deficit. These taxes were 1.93 per cent of the GDP during 1985 (2.18 per cent during the second semester) and only 0.32 per cent in 1987 (Machinea, 1990, p. 64).

After the failure of Grinspun's strategy and the *Austral*, the government realised that economic adjustment, the implementation of a monetarist approach, might be the only tool to resolve the crisis.[14] However, Alfonsín did not want to 'make the adjustment' if this implied that most of its cost would be borne by the working class (Canitrot, 1991, p. 13).[15] Nevertheless, as the government ran out of alternatives, it began to implicitly prepare the ground for a full implementation of economic adjustment. The failures of the Radical government to resolve the economic crisis exacerbated its confrontation with the trade unions.

RELATIONSHIP OF THE GOVERNMENT WITH THE UNIONS IN THE CONTEXT OF THE *AUSTRAL*

With the announcement of the *Austral*, the government abandoned its *concertación* attempt. Indeed, while the *concertación* intended to achieve an agreement between the government, the trade unions and business organisations on economic and social policies, the *Austral* plan was unilaterally implemented by the government.

As a response to the launching of the *Austral*, the CGT published a document entitled 'Defending production and employment in order to defeat inflation' (*Defender la producción y el trabajo argentinos para derrotar la inflación*). This document was known as *Los 26 puntos* (The 26 issues). In the document, the CGT presented an alternative economic policy whose main instruments were: a unilateral moratorium on the interest payments of the external debt, the reorganisation of the financial market, the nationalisation of bank deposits, a tax reform, the promotion of exports and import substitution development, the reactivation of public investment, a promotion of private investment, the defence of democracy, an increase in the education budget and the construction of houses (Beliz, 1988, pp. 228–33). From then on, the CGT would permanently demand the implementation of this economic strategy in order to achieve economic growth. The CGT's document also called for a new general strike, against the implementation of the *Austral*, to be held on 29 August to be followed by a social demonstration (*Ambito Financiero*, 30.8.1985, p. 1).

In July 1985 the government created the Economic and Social Conference (*Conferencia Económica y Social* – CES) whose objectives were similar to those of the *concertación* attempt. Its first meeting was held in August – before the general strike – and was attended by the President, the Ministers for Economy, Labour, Home Affairs and Welfare, three members from the UIA, one from the *Confederación General de la Industria*, one from the *Cámara Argentina de la Industria*, and five members from the CGT (Gaudio and Thompson, 1990, p. 139). Like its predecessor, the CES became an ineffectual talking shop on percentages and could not avoid the organisation of strikes.

Indeed, although the November 1985 election gave the government the impression that it had general support, by December, important groups of workers were holding 'struggle plans'. The metallurgical union (UOM), the construction workers (UOCRA), the textile workers (AOT) and the railway unions (*La Fraternidad, Unión Ferroviaria, Asociación de Señaleros y Jerárquicos*) were pressing for wage increases through national strikes (*Latin America Weekly Report*, 13.12.1985, p. 4).

As a result of the acceleration of the inflation rate at the beginning of 1986 – which went, as stated, from 3.2 per cent in January to 4.6 per cent in March – the government decided that the CES would provide the framework for wage negotiations which would be held sector by sector with the commitment that any increase would not be transferred to price rises. The government estimated an increase of about 6 or 7 per cent. In the negotiations the CGT asked for a general wage increase of 28 per cent, the employers accepted this increase with the condition that they be allowed to transfer it to price rises. The government, however, accepted no more than a 7 per cent increase for the lowest wages. Once again, as during the *concertación* attempt, the CGT left the CES and called for a general strike to be held on 24 January (*Clarín*, 7.2.1986, p. 9). The CGT required an economic emergency plan to promote growth with social justice. It stated that the external debt was unpayable and that Argentina had to service the debt in accordance with its capability (*Clarín*, 7.2.1986, p. 9).

The February 1986 measures were rejected by the CGT, since the government, after recognising the decline in real wages over 1985, gave a compensation of 5 per cent while the decline in real wages was 3 per cent for the private sector and almost 10 per cent for the public sector (Banco Central de la República Argentina, 1992, Table 8.A). Against the February 1986 measures, the CGT called for a general strike to be held on 25 March for a period of 12 hours (Fraga, 1991, p. 25).

The April 1986 measures were mainly criticised by the SRA. During 1986, relations between the agricultural sector and the government deteriorated. The agricultural sector viewed itself as the real loser in the *Austral* plan, owing mainly to the export taxes and the decline in the terms of trade. Regarding the new set of measures of April 1986, Guillermo Alchourón, president of the SRA, complained about the secondary role given to agriculture compared to that given to the industrial sector. He declared that the farmers were disappointed with this second phase of the *Austral* plan because it did not include any measures for the agricultural sector. He argued that the plan did not have the right approach to the promotion of the sector which actually generates Argentina's wealth. Alchourón criticised the government's promotion of industrial exports, while the agricultural exports were subject to an export tax of around 32 per cent (Acuña, 1990, p. 37). In that year agricultural production contracted by 2.8 per cent. As a result of this discrimination against the agricultural sector, 1986 was characterised by *Jornadas de Protesta Agropecuaria* – days of agricultural protests – organised by the SRA, CONINAGRO, FAA and CRA. The protests involved farmers coming from the provinces to Buenos Aires, blocking traffic on national routes, organising lock-outs and demonstrating against the government in *Plaza de Mayo* (*Clarín*, 22.4.1986, p. 9).

After the announcements of the April 1986 measures, a new round of negotiations started within the framework of the CES.

Once again the main discussion focused on the extent of wage increases. Finally, the government decided the percentage independently and applied it by decree. The CGT's response was to call for the sixth general strike for 13 June (Gaudio and Thompson, 1990, p. 153).[16]

Alfonsín's New Strategy

By this time, Alfonsín started to implement a new political strategy in order to neutralise the CGT's opposition. In order to weaken the CGT, he supported wage negotiations between trade unions and employers. Indeed, these negotiations attempted to undermine the role of the CGT, as the peak organisation, which represented all trade unions in its wage negotiations with the government. The most important event was led by the metallurgical union (UOM). Its General Secretary, Lorenzo Miguel, demanded a wage increase over the band determined by the government. The private sector, under pressure from the government, which did not approve the transfer of wage increases to price rises, did not grant the increase. After this refusal, the UOM started an indefinite strike which represented a loss of 1.5 per cent of GDP. Sourrouille himself eventually author-ised the private sector to transfer the costs of the wage increase to price rises. After 33 days of the strike, the agreement determined a wage increase of 48 per cent which would be paid in different steps (Gaudio and Thompson, 1990, p. 154). This event was significant because it showed the continuing weakness of the government *vis-à-vis* the trade unions. In order to avoid social conflict, the government compromised its economic objectives. To transfer the costs of wage increases to price rises fuelled inflation. Moreover, historically, the struggle of the UOM and its results was a test case for other trade unions. Therefore, Alfonsín's strategy to isolate the CGT and negotiate with trade unions threatened the survival of his own economic plan. By August 1986 the government had approved over 50 agreements for wage increases (*Latin America Weekly Report*, 14.8.1986, p. 5).

Despite Alfonsín's new strategy, the CES negotiations continued. In this framework, the CGT[17] mainly demanded a general wage increase. Due to the failure of these negotiations, the CGT called for general strikes on 9 October and on 26 January 1987.[18] After the latter, the government tried to gain some internal confidence among trade unionists in order to attain two different objectives. The political aim was to weaken Peronism by dividing the labour movement. The social aim was to negotiate a 'social peace' – the absence of strikes and demonstrations against the government – in the months prior to the elections. In other words, the government, once again, attempted to control the power of the labour movement. In order to do this, Alfonsín's government began negotiations with the *Grupo de los 15,* a faction of the labour movement. This group was formed by important trade unions such as UOM, Light and Power, plastic sector workers, car workers and commercial workers, and led by 'orthodox' Peronists such as Lorenzo Miguel, Carlos Alderete, Jorge Triaca, José Rodríguez and Armando Cavalieri. All of them had experience of negotiating with governments, from the military dictatorship to Alfonsín.[19] The *Grupo de los 15* had a very different strategy from that of the the CGT. The *Grupo* was negotiating with the government wage increases by sector – most notably, the August UOM's agreement. Within the framework of these agreements, trade unionists were achieving their objectives. Thus, the objective of the *Grupo* was to end the CGT's confrontation since the general strikes did not achieve the trade unions' objectives. Indeed, the *Grupo de los 15* did not want to support more general strikes (Gaudio and Thompson, 1990, p. 170).

As a result of the agreement reached by the government and *los 15*, in April 1987, Carlos Alderete, from the Light and Power workers, was appointed Minister of Labour (*Clarín*, 28.3.1987, p. 2). The terms of the agreement obliged a process of negotiations and dialogue, instead of the confrontation led by the CGT. The government would approve wage accords such as that which the UOM achieved in August 1986, collective wage bargaining would begin in 1988, and the Congress would legislate a new national health system which would involve union participation in the running of workers' social welfare funds (*Obras Sociales*). The trade unionists promised to discourage strikes and to persuade orthodox Peronists in the Chamber of Deputies to support the labour legislation that the government proposed (Beliz, 1988, p. 22).

One of the results of the agreement with *los 15* was that in the next wage increases reached by the UOM there was a three-month no-strike clause (McGuire, 1992, p. 47). During Alderete's six months as Minister of Labour there was no call for a general strike. However, the confrontation with the workers' movement moved to the Cabinet.

As soon as Alderete took office he announced that he was considering with Sourrouille's economic team an emergency wage increase. This was rejected by the Economics Minister (*Clarín*, 30.4.1987, p. 2). After this confrontation, Sourrouille and Alderete agreed an increase of 17.6 per cent of the minimum wage and from June a general increase of 6 per cent (Gaudio and Thompson, 1990, p. 177).

Later, Alderete began to apply a special policy – he was unofficially approving wage accords between trade unions and employers. According to the government's policies the key point of these accords was the promise from the employers not to transfer the wage increase to price rises. Alderete was approving wage accords without that promise (Gaudio and Thompson, 1990, p. 176).

The confrontation between Alderete and Sourrouille changed, focusing on labour legislation. The participants in this struggle were the government, Alderete and the CGT, and the employers organisations such as the UIA and the group of *Capitanes de la Industria*.[20] The labour legislation concerned wage bargaining, union statutes and the administration of workers' social welfare funds. The President received members of the UIA, SRA, *Cámara Argentina de Comercio, Cámara Argentina de la Construcción, Asociación de Bancos Argentinos,* and the *Capitanes* who complained about the legislation. The most controversial point was the extension of strikers' rights (including the work to rule, or *trabajo a desgano,* as one of the strike rights). The employers' organisations argued that this undermined the productivity of the country. Finally, Alfonsín decided to postpone the discussion of the legislation in the Congress until after the September elections (*La Nación*, 14.6.1987, 3rd. section, p. 1).[21]

In seeking to incorporate a Peronist trade unionist into the Cabinet, Alfonsín was attempting to divide and weaken the union movement. Indeed, the CGT, at the beginning, opposed the negotiations between the government and *los 15*. In fact, the CGT vetoed Alfonsín's first candidate, José Rodríguez from SMATA, who, after the CGT's decision, did not accept Alfonsín's offer. Finally, the CGT accepted Alderete's appointment due to the pressure from the *Grupo de los 15* (Gaudio and Thompson, 1990, p. 171). In this sense, Alfonsín's objective was also to neutralise the CGT's confrontation by exacerbating the internal divisions within the labour movement.

Alfonsín's second objective was to avoid confrontation with the trades union movement at the same time as there was internal unrest within the Armed Forces (Alfonsín, 1992, p. 19). This coexistence could, according to Alfonsín, have put democratisation at risk. However, when the Easter military rebellion occurred, Alderete and the CGT's General Secretary were supporting the democratic government. This was the first time in Argentina's history that the CGT actively supported a non-Peronist democratic government threatened by the Armed Forces. In Alfonsín's view this was due to Alderete's incorporation into the Cabinet.[22]

However, Alfonsín's first objective was defeated. He could not control the trade unions. But the trades union movement did achieve some of its objectives: free collective bargaining and the expansion of strikers' rights would be sanctioned. Moreover, the government had given many wage increases as a consequence of the pressure of the trade unions. Finally, Alfonsín's argument about the authoritarian basis of the trades union movement lost validity when, in the Easter military rebellion, trade unionists supported the democratic government.

The powerful role of the trade unions was an important obstacle to the resolution of the crisis of the Argentinian state. Indeed, Alfonsín could not apply an economic adjustment, not even his heterodox proposal, in the context of confrontation with the trade unions. The trade unions were able to block state policies. Indeed, they undermined the *Austral* plan through their endless demands for wage increases.

THE ARMED FORCES

The public judgement of the *Juntas Militares* began a new stage in the relationship between the Radical government and the Armed Forces. On 9 December 1985 the Federal Chamber of Justice passed sentence on the *Juntas Militares*. Lt General Jorge Videla and Admiral Emilio Massera were given life sentences, Lt General Roberto Viola was given 17 years, Admiral Lambruschini eight years, and Brigadier Orlando Agosti four and a half years. Brigadier Omar Graffigna, Lt General Leopoldo Galtieri, Admiral Jorge Anaya and Brigadier Basilio Lami Dozo were acquitted (*Clarín*, 10.12.1985, pp. 2–4, 54). The last three remained under confinement awaiting the outcome of the trial over their management of the

Malvinas war (*Latin America Weekly Report*, 13.12.1985, p. 1).[23]

Point number 30 of the sentence of the Federal Chamber undermined Alfonsín's objectives. The text provided for 'the trial of superior officers who commanded the zones and subzones of defense during the war against subversion and of all those who had operational responsibilities' (*Clarín*, 10.12.1985, p. 55). Point 30 determined that all the evidence that had been presented to the Federal Chamber would be given to the *Consejo Supremo de las Fuerzas Armadas* which would be responsible for setting in motion the judgements (*Clarín*, 10.12.1985, p. 55). Point 30 aborted the government's intention of providing a political solution to the question of human rights violations after the sentence of the Federal Chamber. Indeed, to propose a law which established 'due obedience' would have created tension between the Judicial and Executive Powers. Therefore, Alfonsín had to abandon his proposal of 'due obedience'.

Alfonsín wanted to resolve the question of human rights violations. He well understood that the Armed Forces would not passively accept that their officials – retired or on active duty – were being judged by civilian tribunals for acts committed in 'their war' against guerrillas. The main problem was how to put an end to the question of human rights violations without being accused of weakness *vis-à-vis* the Armed Forces, or even worse, of forgetting the 30,000 *desaparecidos*, their parents, husbands, wives, children and friends who were waiting for justice. Alfonsín could not resolve this predicament.

A double discourse began. On the one hand, Alfonsín was trying to approach the Armed Forces with promises of a political solution – the three levels of responsibility or 'due obedience' – and with the recognition of the need to conclude the trials. On the other hand, Alfonsín was still emphasising his commitment to punish those who had committed human rights violations. Alfonsín's policy towards the Armed Forces became ambiguous. He applied quite different strategies in an attempt to avoid the very thing that eventually occurred: a military rebellion.

Alfonsín's first strategy was to apply the so-called *Instrucciones al Fiscal General del Consejo Supremo de las Fuerzas Armadas* (Instructions to the General Prosecutor of the Supreme Council of the Armed Forces). The Instructions were sent by the Minister of Defence. They established that: (1) subordinates would be punishable when they had been able to decide on their acts, they had known the illegitimacy of the order or they had committed aberrant or atrocious acts; (2) it should be understood that the subordinate was able to decide when not to follow the orders he had been given; (3) it should be considered that the subordinates acted in ignorance of the illegitimacy of the orders; and (4) subordinates were responsible for aberrant or atrocious acts when these acts were in excess of the orders given (*Clarín*, 25.4.1986, pp. 2–3).

After the Instructions were known, Alfonsín faced a crisis within the Judiciary. The Federal Chamber of Justice threatened to resign. Julio Strassera, the General Prosecutor of the trial of the *Juntas Militares* also threatened to resign (Acuña and Smulovitz, 1991, p. 17). Most of the political parties – including the Radical party – and the human rights organisations were against the Instructions. They argued that they were an intrusion of the Executive Power into the judgements and constituted a hidden amnesty. They also called for a social demonstration against the Instructions (Acuña and Smulovitz, 1991, p. 17). Finally, Alfonsín in his speech on 1 May in the Congress announced that he would give new instructions to avoid 'due obedience' protecting those who had committed aberrant and atrocious acts under orders but who in reality had been able to decide not to carry out these commands (*Clarín*, 2.5.1986, p. 10). The Radical government was unable to implement its own policies. Indeed, pressure from organisations of human rights, the Judiciary and the political parties – also the Radical party – blocked and modified Alfonsín's policies.

Before the end of the year, Alfonsín applied his second strategy. He sent a proposal to the Congress to deal with the increasing number of judgements against officials from the Armed Forces. The *Punto Final* ('full stop') law had the objective of ending the trial of human rights violators by establishing a deadline for starting court enquiries of military officials accused of such violations. After the deadline no other trial could be started. The law established a 60-day deadline from the day of its sanction (*Clarín*, 6.12.1986, p. 4). It was passed by the Senate and the Chamber of Deputies by the end of December 1986 (*Clarín*, 31.12.1986, p. 2).[24]

Although January is a holiday month for the Judiciary, the Federal Chambers of Córdoba, Bahía Blanca, Tucumán, Rosario, Mendoza, Comodoro Rivadavia and La Plata suspended the holiday in order to clear the backlog of judgements before the new law came into force. By 23 February 1987 – date of the deadline of the *Punto Final* law – 487 cases had been presented to courts against over 300 officials, 30 per cent of whom were on active duty (*Clarín*, 22.2.1987, pp. 2–3). The *Punto Final* law was intended to put an end to the judgements of Armed Forces officials. However, the Judiciary's reaction modified government expectations.[25] The government thought that less cases would have been presented (*Clarín*, 22.2.1987, pp. 2–3). In this sense, the Radical government saw, once again, the frustration of its objectives.

The Armed Forces were in a situation of internal upheaval. Horizontal divisions – based on ideological and professional differences – had appeared within the Armed Forces under the military dictatorship. However, the Armed Forces were united in their defence of state terrorism. The divisions deepened because of Alfonsín's policies and the reaction of the military hierarchy. Low-ranking officials, although they did not approve of Martínez de Hoz's economic strategy, did support state terrorism and, in fact, they themselves applied it and also went to the Malvinas war. These low-ranking officials were now majors or lieutenant colonels who were being judged by civilian courts for human rights violations. They thought that they were being abandoned by those who had commanded them in the implementation of state terrorism. A strong feeling of solidarity developed amongst them. Before going to face the civilian tribunals, they celebrated in front of farewell masses. They also distributed documents to journalists in which they argued that

> the current military hierarchy was part of the Armed Forces during the war against the guerrilla, occupying significant posts ... The legality that then they did not require of the *Juntas Militares*, they want now to impose on their subordinates who just obeyed their orders ... these judgements affect the dignity and the honour of the Armed Forces and it is not a question of acceptable percentages of convicted or accused. (Fontana and Llenderrozas, 1992, p. 190)

The Army then, was internally divided. Senior officials opposed the Generals and their attitude towards the trials for human rights violations. The Instructions as well as the *Punto Final* law were not enough to placate these officials. On the contrary, they provoked a confrontation between different levels of the Army hierarchy. Senior officials viewed the Generals as accomplices in Alfonsín's attack on the Armed Forces. The Easter rebellion was the outcome of the internal upheaval of the Army.

The First Military Rebellion

On 14 April 1987, Major Ernesto Barreiro refused to present himself to the Federal Chamber of Córdoba and took refuge in the 14th Airborne Infantry Regiment in Córdoba (*Clarín*, 16.4.1987, pp. 2–3). Barreiro had the tacit support of the regiment's commander, Lt Colonel Luis Polo. Three days later, Lt Colonel Aldo Rico barricaded himself and his followers in the *Campo de Mayo* Regiment in Buenos Aires to support Barreiro's action (*Clarín*, 16.4.1987, pp. 2–3). The main demands of the rebels – known as *carapintadas* ('painted faces') – were for a political solution to human rights trials, a change at the top of the Army – they specifically wanted General Eduardo Ríos Ereñú to be removed – and their own pardoning (*Clarín*, 16.4.1987, pp. 2–3).

The Army Chief of Staff, General Ríos Ereñú, ordered troops to repress the rebels but they did not obey him. Therefore, he resigned (*Clarín*, 18.4.1987, p. 44). The Army was divided between the rebels or *carapintadas* and those who, while not supporting the rebellion, refused to repress it. The main point of disagreement between the 'rebels' and the 'legalists' was the method adopted by the former in disobeying internal Army discipline. Alfonsín found himself with the support of generals who did not have any power over their subordinates.[26]

During the days of the rebellion social demonstrations supporting the government were held in all the main squares of Argentina. In Buenos Aires, the *Plaza de Mayo* had been crowded since the very beginning of the rebellion and there were also social demonstrations against the military rebellion in front of the *Campo de Mayo* Regiment (*Clarín*, 18.4.1987, pp. 2–3). The rebels were completely isolated from civil society, and democracy was supported by all the political parties and other institutions such as the Church and the representative organisations of labour and business. An *Acta de Compromiso Democrático* (Democratic Commitment Act) was signed by all the political parties whose leaders were in the House of Government during the days of the rebellions (*Clarín*, 18.4.1987, p. 2). The CGT called for an indefinite strike to support democracy and its General Secretary, Ubaldini, joined the political leaders in the House of Government (*Clarín*, 18.4.1987, pp. 8–9). This was the first time in Argentina's history that the political parties, the representatives of the organisations of labour and business, the Church and society had supported democracy against a military rebellion.

With this popular pressure against the rebellion, Alfonsín went to the *Campo de Mayo* Regiment on 19 April. As Commander-in-Chief of the Army, Alfonsín ordered the rebels to surrender. When he returned to give a speech in the *Plaza de Mayo* he made the mistake of calling some of the *carapintadas* 'heroes of the Malvinas war' (*Clarín*, 20.4.1987, pp. 2–3). Because of this, it was perceived that Alfonsín had negotiated with the rebels. Less than one month later this view seemed to be confirmed when Alfonsín sent his 'due obedience' proposal to the Congress (*La Nación*, 5.6.1987, pp. 1, 4).

The 'due obedience' law had the effect of exonerating all officials at the rank of lieutenant colonel or lower charged with human rights offences – whether or not they had committed excesses – and more senior officers who were not key decision makers (*La Nación*, 5.6.1987, pp. 4).[27] Although the concept of 'due obedience' was one of Alfonsín's initial objectives, its sanction was viewed as a result of military pressures. After three and a half years in office, Alfonsín achieved his objective only after a military rebellion.

The *Semana Santa* military rebellion had many consequences. First, after the rebellion the Army was clearly divided. Although the demands of the rebels were the same as those of the Army proper, the method chosen by the rebels was to break up the Army's internal discipline. Second, the high-ranking officials were against the rebels but did not repress them, showing that despite internal differences the Army was still unified. Third, after *Semana Santa*, in addition to the question of human rights violations, the question of the *carapintadas* added a new conflict to the already tense relationship between the democratic government and the Armed Forces. The final consequence was the legislation of Alfonsín's 'due obedience' proposal.

However, *Semana Santa* had a positive side. It was a military rebellion which was not repressed by force and did not end in a military coup. The President himself ended the rebellion when he went to the *Campo de Mayo* to order the rebels to surrender. Why did *Semana Santa* not give rise to a military coup? One could suggest that the rebels did not want to overthrow the democratic government (Norden, 1990, pp. 168–9) or that the rebels were low-ranking officials unable to unify the Army behind them (Lázara, 1997, pp. 203–10). However, here, it is argued that the deep opposition of Argentinian society to the military rebellion isolated the rebels. The support for democracy from the political parties, the CGT, the SRA, the UIA, the Catholic Church, the *Capitanes de la Industria* and thousands of people in the *Plaza de Mayo* and *Campo de Mayo* was the most important factor in explaining why *Semana Santa* was no more than a rebellion. Last, but not least, the international community also condemned the military action (*Clarín*, 17/18.4.1987).

This support was a consequence of the discrediting of the Armed Forces, partially achieved by Alfonsín's policies towards human rights violations. Therefore, Alfonsín's policies, despite the *Punto Final* and the due obedience laws, did help to consolidate democracy by depoliticising the Armed Forces. However, as stated, due to the intensification of the economic crisis, the human rights violations issue became secondary and it lost the essential domestic support needed to confront the Armed Forces. In other words, the sanction of the *Punto Final* and the due obedience laws were consequences of the failure of the government's economic strategy. The government was gradually losing domestic support because of its inability to stabilise the economy, and thus, it could no longer maintain an open conflict with the Armed Forces.

CONCLUSION

The Radical government, after four years in office, could not resolve the crisis of the Argentinian state. Most clearly, the Radical government, after the failure of Grinspun's strategy to resist the IMF and to prevent high inflation, did not attempt to resolve the crisis of the Argentinian state. It did not intend to radically restructure the state, and at the same time, class relations. The *Austral* plan was not an attempt to modify the economic structure and the structure of class relations in Argentina. Its limited objectives were to prevent hyper-inflation and to reduce the fiscal deficit. As it did not intend to modify the military dictatorship legacy, it maintained it and gradually deepened measures taken by the dictatorship. In this sense, economically, the Radical government inadvertently prepared the ground for a monetarist restructuring of the state and of its relation to the economy.

In its four years in office, the Radical government had applied many strategies to control the power of trade unions. As demonstrated, all its attempts failed. The government yielded to most of the trade unions' demands, since it was unable to undermine their power. The power of unionism was an important barrier to the restructuring of the state and its class relations. As shown, most of the government's economic strategies were undermined by the power of the trade unions.

Finally, the Radical government was threatened by a military rebellion. The government did, however, achieve its objectives in this area. It resisted the military rebellion, and thus, its main political objective – the consolidation of democracy – was strengthened. Despite Alfonsín's concessions to the Armed Forces – the *Punto Final* and due obedience laws – he was able to avoid a military coup for two reasons. First, because of international and domestic support for democracy, and, second, the CONADEP report and the public judgement of the *Juntas Militares*, which uncovered the horrors of state terrorism and discredited the Armed Forces. Thus, while the crisis of the Argentinian state was not resolved by the democratic government, this crisis did not lead to the seizure of state power by the Armed Forces. This was Alfonsín's main political achievement.

As the Radical government did not resolve the crisis, it lost the 1987 elections. The analysis of the government's last two years in office shows that the government began to prepare the ground for the monetarist restructuring of the state, that the trade unions ended their policy of confrontation in order to support the Peronist party for the 1989 general elections, and that the Armed Forces again attempted to retain their historical role by threatening the maintenance of democracy. The downfall of the Radical government was caused by its inability to resolve the economic crisis which became a political crisis, making the monetarist restructuring of the state and of its class relations seem inevitable.

NOTES

1. The economic team argued that, in a highly inflationary situation, future inflation is a function of past inflation. They believed that 'inertial' inflation cannot be solved by orthodox policies. Sourrouille's economic team believed that the way to end this vicious circle was to abandon indexation (Dornbusch and De Pablo, 1988, p. 116).
2. As stated above, the September 1984 agreement with the IMF had been cancelled in January 1985 by the Fund, since Argentina did not achieve the targets of the agreement due to a monthly inflation rate of 25 per cent. As the Radical government had decided to service the debt it had to agree with the Fund on the domestic economic strategy which would allow the interest payment. This was the main objective of the IMF 'letter of intent'. The government would apply a specific economic strategy, and pay the debt, so that it could receive fresh money from the Fund mainly to pay the interest on the debt. As the 1984 agreement was cancelled, Argentina began new negotiations with the Fund. For more details on the 'conditionality' of the IMF agreements, see Mosley (1987) and Sachs (1989a).
3. Interview with senior official from Alfonsín's government, 19.10.1993, Buenos Aires.
4. Interview with senior official from Alfonsín's government, 25.10.1993, Buenos Aires.
5. Interviews with senior officials from Alfonsín's government, 19.10.1993 and 25.10.1993, Buenos Aires.
6. Interview with senior official from Alfonsín's government, 19.10.1993, Buenos Aires.
7. Interview with senior official from Alfonsín's government, 19.10.1993, Buenos Aires.
8. 'Over-indexed' means that the increase of public service prices was above the inflation target.
9. My italics.
10. Interview with senior official from CEPAL, 10.9.1992, Buenos Aires.
11. A very useful work on this topic is Basualdo and Azpiazu (1990).
12. Interview with senior official from Alfonsín's government, 19.10.1993, Buenos Aires.
13. In 1984 the volume of grain was 40 million (Sociedad Rural Argentina, 1992, p. 93). 1985 constituted a record which Argentina would not reach in future years.
14. Interviews with senior officials from Alfonsín's government, 19.10.1993 and 25.10.1993, Buenos Aires.
15. Interviews with senior officials from Alfonsín's government, 19.10.1993 and 25.10.1993, Buenos Aires.
16. The four strikes mentioned had total adherence in the industrial sector and partial in the tertiary sector (Fraga, 1991, p. 25).
17. By this time the CGT was organising its first delegates congress for ten years. Under the dictatorship, the CGT operated under informal leadership. Once the democratic government took office, the CGT started to organise its internal 'normalisation' but this was postponed due to

internal struggles. The congress eventually took place on 7 November and the General Secretary, Saúl Ubaldini, retained his post (Gaudio and Thompson, 1990, p. 131).

18. Both strikes had total adherence in the industrial sector (Fraga, 1991, p. 25).
19. As explained above, during the presidential electoral campaign Alfonsín announced that some trade unionists had reached a pact with some military officials. They were the same trade unionists with whom Alfonsín now wanted to make a pact.
20. In the transition to democracy, a new group of businessmen was created in opposition to the *Consejo Empresario Argentino*, a business organisation which had been closely connected to the military dictatorship. During the transition some businessmen understood that a democratic government would require a different form of business organisation. This group was known as *Grupo de los nueve* (Group of the nine). Its objective was to support industrial development in order to weaken the agricultural sector. The *Grupo de los nueve* declared its support for democratisation. The *Grupo de los nueve* was the antecedent of the *Capitanes de la Industria* (captains of industry). They were Manuel Gurmendi from ACINDAR (steel company), Ricardo Gruneisen from ASTRA (petrol and petrochemical companies), Jaime Nuñez from Bagley (food company), Sebastián Bagó from Laboratorios Bagó (pharmaceuticals), Julio Hojman from BGH (electrical products), Carlos Bulgheroni from BRIDAS (GEN), Miguel Roig from Bunge y Born (multinational company), Gerardo Cartellone from Cartellone (construction), Guillermo Kühl from Celulosa Jujuy (paper production) and SAAB Scania, Martín Blaquier from Ledesma (sugar company), Amalia Lacroze de Fortabat from Loma Negra (cement company), Francisco Macri from SEVEL (automobile company), Amín Massuh from Massuh (paper production), Vittorio Orsi from Perez Companc (GEN), Enrique Pescarmona from IMPSA/Pescarmona (GEN), Javier Gamboa from Alpargatas (textile company) and Roberto Rocca from Techint (multinational company). Alfonsín promoted and supported the *Capitanes de la Industria*. There was frequent communication between the *Capitanes* and the government. The *Capitanes'* aim was to organise a group to influence the government. The *Consejo Empresario Argentino* could not do this because of its links with the military dictatorship. The *Capitanes* wanted also to distance themselves from the 'liberal' point of view of the *UIA*. Both organisations, the *UIA* and the *Consejo Empresario Argentino*, were discredited due to their support of the military dictatorship. The *Capitanes* wanted to show that the bourgeoisie could prosper and be influential in a democracy. From Alfonsín's point of view, the *Capitanes* were a significant support. He wanted to integrate the bourgeoisie into the redemocratisation process. As the bourgeoisie had traditionally supported military coups, Alfonsín wanted to dispel the perception that democracy was against business. For more details see Ostiguy (1990), Sguiglia (1992), Majul (1992), Acuña (1995) and Acevedo *et al.* (1990).
21. For more details see Acuña (1995).
22. Interviews with senior officials from Alfonsín's government, 19.10.1993 and 25.10.1993, Buenos Aires.

23. In 1986 Galtieri was given 12 years, Anaya 14, and Lami Dozo eight years for their responsibility in Argentina's defeat in the Malvinas conflict (*Latin America Weekly Report*, 9.5.1986, p. 2).

24. In the Senate the bill was passed by 25 votes in favour, 10 votes against (8 Peronist senators and the two representatives of the *Movimiento Popular Neuquino*); 11 Peronist senators did not attend. In the Chamber of Deputies the bill was passed with 126 votes in favour, 16 votes against and 1 abstention; 111 deputies did not attend. The absence of the Peronist deputies made it easier for the bill to be sanctioned with the two-thirds required for its direct treatment. Therefore, in both Houses the Peronist party co-operated with the government to pass the bill (De Riz, 1991, p. 24).

25. For more details on the Judiciary's reaction see Pion-Berlin (1997) and Lázara (1997).

26. The Air and Naval Force supported the democratic government but because they perceived that the rebellion was not an attempt to overthrow the democratic government but an internal problem of the Army, they did not want to repress the rebels (*Clarín*, 18.4.1987, p. 2).

27. The law was passed in the Chamber of Deputies with 119 votes in favour and 59 votes against. The Senate modified the law and passed it with 23 votes in favour and 4 votes against. Finally, the Senate's modifications were passed by the Chamber of deputies with 125 votes in favour and 54 against (Acuña and Smulovitz, 1991, p. 20).

5

The Downfall, 1987–89

After the failure of the *Austral* plan and the September 1987 electoral defeat, the Radical government attempted to avoid an exacerbation of the economic crisis. Economically, the launching of the *Plan Primavera* was an attempt to temporarily stabilise the economy as a means of winning the 1989 general elections. However, the plan intensified the economic crisis mainly due to its policies discriminating against international creditors and agricultural exporters. With the collapse of the plan, the economic crisis became a political crisis. In order to avoid the breakdown of democracy, Alfonsín resigned, bringing forward the presidential hand-over.

In this context, the level of confrontation with the trade unions decreased. The CGT was more concerned over the internal elections of the Peronist party. The *sindicalismo Peronista* was divided; while the CGT supported Antonio Cafiero, governor of Buenos Aires province, the *grupo de los 15* supported Carlos Menem, governor of La Rioja province. After Cafiero's defeat in the internal elections of the Peronist party, the role of the CGT was neutralised. The *grupo de los 15* and Carlos Menem criticised the CGT's confrontational policy. Thus, during the last two years of the Radical government the role of the CGT was gradually undermined by the Peronist presidential candidate, Carlos Menem. This explains the CGT's indifference during the hyper-inflation process and the phase of wide-scale looting.

Finally, two military rebellions and a guerrilla attack on an Army unit slightly modified the confrontation with the Armed Forces. The two military rebellions were consequences of the Easter rebellion since their main objective was that the *carapintadas* should not be judged for having disobeyed the Army's internal discipline. The guerrilla attack on an Army unit actually benefited the Armed Forces, the latter being allowed back to participate in the resolution of internal conflicts which was the basis of state terrorism.

This chapter is divided into four sections. The first section analyses the economic crisis and the political causes of its intensification. The second section analyses the reason for the CGT's change of policy and its neutralisation by the Peronist presidential candidate, Carlos Menem. The third section deals with the two military rebellions and the guerrilla attack, analysing their main causes and consequences. The fourth section concludes by briefly analysing the reasons for the intensification of the economic crisis and the downfall of Alfonsín's government.

NEW ECONOMIC MEASURES

After the failure of Grinspun's strategy and the *Austral* plan, the Radical government had no economic strategy to resolve the economic situation. Rather it attempted to control the crisis using short-term measures. However, regarding the external debt, the government modified its policy. In April 1988 the government began to delay interest payments on the external debt. Although it did not declare a unilateral moratorium, it announced its decision to suspend interest payments until after the 1989 general elections. This return to Grinspun's strategy confronted the government with Argentina's international creditors, intensifying the economic crisis. In this context, Alfonsín was forced to resign in order to avoid a political crisis ending with the collapse of democracy.

After the 1987 electoral defeat a new set of economic measures was applied: prices, wages, the exchange rate and public utility rates were all frozen. A two-tier market was implemented to eliminate the black market. This measure implied that the price of the dollar was, in the financial market, freely determined while, for commercial transactions, it was fixed by the Central Bank (*La Nación*, 14.10.1987, p. 1).

After the elections, crucial international support was obtained from the US government. Sourrouille managed to win the support of James Baker, Treasury Secretary, and the World Bank for the new set of measures applied in October. A bridging loan of US$1.95 billion in fresh funds was announced in Washington by the Chairman of the creditors' steering committee (*Latin America Weekly Report*, 8.10.1987, p. 4). This credit gave a breathing-space for Alfonsín's government after its electoral defeat.

As a consequence of the October measures, by the end of December, the inflation rate was 3 per cent – in October it had reached 20 per cent. The freeze was abandoned, however, when the exchange rate was devalued by 7.5 per cent in the last week of December. In order to avoid distortions of relative prices the freeze had to be abandoned. Fiscal deficit of the public sector reached 6.3 per cent of GDP for the last quarter of the year (Machinea, 1990, p. 69).

The first half of 1988 proved the government's inability once again, to reduce the fiscal deficit, to prevent increases in the inflation rate, and to reach an agreement with the IMF and the commercial banks. Regarding the latter, due to Argentina's incapacity to meet the IMF's target for 1987 – that is, the reduction of the fiscal deficit to 1.14 per cent of GDP for the last quarter of the year (*Clarín*, 11.7.1987, p. 2) – the Fund stopped a withdrawal of US$225 million. In January after several meetings between the government and the IMF staff, an agreement could not be reached. The main disagreement was over Argentina's efforts to bring down the fiscal deficit. The negotiations broke the stalemate after the January 1988 military rebellion. The IMF changed its position in order to demonstrate its support for democracy.[1] Thus, after the rebellion, in February, an agreement with the IMF was reached. The agreement was based on periodical increases in public utility rates as well as the establishment of new taxes in order to reduce the fiscal deficit (*Clarín*, 15.2.1988, p. 2).

In April 1988, Argentina suspended the interest payments. The Radical government, after four and a half years in office, decided to unilaterally suspend the service of the debt without declaring a unilateral moratorium. The government suspended the payments mainly due to a very low level of international reserves, which by the end of 1987 was around US$1 billion (Machinea, 1990, p. 70). This low level was caused by the large current account deficit of 1987[2] and delays in the disbursements from the commercial banks (Machinea, 1990, p. 69). As explained above, the Radical government implemented this strategy of delaying interest payments at the beginning of 1984 when the level of international reserves was also US$1 billion. By mid-1984 they stood at US$3.5 billion. Therefore, one of the main objectives of the 1988 *de facto* moratorium was to increase the level of international reserves which, as explained below, was essential for the launching of the *Primavera* plan.

In order to avoid a confrontation with the international creditors, the government did not declare a unilateral moratorium, but continued negotiations. Thus, the *de facto* moratorium was never presented as a political issue, rather it was explained as being based on economic difficulties. However, the launching of the *Primavera* plan explained that the *de facto* moratorium was preparing the ground for measures to be applied in the exchange market.

By this time, the increase in public utility rates – which reached 22 per cent from February to March (*Clarín*, 9.4.1988, p. 17) – the rise in the international prices of grains[3] and the uncertainty in the exchange market because of the low level of international reserves caused an acceleration of the inflation rate. From January to March the CPI growth went from 9.1 to 14.7, and from April to August from 17.2, 15.7, 18, 25.6 to 27.6 per cent (*Ambito Financiero*, 8.7.1988, p. 2 and 8.9.1988, p. 1).

On 9 July internal elections were held in the Peronist party. Carlos Menem,[4] governor of La Rioja province, became the presidential candidate of the Peronist party in opposition to the candidature of Antonio Cafiero, governor of Buenos Aires province (*Clarín*, 11.7.1988, p. 1). This meant that the campaign for the general elections of 1989 began approximately one and a half years earlier than the date of the elections. The campaign was focused mainly on the economic situation, and both candidates, from the ruling party and the opposition, criticised the economic team and the President himself. After the internal elections of the Peronist party, the Radical government, in its last attempt to resolve the economic crisis and win the 1989 general elections, implemented a new set of economic measures.

THE *PRIMAVERA* PLAN

The *Plan Primavera*, launched at the beginning of August, was based on a price agreement with the UIA and the *Cámara Argentina de*

Comercio (Argentinian Chamber of Commerce, CAC) to be periodically renewed. In order to obtain the UIA's support, the government made some concessions. VAT was reduced from 18 to 15 per cent which represented a total revenue loss of 0.5 per cent of GDP. The plan included a price agreement for 180 days, a devaluation of the *austral* against the dollar by 11.4 per cent, and an increase in the public utility rates. The wholesale prices could be increased by 5 per cent until the end of September. Public utility rates would remain unchanged until the end of September. In October they would increase by 3 per cent, and afterwards they would be indexed at slightly below the inflation rate (*Ambito Financiero*, 4.8.1988, p. 1).

Although the two-tier market continued, some changes were implemented: the imports and private interest payments would be paid by the free market, the proceeds from agricultural exports and 50 per cent of the proceeds from industrial exports by the official market, and the other 50 per cent would be sold in the free market. The Central Bank's strategy was that the gap between both exchange rates should not be larger than 25 per cent and that, in order to maintain it, the Bank would use monetary policy. The exchange rate system implied a tax on agricultural products which was going to be collected by the Central Bank, buying dollars at the official exchange rate and selling them in the free market. The tax was equivalent to the difference between the exchange rates in both markets (*Ambito Financiero*, 4.8.1988, p. 1). The government decided this policy due to its promise of not increasing taxes on agricultural exports. However, as the two-tier market implied a tax, the agricultural sector did not support the plan (*Ambito Financiero*, 4.8.1988, p.1).

World Bank Support: Argentina's Lifeline

The Alfonsín administration obtained the support of the World Bank for the *Plan Primavera* through an unprecedented loan package. The President of the World Bank, Barber Conable, went to Buenos Aires to negotiate the loan and to support the plan pointing out that 'Argentina is implementing a programme which can be beneficial for the people of that country' (*Latin America Weekly Report*, 29.9.1988, p. 3). At the September meeting of the IMF and the World Bank, held in Berlin, Mr Conable announced his decision to recommend US$1.25 billion in new loans for Argentina (*Ambito Financiero*, 26.9.1988, p. 1). This announcement was highly controversial because the loan was approved before Argentina had reached an agreement with the IMF.

The *Financial Times* (27.9.1988, p. 4) pointed out that, regarding the debt problem, this loan would change the relationship between both institutions. It argued that, in the Argentinian case, the World Bank was taking the lead, incorporating in the agreement some macroeconomic conditions which were usual in an IMF letter of intent. In the words of the *Financial Times*, the World Bank was 'usurping' the role of the IMF. The newspaper suggested that this was a result of pressure from the US government: 'the US administration anxious for the debt crisis not to blow up during the election period has pushed the World Bank into this more central role' (*Financial Times*, 27.9.1988, p. 4). This was also suggested by *The Economist* (11.3.1989, p. 20), which also highlighted that the support which Argentina obtained from the World Bank was unusual, considering that the country was, as a borrower, as 'bad' as any. The article also emphasised that this agreement was made with the country which, since 1982, had rescheduled its debt three times and taken US$7.7 billion in new cash from the banks. It also pointed out that the agreement with the World Bank was based only on Argentina's promise to reduce its fiscal deficit from 4.6 per cent of GDP to 2.4 per cent for 1989.

It was suggested (*Latin American Regional Reports Southern Cone*, 1988, 17.11.1988, p. 5 and Lázara, 1997, pp. 151–52) that the US government put pressure on the World Bank to support the Radical administration, fearing the possibility of a Peronist victory in the approaching general elections. Machinea, who was then President of the Central Bank, points out (1990, p. 125) that the 1988 agreement 'produced frictions among some developed countries and inside the US government, as well as a lot of trouble to some members of the World Bank'. There were two different sides within the US government. On the one hand, George Schultz, Secretary of State, and James Baker, Secretary of the Treasury wanted to support Argentina's democracy and Alfonsín's government. They put pressure on the World Bank to grant the September loan. On the other hand, David Muldford, Under-Secretary of the Treasury, Michel Camdessus, Director of the IMF, and the commercial banks, were against such agreement on the grounds that from April 1988,

Argentina stopped paying interest (Morales Solá, 1990, p. 41). The commercial banks soon gave a reply to the World Bank's attitude. In October the Chase Manhattan Bank announced that it would transfer US$550 million of Argentina's credit to the 'non-performing category' – that is that the Chase recognised that this money would not be paid back. After this, some other commercial banks threatened to do the same if Argentina did not suspend its *de facto* moratorium (Morales Solá, 1990, p. 41). However, this did not affect Argentina's international position due to the World Bank's support.

Turning to the domestic sphere, the *Primavera* plan initially performed better than expected as the CPI growth went from 11.7 per cent in September to 6.8 per cent in December (*Ambito Financiero*, 11.1.1989, p. 4). The price agreement with the UIA and the CAC was renewed. The exchange market seemed under government control. The Central Bank increased its reserves due to the mechanism implemented through the exchange market. Likewise, from September the government began to implement reductions on tariffs, starting to open up Argentina's economy as had been agreed with the World Bank (*Ambito Financiero*, 5.9.1988, p. 1).

In October, with the better performance of the economy and international support, the government announced that the general elections would take place on 14 May (*Ambito Financiero*, 8.9.1988, p. 1). This meant there would be considerable time between the elections and the presidential change-over which would occur on 10 December. The earlier positive results of the plan and its international support were the main reasons why the government decided on such a long transition (Alfonsín, 1992, p. 8). The government knew the limits of the plan and after May an electoral defeat would have been highly probable. Therefore, the main political objective of the *Primavera* plan was to stabilise the economy in order to win the 1989 general elections. In this sense, the *de facto* moratorium was also a tool to win the elections by improving the economic situation.

November was the best period of the *Primavera* plan. The CPI growth was 5.7 per cent and the WPI growth was only 3.9 per cent (*Ambito Financiero*, 11.1.1989, p. 4). However, in the exchange market the situation was not so good. Between August and November the official dollar was adjusted by only 7.98 per cent while the inflation rate was 58.2 per cent (Garfunkel, 1990, p. 38).

The *atraso cambiario* – the overvaluation of the *austral* – was the focus of criticism of the plan and would later provoke its abandonment. The *atraso* was strongly criticised by the agricultural sector and the exporters, since they had to deal with a low dollar (compared with the black-market dollar) and the domestic inflation rate.

By the time of the implementation of the *Primavera* plan, the economic team had lost direction, but they did not leave the government due to their loyalty to Alfonsín, who did not have any other economic team to replace them.[5] As stated, the main objective of the plan was to control short-term variables in order to win the general election. International support from the World Bank was essential to obtain domestic credibility. Indeed, the exchange market mechanism was very risky, even though international support was supposed to enable the Central Bank to maintain the level of international reserves. The US government and World Bank appeared to be Alfonsín's lifeline.

However, in January 1989, due to Argentina's inability to meet the World Bank's target, the Bank announced that the disbursement of US$350 million scheduled for the end of February would not take place (*Ambito Financiero*, 3.3.1989, p. 1). The unprecedented loan became a dead letter. The government thereby lost its international lifeline. The main reasons why the World Bank and the US Government left Argentina without support were the presidential change in the US and Menem's international campaign to change his image, led by a Peronist MP and one of his economic advisers, Domingo Cavallo.[6]

Under the Bush administration, Nicholas Brady was appointed Secretary of the Treasury and David Muldford was confirmed as Under-Secretary. James Baker replaced George Schultz as Secretary of State. These changes, together with the power vacuum created as a result of the change of administration, undermined the US government's support for Alfonsín. The *Wall Street Journal* (18.5.1989, p. 10) stated that it was not altogether clear whether the change in US policy was a political decision or the consequence of the US presidential change. In addition, Domingo Cavallo, a Harvard economist, began an external campaign on behalf of the Peronist candidate, especially in Washington, to modify Menem's image. He was to convince US policy makers that the Menem presidency would not be 'dangerous' either for the US government or for the commercial banks. He also had to prove that the loans asked for by Alfonsín had an electoral objective (Morales Solá, 1990, 51). In other words, Cavallo aimed to prepare a favourable international context for a Peronist victory. He was, at least in part, successful and the international support given to Alfonsín's government – mainly from the World Bank – weakened. Morales Solá suggests (1990, p. 51) that Cavallo's mission undermined Alfonsín's international support by clarifying Menem's strategy – which, rather than being dangerous, would become a guarantee for the international creditors and the US government.

By this time, the President of the Central Bank, Machinea, announced that Argentina would not pay the arrears of the debt until an IMF agreement had been reached. He criticised Peronist contacts with international creditors – especially bankers – who had expressed that if the Radical government was not forced to pay the arrears, a Peronist government would adopt the same policy of delaying payments (*Ambito Financiero*, 6.2.1989, p. 4). Cavallo, who made these Peronist contacts, affirmed that while the government delayed interest payments, it was wasting Argentina's international reserves in trying to control the exchange market. He confirmed that a Peronist government would not service these arrears (*Ambito Financiero*, 6.2.1989, p. 4). The electoral campaign was also played out in New York and Washington. This Peronist attitude became crucial.

Indeed, Carlos Menem was the most probable victor in the approaching general elections yet, despite the international and national efforts to modify his image, his economic strategy was unclear, apart from two slogans: a *salariazo* (a massive wage increase) and a *revolución productiva* (a productive revolution) (*Ambito Financiero*, 27.2.1989, p. 1). Uncertainty over the general elections and the ambiguity of Menem's economic positions, together with the precariousness and vulnerability of the economic situation, unleashed a run on the *austral* to the dollar at the end of January. Nevertheless, the crucial element was, once again, the international creditors.

As stated above, US government and World Bank support were Alfonsín's lifeline. Therefore, when both adopted a 'hands off' approach, Argentina's economy began to collapse. The instability of the economic situation, together with the normal uncertainty provoked by general elections, could have been controlled if the

World Bank had not suspended its loan. Without this international support, it was assumed that the Central Bank could not maintain the exchange rate mechanism. Uncertainty over a 'dollarised' economy unleashed a run on the *austral*.[7]

Argentina's Black Monday

In order to maintain the gap between the two exchange rates, the Central Bank sold US$12.1 million in December, US$668.1 million in January and US$242.3 million in the first three days of February (Garfunkel, 1990, p. 82). From 30 January to 3 February, the Central Bank lost US$495 million. On the last weekday of the *Plan Primavera*, the commercial dollar was 14.06 *australes* and on the black market, 17.67 *australes* (Garfunkel, 1990, p. 82). It was then that the government decided to change the exchange market. The 6th February marked the end of the *Primavera* plan and the beginning of the end of the Radical government.

Black Monday resulted in big losses for important enterprises[8] which, following the advice of some of the members of the economic team, did not abandon the *austral*, believing that the international reserves of the Central Bank were high enough to maintain the exchange market system. They were not the only losers. The other side of the coin shows that the *austral* was devalued 60 per cent in only 26 days, thereby depreciating the salary of the workers (Garfunkel, 1990, p. 32).

The reasons for the collapse of the *Primavera* plan were first, the end of the World Bank's support, second, a run against the *austral* due to the approaching elections and the uncertainty of the economic strategy of Carlos Menem, and finally, the reluctance of exporters to sell foreign exchange, speculating on an adjustment of the exchange market.[9] The chaos provoked by the end of the plan was mainly caused by the reluctance of the exporters to sell foreign exchange which provoked an indefinite rise of the dollar because demand was rising and supply was lacking. The exporters no longer wanted to pay the cost of the combination of an inflation rate of 81.5 per cent from August 1988 to January 1989 with an adjustment of the commercial dollar of only 17.17 per cent for the same period (Garfunkel, 1990, p. 41). The Central Bank continued losing reserves while exporters did not sell foreign exchange, expecting a new exchange market modification and speculating with the next government's strategies. Exporters began to sell foreign exchange in Montevideo, Uruguay (*Clarín*, 27.2.1989, p. 10).

While the dollar supply was very low, its demand was excessively high. A government research paper explained that some of the most powerful banks were buying dollars, making demand rise. These banks had as customers the most important transnational companies operating in Argentina. According to this document, the Republic of New York Bank bought US$35 million; the French Bank, US$24; Morgan, US$24; Citibank, US$20; Chase Manhattan, US$8; and among the national banks, *Crédito Argentino* bought US$14 million, and *Provincia de Buenos Aires*, US$7 million (Majul, 1990, p. 19). From the government's point of view, this was a strategy of Argentina's international creditors, mainly the commercial banks, to undermine the precarious stability reached by the *Primavera* plan and prove that – whoever governs – Argentina had to pay its debt in order to attain any permanent stability.

The exchange market modification of February attempted to minimise the impact of the run against the *austral* on prices. The new exchange market determined that the exchange rate for all commercial transactions would be set by the government while the financial transactions would operate in the free market (*Ambito Financiero*, 7.2.1989, p. 1). There was a commercial dollar (14.41 *australes*) for agricultural exports, a special dollar (18.01 *australes*) for imports and a free dollar which was estimated by the government to be 20 per cent over the special dollar (Garfunkel, 1990, p. 83). In a few days the free dollar jumped 45 per cent, reaching 27 *australes*. It also jumped and fell 12 per cent in only one day, with margins of 26 per cent between the purchase and the sale (Garfunkel, 1990, p. 87). These oscillations represented a spectacular wealth transfer within the private sector and between private and the public sector.

At the end of February, new measures were implemented in the exchange market. Eighty per cent of the proceeds from agricultural exports were to be sold in the commercial market, and 20 per cent in the free market; of those from the industrial exports, 30 per cent would be sold in the commercial market, 50 per cent in the special one and 20 per cent in the free market (*Ambito Financiero*, 21.2.1989, p. 1). Despite this measure, the run against the *austral* and the strengthening of the dollar continued.

The price agreement between the government, the UIA and the CAC was broken by the unilateral decision of the government to allow a price increase of 7.5 per cent (*Ambito Financiero*, 24.2.1989, p. 1). The government's decision was not so different from the previous agreement. However, the unilateralism of the decision was a good excuse for the UIA and CAC to break the agreement (*Página/12*, 1.3.1989, p. 1). Soon after, Terrabusi, an enterprise belonging to Gilberto Montagna, a representative of UIA in the team which negotiated the previous agreement, increased its prices by 30 per cent (Majul, 1990, p. 49).

Despite the run against the *austral*,[10] the CPI growth was 8.9 per cent in January and 9.6 per cent in February and the WPI growth, 6.9 per cent and 8.3 per cent respectively (*Ambito Financiero*, 7.3.1989, p. 5).

At the end of March, when the dollar reached 48.40 *australes* (*Ambito Financiero*, 30.3.1988, p. 1), Eduardo Angeloz, the Presidential Candidate of the Radical party, publicly demanded the resignation of the economic team (*Ambito Financiero*, 30.3.1989, p. 12). After four years in office, Sourrouille and his team left Alfonsín's government. Sourrouille's letter of resignation stated that his failure was mainly based on the lack of a political and social pact to neutralise the actions of those who wanted to obstruct an economic reform and the stabilisation of the economy (*Ambito Financiero*, 3.4.1989, p. 1). However, such a political and social pact was never the government's objective. As explained, the *concertación* attempt was interrupted by the government's unilateral decision to implement the *Austral* plan. Moreover, the Radical government did not fully attempt to implement an economic reform. While it did intend to stabilise the economy through the *Austral* plan, this was, as stated, not a comprehensive economic reform programme. Therefore, as Sourrouille put it 'those who wanted to obstruct an economic reform and the stabilisation of the economy' were, in fact, asking for a specific economic reform: the monetarist restructuring of the state and of its relation to the economy. This was sought mainly by Argentina's international creditors and the upper bourgeoisie.

After four years as a member of the economic team, Machinea stated that 'the external debt is unpayable' (*Página/12*, 19.3.1989, p. 6). He affirmed that the interest payments represented 7 per cent of the GDP. Argentina, under the Radical government, had paid only 50 per cent of the interest. He argued that for the middle and long term the only solution was a unilateral moratorium, however this measure was highly risky for the short term (*Página/12*, 19.3.1989, p. 7). From Machinea's point of view, Argentina's main economic problem was the payment of the external debt which constrained Argentina's economy. As the debt was viewed as a fiscal problem, the 'only' solution to it was a restructuring of the state. Thus, the 'only' solution seemed to be the implementation of the monetarist approach of the 'Washington consensus', since the Radical government had no viable strategy.

The Political Significance of Black Monday

Black Monday was the event which signalled that the economic crisis had become a political one. As the Radical government proved unable to resolve the crisis of the Argentinian state, the crisis deepened and class struggle intensified. By this time, the state appeared to 'all social forces as the primary barrier to the resolution of the crisis and the realisation of their particular aspirations' (Clarke, 1990, p. 27). Black Monday was provoked to show that the 'monetarist' restructuring of the state was inevitable. It was provoked by the 'hands off' approach of the international creditors, the reluctance of agricultural exporters to sell the proceeds from exports and the run against the *austral* unleashed by the banks. The objective of these groups was to demonstrate that the incoming government – either from the ruling party or the Peronist party – had to resolve the crisis of the Argentinian state by a monetarist restructuring. That is, to fully apply an orthodox IMF programme whose main measures were 'fiscal discipline and the reduction of some public expenditures such as subsidies, tax reform, market-determined interest rates, competitive exchange rate, import liberalisation, promotion of foreign direct investment, privatisation, deregulation, and new laws on property rights' (Williamson, 1990, p. 1). This was the set of policies promoted by the 'Washington consensus'. These market-oriented policies would resolve the political crisis of the state by restructuring both the state and the working class. It was, thus, to deepen the military dictatorship's *disciplinamiento social* by subordinating the working class economically and politically. Thus, Black Monday, together with the consequences which provoked Alfonsín's resignation, was the price that the Radical government paid for non-implementation of an IMF plan. That is, it was the result of the government's reluctance to apply a monetarist restructuring of the state and of its class relations. Black Monday also represented a redistribution of income against the working class, since the devaluation of the *austral* constituted a depreciation of wages.

Argentina after Sourrouille

In April, Juan Carlos Pugliese, a veteran member of the Radical party, who had been Minister of Economy under Illia's administration, was appointed to replace Juan Sourrouille. Enrique García Vázquez was again appointed as President of the Central Bank (*Ambito Financiero*, 3.4.1989, p. 1). Owing to pressure from exporters and the low level of international reserves, the exchange market was modified to an exchange rate system where 50 per cent of goods transactions would operate in the free market.[11] This implied a devaluation of 60 per cent for agricultural exports, and that import and food prices would be tied daily to the exchange rate oscillations (*Ambito Financiero*, 5.4.1989, p. 1). Thus, inflation accelerated. Interest rates increased to 100 per cent per month. By the end of April, nothing could stop the rise of the dollar which reached 90 *australes* (Garfunkel, 1990, p. 143). The CPI growth was 33.4 per cent in April and the WPI growth was 58 per cent (*Ambito Financiero*, 5.5.1989, p. 1).

After two weeks, the exchange market was again modified. The proceeds from all the exports were sold in the free market with a deduction determined by the difference between the free dollar and the dollar fixed daily by the government – which was, at the beginning, determined at 36 *australes* (*Ambito Financiero*, 14.4.1989, p. 1).

The *Grupo de los Ocho*[12] proposed to the government a set of economic measures which had two main pillars: an improvement for exporters and the reduction of the fiscal deficit. Rumours that Roberto Alemann would be appointed Minister of Economy appeared.[13] A meeting was held between Alfonsín and the representatives of the *Grupo de los Ocho* (*Ambito Financiero*, 27.4.1989, p. 1) The outcome of this meeting was a new economic plan. Prices were frozen and public utility rates increased by 20 per cent. The exchange market underwent the most 'expected'[14] and crucial modification: its unification and liberalisation (*Ambito Financiero*, 27.4.1989, p. 1).

The general elections took place on 14 May. Carlos Menem won with 41 per cent of the total vote cast, the Radical candidate obtained 37 per cent (*Clarín*, 15.5.1989, p. 1).

Five days after the general elections, the dollar reached 175 *australes* (*Ambito Financiero*, 19.5.1989, p. 1). The government tried to reach an agreement with the Peronist party to accelerate the Presidential change-over, scheduled for 10 December. These negotiations failed: Peronism did not want to be seen co-operating with the government.[15] After winning the general election, Menem had announced some modifications to his economic strategy. Most notably, he now proposed the unification of the exchange market, the reduction of export taxes and the payment of the external debt (*Ambito Financiero*, 4.4.1989, p. 9). These three policies were mainly the demands of those actors who had opposed Alfonsín. The unification of the exchange rate and the reduction of export taxes were demands from the agricultural and industrial sectors, while the payment of the external debt was, of course, demanded by the international creditors. Menem went from proposing a *salariazo* (massive wage increase) and a *revolución productiva* (productive revolution) to these new announcements which showed that the incoming Peronist government had understood the true objectives of Black Monday. The Peronist government would begin the monetarist restructuring of the state and its class relations.

As Pugliese could not stop the run against the *austral* he was replaced by Jesús Rodríguez (*Ambito Financiero*, 26.5.1989, p. 1), a young man from the *Coordinadora* – the internal faction of the Radical party that, despite foreseeing a defeat, was still loyal to Alfonsín. Soon after taking office, Rodríguez implemented a new set of measures to be applied after 10 days' suspension of most banking activity. Exchange rate control was reapplied, a crawling peg was announced, the export tax was fixed at 35 per cent for agricultural goods and 20 per cent for industrial goods and public utility rates were adjusted. The Congress approved new taxes which included the suspension of industrial promotion benefits. The exchange rate was fixed at 177 *australes* to the dollar (*Ambito Financiero*, 29.5.1989, p. 1).

During the first ten days of the Rodríguez plan hyper-inflation was at its peak. Price lists in dollar terms, purchases with dollars notes, non-acceptance of credit cards, daily price increases, the closure of shops due to the impossibility of determining prices, workers unable to go to work because the transport cost was almost 90 per cent of their salary, and looting were some of the main features of the hyper-inflation process.

From 24 to 31 May looting became the principal political issue (*Ambito Financiero*, 31.5.1989, p. 1). Looting was spontaneous, and took place mainly in Rosario, Córdoba, Mendoza and Greater Buenos Aires. The government established a state of emergency for 30 days in an attempt to prevent an escalation of violence (*Ambito Financiero*, 30.5.1989, p. 1). Initially the looting was non-violent, women and children merely taking food from supermarkets. However, in Rosario violence increased as shopowners began defending themselves with guns. The police had to be helped by the *Gendarmería* (Frontier Police Corps) to prevent an escalation of violence at Rosario. Bombs in the centre of Buenos Aires, in some Radical party's offices and some Communist party's offices provoked panic. Violence increased in Greater Buenos Aires, six people died in San Miguel and approximately 80 were injured. In Rosario five people died and hundreds were arrested (*Clarín*, 1.6.1989, p. 2).

The looting was the workers' reaction to hyper-inflation. While the bourgeoisie was speculating against the *austral*, making prices rise, the workers were trying to survive. The looting was the other side of Black Monday. It showed workers' reaction to Black Monday's redistribution of income. It also showed the capacity of the working class to defend its interests independently from the trades union movement: the CGT did not call a general strike nor did it organise a social demonstration. Despite this, the workers organised themselves to demonstrate that they would not passively accept any economic strategy. Black Monday and the looting were the two sides of the income distribution struggle in Argentina. They represented the intensification of Argentina's class struggle.

Hyper-inflation

In the first week of June the dollar reached 370 *australes*, the monthly interest rate was over 100 per cent, the CPI growth for May was 78.5 per cent and the WPI growth was 103.7 per cent (*Ambito Financiero*, 8.7.1989, p. 1). These were records even for Argentina's history of high inflation.

The Economist (13.5.1989, p. 95) pointed out that:

At first sight it seems ridiculous to argue that it might do a country good to have, like Argentina, a collapsing currency and a monthly inflation rate of more than 40 per cent. That is equivalent to an annual rate of 6000 per cent, high enough to satisfy the most stringent definition of 'hyperinflation' ... High-but-stable inflation, though extremely damaging, is tolerable ... Hyperinflation, on the other hand, is intolerable. At the limit, money ceases to mean anything and transactions are conducted in foreign currency, or by barter. As the economy opts out of the domestic monetary system the government has a chance to start afresh. In the midst of a real crisis (as opposed to the countless phoney crises that preceded it), the government is more likely to be believed. If an election and a change of government is in the offing at just the right time, so much the better.

For Argentina, it seemed, according to *The Economist*, to be the right time and at right stage. Domingo Cavallo, who had been appointed by the elected President, Carlos Menem, as Foreign Affairs Minister,[16] agreed with *The Economist*'s point of view. Cavallo advised Menem not to establish an agreement with the Radical government which would undermine Menem's public image. Cavallo thought, as *The Economist* suggested, that after the hyper-inflation process, the Peronist government would be able to apply the, in his opinion, necessary adjustment. Machinea (1990, p. 118) also points out that an alternative would have been to let the situation explode in order to introduce a completely new programme afterwards. However, he states that for the government this was not a viable option, since hyper-inflation was considered one of the greatest dangers for the consolidation of democracy. He suggests that after hyper-inflation – considering also the general political and social situation – the Radical government would not have the necessary credibility to implement a new economic strategy.

By June, it was clear that the government could not deal with the economic, social and political aspects of the crisis. Alfonsín began a negotiation process to move forward the presidential hand-over. When Alfonsín and Menem's team were discussing the new date, one of Menem advisors announced that a very high exchange rate would be fixed under the Peronist administration (*Página/12*, 11.6.1989, p. 3). This provoked a new run against the *austral*. As Menem did not deny this statement, Alfonsín interrupted the negotiation process. On 12 June, Alfonsín announced that he would resign on 30 June (*Clarín*, 13.7.1989, pp. 2–3).

ALFONSÍN'S ECONOMIC LEGACY

Alfonsín's downfall began in September 1987 when the Radical party lost the elections. The government's inability to resolve the economic crisis was the immediate cause of its fall. Under Alfonsín, GDP never reached its 1980 level. Table 8 shows the performance of the Gross Domestic Product under the democratic regime.

TABLE 8
Gross Domestic Product

Year	%
1981	93.6
1982	88.8
1983	91.5
1984	93.9
1985	89.8
1986	94.9
1987	97.0
1988	94.5
1989	90.2

Source: Sociedad Rural Argentina (1992).

Note: 1980 = 100.

By the end of Alfonsín's term of office, GDP was 10 per cent a year lower than it had been at the beginning of the 1980s. Moreover, after the failure of the *Plan Austral* the Radical government could not prevent price increases. In June 1989, the last month of Alfonsín's administration, the CPI growth was 114.5 per cent and the WPI growth, 132.3 per cent. In the last twelve months the first index grew 1,472 per cent and the second, 1,983 per cent. Table 9 shows the price evolution under the Alfonsín administration. Table 9 demonstrates that the best performance was in the first year of the *Plan Austral*. As soon as the plan was abandoned prices began to rise. Regarding the fiscal deficit, the table confirms this tendency.

TABLE 9
Price indices
(from December to December)

	1984	1985	1986	1987	1988	1989
CPI	688.0	385.4	81.9	174.8	387.7	4923.8
WPI	585.0	363.9	57.9	181.8	431.6	5386.4

Source: CEPAL (1991).

TABLE 10
Fiscal deficit as a percentage of GDP

Year	%
1984	12.5
1985	5.4
1986	4.3
1987	6.4
1988	8.6*
1989	7.2*

Source: Argentinian Central Bank (*Banco Central de la República Argentina*), unpublished data.

Note: * from Economic Commission for Latin America and the Caribbean (1990).

The fiscal deficit also began to rise after dropping 65.6 per cent between 1984 and 1986. As indicated earlier, one of the causes of this rise was the increasing interest payments on the external debt.

TABLE 11
External debt (US$ million)

Year	US$ million
1984	46903
1985	49326
1986	51422
1987	54700
1988	57000
1989	63314*

Source: Argentinian Central Bank (*Banco Central de la República Argentina*), unpublished data.

Note: * from Economic Commission for Latin America and the Caribbean (1990).

TABLE 12
Total debt as a percentage of GNP

Year	%
1984	67.5
1985	84.2
1986	70.5
1987	76.4
1988	66.5
1989	121.9

Source: Organización de Estados Americanos (1992).

TABLE 13
Interest paid as a percentage of GNP

Year	%
1984	5.8
1985	8.4
1986	5.8
1987	5.3
1988	3.5
1989	4.0

Source: Organización de Estados Americanos (1992).

As the above tables demonstrate, Argentina's growth potential was severely constrained by the servicing of the external debt. The *Austral* plan contained inflation and the fiscal deficit, but after its abandonment no substitute measures were found to stem the worsening economic crisis and the deterioration in workers' conditions.

TABLE 14
Real wages by sector
1986 = 100

Year	Private Sector	Public Sector
1984	115.83	119.51
1985	112.45	107.05
1986	100.00	100.00
1987	92.06	92.26
1988	88.74	92.73
1989	72.23	84.84

Source: Banco Central de la República Argentina (1992).

As shown in Table 9, the CPI and the WPI indexes increased after the failure of the *austral,* which led to the decrease in real wages and produced a decline in the workers' purchasing power.

TABLE 15
Purchasing power by sector
(1986 = 100)

Year	Private Sector	Public Sector
1984	101.62	105.29
1985	98.50	100.17
1986	100.00	100.00
1987	89.63	89.78
1988	81.40	84.98
1989	64.63	67.95

Source: Banco Central de la República Argentina (1992).

From 1986 to 1987 purchasing power fell by 10.37 per cent for the private sector and 10.22 per cent for the public sector. This shows that the *disciplinamiento social* achieved by the military dictatorship was intensified under the democratic government. Although the democratic government could not politically subordinate the working class, it maintained its economic subordination. Indeed, the unemployment and underemployment rates confirm that the democratic government did not improve the workers' situation.

TABLE 16
Unemployment (1) and underemployment[17] (2) rates
(October each year)

	1981	1982	1983	1984	1985	1986	1987	1988	1989
1	5.3	4.6	3.9	4.4	5.9	5.2	5.7	6.1	7.1
2	6.0	6.4	5.9	5.9	7.1	7.4	8.5	8.0	8.6

Source: Banco Central de la República Argentina (1992).

After the democratic government 1 dollar cost 560 *australes.* After Black Monday, it rose by 3,069 per cent. The interest rate was 84.36 per cent per month. The internal debt was US$3,000 million, US$2,000 million of bank reserves and US$1,000 million of government bonds. External debt was US$67,000 million and the arrears on interest payments reached US$6,500 million (Majul, 1990, p. 249).

Domestic investment declined from an average of 21.4 per cent of GDP in the 1970s to 12.2 per cent in 1988. Subsidies from the state to the private sector – such as industrial promotion or tax exemption – represented US$3,134 million per year (Verbitsky, 1990, p. 102). The industrial sector's physical output declined by 11.9 per cent from 1974 to 1983; from 1983 to 1988 the growth in production was only 0.6 per cent. From 1974 to 1983, the number of workers employed in manufacturing declined by 39.4 per cent; from 1983 to 1988 the decrease was 5.2 per cent.

Under the democratic government, economic stagnation and inequality became more firmly rooted. Thus, the reasons for the CGT's opposition were to be found in the government's inability to transform the economic structure and the *disciplinamiento social* implemented by the *Proceso*.

CGT OPPOSITION

After the September 1987 electoral defeat, the replacement of Carlos Alderete by Ideler Tonelli signalled the collapse of the government's alliance with the *Grupo de los 15* (*Clarín*, 12.9.1987, p. 1). It also represented the beginning of a new period of confrontation between trade unions and the government. Finally, it meant that the main objective of the alliance between the government and the *Grupo de los 15* – that is, the neutralisation of the CGT's confrontational policy – was defeated. Nevertheless, Alderete had actually achieved his objective: free collective bargaining would begin in 1988 (Beliz, 1988, p. 22).

After Alderete's replacement and the October economic measures, the CGT called a general strike for 4 November (*La Nación*, 5.11.1987, p. 1). The strike was successful, with almost 90 per cent adherence in the industrial sector (*La Nación*, 5.11.1987, p. 1). The demonstration at which Ubaldini gave a speech was not so successful – 15,000 people attended according to Federal Police estimates (*La Nación*, 5.11.1987, p. 1). This would deepen internal divisions within the trades union movement over the organisation of general strikes and social demonstrations. As explained above, one of the most important differences between the CGT and the *Grupo de los 15* was over the utility of general strikes and social demonstrations in achieving the labour movement's objectives. The *Grupo de los 15* had achieved most of its objectives by negotiating with the government, while the CGT's more confrontational policy was much less fruitful. An example was the free collective bargaining legislation achieved by Alderete's appointment which was agreed by the *Grupo de los 15* and the government.

Despite these internal divisions, Alfonsín's refusal to meet the CGT's leadership to discuss wage increases (*La Nación*, 9.12.1987, p. 1) provoked the CGT to organise another general strike for 8 and 9 December (*La Nación*, 10.12.1987, p. 1). The strikes had total adherence in both the industrial and the tertiary sectors (Fraga, 1991, p. 25).

In February 1988, the government provided regulations for the free collective bargaining law which would begin to be applied in March (*Clarín*, 14.2.1988, p. 2). By April, the government passed the labour legislation which had been opposed by the employers' organisations before the September 1987 elections (*Clarín*, 15.4.1988, p. 11; Acuña, 1995, p. 300). Despite all these measures, the CGT organised another general strike for 14 April, demanding economic measures to prevent the rise of inflation – in the first three months of 1988 the CPI increased by 38.2 per cent (*Clarín*, 9.4.1988, p. 17). The general strike in April had total adherence in the industrial sector (Fraga, 1991, p. 25). This month also saw a teacher's strike which lasted 33 days, seriously disrupting the school year (*Clarín*, 20.4.1988, p. 2).

After the internal elections of the Peronist party, the role of the CGT was undermined. There were two presidential candidates, Antonio Cafiero and Carlos Menem. Cafiero's policies were viewed as a continuation of Alfonsín's policies. Cafiero emphasised, as Alfonsín did at the beginning of his government, the importance of an agreement between the government, the labour movement and the business organisations as an instrument in resolving the crisis (Gaudio and Thompson, 1990, p. 224). By this time, Menem's policies were viewed as populist. They promoted a redistribution of income as a tool to achieve economic growth. Menem's policies were based on a massive wage increase (*salariazo*) which would promote a *revolución productiva* (productive revolution). The *sindicalismo Peronista* was divided between the two candidates. The

CGT supported Cafiero and the *Grupo de los 15* supported Menem (Gaudio and Thompson, 1990, p. 217). The main agreement between the CGT and Cafiero was that the latter was promoting a unilateral moratorium on the external debt, and an agreement between the government, the trade unions, and the business organisations as a means to attain economic growth (*Clarín*, 25/25.4.1988).

After Cafiero's defeat, the influence of the CGT was undermined. The *Grupo de los 15* and Carlos Menem argued that their victory was a response to the CGT's confrontational policy (Gaudio and Thompson, 1990, p. 230). Once again, the *Grupo de los 15* affirmed that the CGT's confrontational policy did not achieve the trades union movement's main objectives. Therefore, the CGT decreased its level of confrontation mainly by stopping the organisation of general strikes. Likewise, the CGT began to prioritise the issue of the general elections and therefore became more passive in order to facilitate Menem's electoral campaign. The CGT's new objective was to avoid Menem being accused of giving power to trade unions, an accusation which could be used by the Radical party to undermine Menem's image, bringing back memories of Isabel's government.

In August the government launched the *Primavera* plan. After the launching, the CGT began discussing with the government an increase in the minimum wage (*salario mínimo*). As they could not agree on the size of the increase, the CGT called a general strike to be held on 9 September (*Ambito Financiero*, 10.9.1988, p. 1). The general strike was followed by a social demonstration at the *Plaza de Mayo*. Although the strike was widely criticised among trade unionists, and the Peronist presidential candidate refused to participate in the social demonstration (*Clarín*, 7.9.1989, pp. 2–3), it became the most important action and led to a further general strike being called for 12 September (*Ambito Financiero*, 10.9.1988, p. 1). The meeting at *Plaza de Mayo* ended with a violence previously unseen during Alfonsín's government. The Federal Police were particularly brutal and 100 people were injured (*Ambito Financiero*, 13.9.1988, p. 1). After the demonstration, there were accusations made among the government, the CGT and the Peronist party regarding the results of the strike. For the CGT and the Peronist party, the government agitators had promoted the violent break-up of the demonstration in order to prove that a Peronist government

– closely related to trade unions – would represent a return to the violence of the early 1970s. The government held that the police had to intervene due to looting in the area of the square (*Clarín*, 14.9.1988, p. 2).

Carlos Menem did not support the general strike of 12 September. He argued that the Peronist party did not agree with the CGT's decision (Gaudio and Thompson, 1990, p. 34). The CGT confrontational policy was criticised by the Peronist party and, therefore, divided the *sindicalismo Peronista*. Due to this, and despite the hyper-inflation process and the looting, the CGT did not organise more general strikes or social demonstrations. The CGT became a passive actor.

Despite the CGT's change of policies, there were national strikes. In October, railway services were virtually paralysed; postal workers began a work-to-rule campaign and planned an indefinite strike for December; gas workers went on strike from November; and other sectors such as customs, hospitals and the prison service organised strikes (*Clarín*, 5, 6, 10, 15, 27.11.1988). Thus, despite the neutralisation of the CGT, the Radical government was still unable politically to demobilise the labour movement. The last two years of the Radical government showed the gradual neutralisation of the CGT role by the Peronist presidential candidate, Carlos Menem. Despite this, the working class was able to organise itself against the consequences of Black Monday. Therefore, the Radical government was unable to demobilise politically not only the trades union movement but also the working class.

In economic terms this was not the case. Under Alfonsín's government real wages had dramatically fallen; if in January 1984 real wages were 100, in June 1989 they were 55.14. The purchasing power of real wages was, starting from of a base of 100 for January 1984, 44.60 in June 1989 (Garfunkel, 1990, p. 72). Per capita GDP was 12 per cent less in 1988 than in 1975. In 1975, wages and salaries accounted for 53.8 per cent of GDP; in 1983, 41 per cent, and in 1988 only 30 per cent of GDP (Smith, 1990, p. 30).

As the CPI and the WPI began to increase after the failure of the *Plan Austral*, real wages decreased. From 1986 to 1989, the CPI rose by 5,911.9 per cent, and the real wage in the private sector decreased by 27.77 per cent and in the public sector by 15.16 per cent.[18] From 1988 to 1989 purchasing power fell by 20.60 per cent for the private sector and 20.04 per cent for the public sector as a result of hyper-inflation.[19] The situation of the workers was damaged by the failure of the *Plan Austral* and the inability of the democratic government to prevent high inflation rates. This damage was done after the overwhelming redistribution of income at the beginning of the military dictatorship; as said above, from 1974 to 1976 the inflation rate increased by 772.5 per cent while the real wage of the industrial sector fell by 37 per cent. The workers' situation deteriorated progressively under both the dictatorship and the democratic government.

By 1989, unemployment and underemployment rates had risen. Combining both rates, the 1989 level reached approximately 16 per cent of the population of working age. Under the military dictatorship, the figure had been only 11 per cent. In 1974, the industrial unemployment rate was 1.3 per cent; for the construction sector, 2.4 per cent; for the commercial sector, 3.1 per cent; and for services, 1.4 per cent. In October 1989, the rates were 6 per cent, 18.1 per cent, 5.5 per cent and 4.4 per cent, respectively (Morales Solá, 1990, p. 293). The labour force in 1989 was 12.2 million: 7.69 million were employed, 3.6 million were underemployed, and 910,000 were unemployed (*Página/12*, 10.6.1990, p. 11).

From a population of 32 million, 10 million were, after Alfonsín's administration, living beneath the poverty line – that is a family income of US$100 or less per month. Fifteen million were living only slightly above the line. In Greater Buenos Aires, out of a population of 7.3 million people, 36.7 per cent of all households – and 44.3 per cent of individuals – lived in poverty. Of the poor householders, 31.3 per cent were structurally poor and 68.7 per cent were *pauperizados* (Smith, 1990, p. 31).

Fifty per cent of the national income was concentrated in the hands of 20 per cent of the population. In 1974, the richest 20 per cent possessed 39.5 per cent of the national wealth, and the poorest 20 per cent, 8.8 per cent. Under Videla the gap widened, the figures being 42 per cent and 7 per cent, respectively. The last year of the dictatorship, the richest 20 per cent reached 47.7 per cent and the poorest 20 per cent took only 5.9 per cent of the national wealth. By 1988 the gap had widened even further, with figures of 52.4 per cent for the wealthiest fifth, 5.3 per cent for the poorest fifth of the population (Verbitsky, 1990, p. 244).

The economic legacy of the Alfonsín government was a further impoverishment of the working class. The government did not politically demobilise the workers but it did, economically, subordinate them.

TABLE 17
Income distribution
(September each year)

Year	30 % lowest	60 % middle	10 % highest
1974	11.40	60.60	28.10
1976	12.10	59.80	28.00
1978	10.20	53.70	36.10
1981	10.50	54.50	35.00
1985	9.90	56.80	33.30
1988	9.20	54.90	35.90
1989	7.90	50.50	41.60

Source: Boron, A. (1992).

The CGT's confrontational policy maintained the politically powerful role of the trades union movement but it could not avoid a deepening of the *disciplinamiento social* begun under the military dictatorship.

FROM MILITARY REBELLIONS TO GUERRILLA ATTACK

Military Rebellions

In January 1988 a second military rebellion occurred, provoked by Aldo Rico's refusal to accept the detention imposed by a military judge (*Clarín*, 15.1.1988, p. 2). This detention was due to the fact that Aldo Rico had led the former military rebellion. This time, Rico took an infantry regiment in Monte Caseros, located in the Corrientes province, and repudiated General Caridi's authority. Rico demanded a solution for the human rights violations judgements, since the *Semana Santa*'s agreements had not been fulfilled (*Clarín*, 17.1.1988, pp. 2–3). General Caridi was ordered to mobilise a number of key army units from several provincial locations. The repression was periodically interrupted by rains and the information that Rico's followers had laid mines on access bridges – these mines injured three loyal officials (*Clarín*, 18.1.1988, pp. 2–3). After four days, without resisting, Rico surrendered unconditionally (*Clarín*, 19.1.1988, p. 1).

The reason why Rico failed in his second attempt was that the main objective of the rebellion was his refusal to accept the military court's decision. After the passing of the 'due obedience' law the demand for suspending the human rights trials lost most of its followers within the Army. An attack on the Army's hierarchy based on a rejection of a military court's decision did not find many sympathisers. Rico could convince few people that Monte Caseros had any objective other than his own judicial predicament.

After Monte Caseros, 396 members of the Army were accused of undermining the hierarchy of the Army, and 127 of them were imprisoned (*Clarín*, 22.1.1988, p. 2). However, the main consequence of the January rebellion was the 'politicisation' of a faction of the *carapintadas*. This was a result of the defeat of Monte Caseros. Rico and his followers understood that either they began to fight against their comrades – taking the risk of losing support when they began to kill – or they began a 'politicisation' process to confront the hierarchy of the Army and to win civilian support. The latter was chosen and so the *carapintadas* started to publicly criticise the Army hierarchy, the economic strategy of the government, education policy, increasing poverty, corruption and the lack of political leadership. Rico became a political actor who began to play a role inside the democratic game (Acuña and Smulovitz, 1991, p. 25).

In April, new defence legislation was approved (*Ambito Financiero*, 14.4.1988, p. 10). One of the objectives of this law was to annul the previous legislation established by the military dictatorship of Lt General Juan Carlos Onganía. Onganía's law represented the institutionalisation of the National Security Doctrine which defined the participation of the Armed Forces in internal matters. This law gave the Armed forces the 'right' to fight against the armed urban guerrillas, and to concentrate their intelligence services on the investigation of Argentinian citizens. This law was supposed to be the juridical framework of state terrorism. Therefore, the new defence legislation attempted to abolish Onganía's law in order to prevent military coups and human rights violations. The new law defined a different role for the Armed Forces. It established that the Armed Forces would act to confront aggressions of *external* origin. It also refused the military a seat on the *Consejo de Defensa Nacional* (National Defence Council), which consisted of the vice-president, ministers and the head of the Intelligence Service (*Ambito Financiero*, 14.4.1988, p. 10). Finally, the law clearly stated that 'matters related to the country's domestic politics can not, in any case, constitute working hypotheses for military intelligence organisms' (*Latin America Weekly Report*, 28.4.1988, p. 2). The main objective of this law was to limit the actions of the Armed Forces to the defence of the country from external aggression and to avoid their participation in domestic political matters – which was, historically, their main activity.

At the end of 1988, another personal situation provoked a military rebellion. This time, Colonel Mohamed Ali Seineldín, who was in Panama training a special force of Manuel Noriega's Army, began a rebellion due to the Army's refusal to promote him to General (*Clarín*, 5.12.1988, 4). Seineldín was supposed to be the moral leader of the *carapintadas*, therefore the refusal was viewed as another measure to neutralise the role of the movement within the Army. On 30 November, members of the *Albatros* unit of the *Prefectura Naval* left their base armed and in combat gear (*Clarín*, 1.12.1988, pp. 2–3). Two days later they took the infantry school at *Campo de Mayo*, and announced that they were under Seineldín's orders. The Colonel left Panama to lead the rebellion in Buenos Aires (*Clarín*, 5.2.1988, p. 4). The *carapintadas'* main demand was an amnesty for those accused of human rights violations and of participating in the previous rebellions. General Caridi, in a meeting with Seineldín, accepted this demand as a general demand of the Army. Alfonsín refused to establish an amnesty, and ordered the Army to quash the rebellion (*Clarín*, 6.12.1988, pp. 2–3). The Congress called for an emergency session which was attended by several ambassadors showing their support for the democratic government (*Clarín*, 6.12.1988, p. 2). The CGT and business organisations called for a general strike to support democracy while the population was demonstrating against the rebellion in the main squares of Argentina (*Clarín*, 6.12.1988, pp. 2–3).

Once the repression began, the rebels went from *Campo de Mayo* to *Villa Martelli* barracks, located in a suburb close to Buenos Aires. Once at *Villa Martelli*, Seineldín announced his demands which went from budget increases to the establishment of an amnesty. General Isidro Cáceres was leading the repression, when he arrived with his troops at *Villa Martelli*, he – with the approval of General

Caridi – went into the barracks to meet Colonel Seineldín (*Clarín*, 6.12.1988, p. 1). Outside the barracks, there was a social demonstration against the *carapintadas*. This provoked fights between the population and the *carapintadas*, leaving three people dead and 43 injured (*Clarín*, 5.12.1988, p. 5). As Argentina was waiting for the fight to start, General Caridi announced that the operations had ended (*Clarín*, 6.12.1988, p. 1).

Soon after the end of the rebellion, the *carapintadas* publicly announced the terms of the agreement reached with General Cáceres: the replacement of General Caridi by General Cáceres before 23 December, a wage increase, that the *carapintadas* not be judged, the recognition of the 'dirty war' as a positive event and a general amnesty between the elections and the change of administration (Acuña and Smulovitz, 1991, p. 27).

After *Villa Martelli*, the hierarchy of the Army decided on a new strategy to neutralise the *carapintadas*' power. It decided to make the main demands of the *carapintadas* its own, leaving the latter with only the plea that they be spared from trial. Therefore, the *carapintadas* would only deal with their particular juridical situation, while the Army as a whole would lead the negotiations with the government to achieve the main demands (Acuña and Smulovitz, 1991, p. 28). The government, in order to decrease the level of confrontation with the Army, increased the wages of the members of the Armed Forces and replaced General Caridi by General Gassino, a follower of Caridi's strategy (Acuña and Smulovitz, 1991, p. 28).

The Guerrilla Attack

The reappearance of the guerrilla issue would, finally, improve the public image of the Armed Forces and give them, once again, a role in the internal security of the country. On 23 January, an armed group occupied the barracks of an infantry regiment in *La Tablada* (*Ambito Financiero*, 24.1.1989, p. 1). The attack was led by the *Movimiento Todos por la Patria* (MTP) (Movement of All for the Fatherland) constituted mainly by members of the ERP (People's Revolutionary Army) one of the main guerrilla movements of the early 1970s. Apparently, Enrique Gorriarán Merlo, a well-known ERP member who had collaborated in the Nicaraguan Revolution and is supposed to have killed Anastasio Somoza in Paraguay, was leading the attack and escaped before the defeat (*Página/12*, 25.1.1989, p. 6). Paradoxically, the MTP was known as an organisation for the defence of human rights. One of its leaders, Jorge Baños, was a lawyer who had represented relatives of the *desaparecidos* and had promoted the defence of human rights. Baños was found dead in *La Tablada* (*Página/12*, 25.1.1989, p. 6). A few days before the attack, Baños had appeared on the government-owned TV channels alleging an alliance between the *carapintadas* and Menem against Alfonsín's government (*Página/12*, 20.1.1989, p. 6). Due to this, Menem accused Alfonsín's government of being connected with the guerrilla attack, as a means of undermining Menem's possibilities of winning the elections (*Ambito Financiero*, 27.1.1989, p. 6).

The real objective of the attack was never clarified. As the survivors explained, the objective of the attack was to avoid a new military rebellion. However, documents suggested that it tried to simulate a military rebellion, scattering pamphlets praising Colonel Seineldín. Once the participants had taken the barracks they called for rebellion, announcing that they had become the representatives of the popular resistance, since they had managed to abort the military rebellion. Finally, they would call for a popular demonstration at *Plaza de Mayo* to ask Alfonsín to place himself at the head of this 'armed popular movement' (*Página/12*, 25.1.1989, pp. 6–9).

The real victor of *La Tablada* attack was the Army. First, the Generals repaired their image as soldiers after having been accused by the *carapintadas* of being 'desk Generals'. Second, the Army would, again, participate in internal conflicts and internal intelligence activities. Finally, as the organisations for human rights had been discredited by the participation of some of their members in the attack, the Army began to accuse them of guerrilla activities (*Página/12*, 24.1.1989, p. 1).

A few days after the attack, Alfonsín created the *Consejo Nacional de Seguridad* (National Security Council) constituted by the Ministers of Defence, Home Affairs and Foreign Affairs, the head of the Intelligence Services, the chiefs of staff of the three Armed Forces and the chief of the Armed Forces (*Ambito Financiero*, 26.1.1989, p. 1). The objective of the Council was to advise the government on guerrilla matters. Alfonsín also established by decree permission to use the Armed Forces against internal attacks that could not be repelled by the police or by security forces (*Ambito Financiero*, 26.1.1989, p. 1). The decree stated that guerrilla actions whose objective was the destruction of the constitutional order would warrant defence measures 'that will be graduated, depending upon the magnitude of the aggression' (Pion-Berlin, 1991, p. 568). This represented a setback for the government's position, which had been expressed in the Defence Law approved in April 1988. No one had so far done so much to achieve the vindication of the dirty war and the Armed Forces than the MTP and its incomprehensible attack on *La Tablada*.

Between the guerrilla attack and the change of administration, the conflict with the Armed Forces was at an impasse. The amnesty question would arise in the meetings between Alfonsín and Menem. The former wanted Menem to sign a joint decree establishing the amnesty for officials accused, but not yet condemned, of human rights violations. Therefore, the Commander-in-Chief would remain in prison. Menem wanted to include the *carapintadas*, something that Alfonsín would not accept since they had threatened the democratic regime three times in two years. Nevertheless, Menem did not accept Alfonsín's proposal mainly because he wanted to keep this measure for his government and to monopolise its benefits. Such a decision would facilitate Menem's relationship with the Armed Forces.

The Gradual Neutralisation of the Carapintadas' *Power*

After *Villa Martelli*, the *carapintadas* had lost support within the Armed Forces. Their confrontation was based on personal grievances rather than general demands for the Armed Forces. The 'due obedience' law neutralised the role of the *carapintadas* since it had given them what they required: the end of human rights trials.

In order to avoid the collapse of the democratic system, Alfonsín made concessions to the Armed Forces. From the *Punto Final* to 'due obedience', he conceded more than he actually wanted to. Aldo Rico's example showed the outcome of these concessions. He threatened democracy with the *Semana Santa* rebellion and then achieved his real objective: the 'due obedience' law and the end of the trials. As he achieved his objectives the *carapintadas* movement lost its power, as evidenced in the failure of *Monte Caseros*. The only way to have a voice was, then, by joining the democratic game. The cost of Aldo Rico's integration into the democratic process was very high: the freedom of torturers and killers. However, the earlier defeat of Alfonsín's objectives – that is, the *Consejo Supremo* sentence and the Sapag amendment – rendered the relationship with the Armed Forces very difficult. This defeat meant that Alfonsín could no longer control the policy towards the Armed Forces. His government started to react rather than to decide. The defeat also signified that Alfonsín could not move quickly and decisively when, at the beginning of his government, public opinion supported him (Huntington, 1993, p. 224).

Gradually the economic crisis became more important than human rights violations. Public opinion turned against the government. The economic crisis also strained the government's relationship with the trade unions. Thus, Alfonsín did not have sufficient domestic support to confront the Armed Forces. He could not maintain an open conflict with the Armed Forces indefinitely. However, he was also unable to put an end to all human rights trials. Alfonsín faced a dilemma: to prosecute and to punish or to forgive and forget (Huntington, 1993). He chose a compromise path between these extremes. He prosecuted and punished the Commanders-in-Chief, while excusing the crimes of low-ranking officials. What became difficult, or almost impossible, was to achieve domestic support to forgive the latter. When – through the CONADEP report and the public judgement of the *Juntas* – the truth about the 'dirty war' emerged, Argentinian public opinion, the organisations of human rights and political parties – among them the Radical party – required, through social mobilisations, punishment for low-ranking officials. The Judiciary, anyway, did just this, through Point 30 of the sentence for the Commanders-in-Chief.

It was after the Easter rebellion when Alfonsín achieved his objective of passing the 'due obedience' law. However, this undermined his power over the Armed Forces and his political credibility.[20]

The concessions that Alfonsín made have to be understood in the context of Argentina's history and the circumstances of the new democracy. Without domestic and trade union support, due to the economic crisis, an open conflict with the Armed Forces seemed to be a real threat to the consolidation of democracy. For Alfonsín, it was crucial that during the Easter rebellion, he obtained the support of the CGT. If the CGT had not repudiated the rebellion, it could have finished in a very different fashion. Although the appointment of Alderete complicated the economic strategy, Alfonsín believed that this was necessary in order to consolidate democracy.[21]

The economic crisis reduced Alfonsín's margin of manoeuvre: his domestic support was undermined and the conflict with the trade unions was intensified. Therefore, in order to consolidate democracy, he had to make some concessions. His policy towards the Armed Forces gave many concessions. Here it is argued that after having imprisoned the Commanders-in-Chief, he could not go further in his confrontation with the Armed Forces without threatening democracy. The economic crisis and trade union opposition limited Alfonsín's ability to maintain an open conflict with the Armed Forces.

CONCLUSION

During its last two years, the Radical government did not attempt to resolve the crisis of the Argentinian state, intensifying the economic crisis and accelerating the implementation of a monetarist restructuring of the state. The government deepened the economic subordination of the working class without politically demobilising it. Finally, it managed to prevent the seizure of state power by the Armed Forces. The consolidation of democracy was its main achievement. However, democracy was consolidated by deepening the military dictatorship's *disciplinamiento social*. In this sense, the military dictatorship succeeded since its economic structural reform and the *disciplinamiento social* lasted longer than the dictatorship itself, and the democratic government succeeded since democracy was consolidated. By the end of the first democratic government, although the crisis of the Argentinian state was acute, one of its main political features had been modified: the democratic regime was not threatened by the Armed Forces.

NOTES

1. Interview with senior official from Alfonsín's government, 25.10.1993, Buenos Aires.

2. The current account deficit amounted to US$4,236 million (Banco Central de la República Argentina, unpublished data).
3. Machinea points out (1990, p. 71) that from the second quarter of 1987 to the second quarter of 1988 international prices rose around 30 per cent mainly as a result of the drought in the US and the large devaluation of the dollar in the two previous years. This had a beneficial effect in the balance of payments, however, as Argentina 'eats' the same goods that it exports; it also had a negative impact on food prices in the domestic market.
4. Carlos Menem, a lawyer from the University of Córdoba, belonged to the non-union wing of the Peronist party which is particularly strong in the provinces. He was three times governor of La Rioja. He had been imprisoned under Videla's presidency and rearrested in 1982 for joining an anti-government demonstration. Menem, together with Antonio Cafiero and Carlos Grosso, represented the Peronist *Renovación*, one main pillar of which was to be a non-union sector of Peronism. Menem and Cafiero both wanted to be the Peronist presidential candidate for the 1989 general election. For the first time in its history, on 9 July 1988, Peronism nominated its presidential candidate by direct primary election. Cafiero had the support of the CGT, while Menem was supported by *los 15*. Menem obtained 53 per cent of the total vote cast and Cafiero, 46 per cent (McGuire, 1992, p. 48).
5. Interviews with senior officials from Alfonsín's government, 19.10.1993 and 1.11.1993, Buenos Aires.
6. As indicated earlier, Domingo Cavallo was President of the Central Bank during the last period of the military dictatorship. He implemented the last step of the nationalisation of the private external debt. Lázara (1997, p. 355) argues that the international creditors abandoned the Radical government because they were tired of its attitude towards the external debt.
7. According to Lázara (1997, p. 40) the run against the *austral* was also a consequence of the guerrilla attack on an Army unit in January 1989.
8. Most of the enterprises were those which constituted the group of *Capitanes de la Industria* such as Grupo Macri, Loma Negra, Grupo Bulgheroni as well as transnational corporations such as Bunge y Born and Techint.
9. According to Lázara (1997, p. 358), the sale of exports during the first three months of 1989 was 46.3 per cent less than that of 1988.
10. Between 500 and 600 million dollars left Argentina between 6 and 27 February (Lázara, 1997, p. 357).
11. The February measures meant that 80 per cent of the proceeds from agricultural exports were to be sold in the commercial market with an exchange rate set by the government, and 20 per cent in the free market.
12. The *Grupo de los Ocho* succeeded the *Grupo de los Once;* it was constituted by the UIA, CAC, ADEBA, Chamber of Construction, Commerce Stock, Union of the Construction, SRA and ABRA.
13. He was Minister of Economics during the military dictatorship, under Galtieri's presidency during the Malvinas conflict.

14. Roberto Alemann explained the reasons why the liberalisation was 'expected' by the economic establishment in an article in *La Nación*, 7.8.1988, p. 1, Suplemento Económico. See also Lázara (1997).
15. For more details on these negotiations see Lázara (1997).
16. After the failure of his first economic strategies, Menem named Domingo Cavallo as Economics Minister.
17. 'Under-employees' (*subempleados*) means those who work less than eight hours per day. They are also without any kind of social security since they are 'black employees' (*trabajadores no efectivizados*).
18. Calculated from Tables 9 and 14.
19. Calculated from Table 15.
20. Cheresky (1998, p. 54) points out how the concessions made to the Armed Forces affected Alfonsín's public image.
21. Interviews with senior officials from Alfonsín's government, 25.10.1993 and 19.10.1993, Buenos Aires.

Conclusions

*'... me ocurrió lo peor que le puede pasar a un luchador: sentí lástima de mí.
Recordé la ley de obediencia debida, la entrega anticipada del gobierno ... Por
qué siempre he de ser yo quien pague el precio de la defensa de la democracia?'*

*[... the worst thing for a fighter happened to me: I felt sorry for myself. I
remembered the due obedience law, the early hand-over of the government ...
Why does it always have to be me who pays the price for defending democracy?]*
Raúl Alfonsín quoted by Lázara, 1997, p. 381

SOME FINAL CONSIDERATIONS ON THE STATE AND ITS CRISIS

In order to conceptualise the capitalist state, the usual distinction
which orthodox political science draws between 'economics' and
'politics' must be reassessed. This book argues that to understand
fully the development of the Argentinian capitalist state, the state
must be conceived of as a social relation expressing the instability of
the capital–labour relation. A purely economic analysis of the
Alfonsín government would miss the conceptualisation of the
working class as a barrier to the successful implementation of
economic reforms. A purely political analysis would miss the
consequences of the economic crisis and the constraints of the
external debt. This book argues that understanding the capitalist
state as a social relation offers a more comprehensive framework for
the analysis of contemporary crisis.

This conceptualisation of the capitalist state includes, crucially,
the notion of class struggle. This book suggests that class struggle
not only impinges on the development of the capitalist state but that
the state itself is an aspect and a site of class struggle. The income
distribution struggle between, on the one hand, Argentina's
international creditors and its upper bourgeoisie and, on the other
hand, the working class, was the ultimate reason why the Radical
government was unable to resolve the crisis of the Argentinian state.

Finally, the book suggests that it is necessary to view the state as
embedded within an international state system in the context of a

globalising economy. It affirms that the capitalist state can no longer be studied in isolation. This is clearly demonstrated by the analysis of the Alfonsín government. The external debt crisis severely constrained the decision making capacity of the Radical government. The debt crisis was subsequently employed as a means of imposing and legitimising the imposition of monetarism upon debtor countries. Thus, the development of the capitalist state must be studied in relation to the development of the global economy itself.

Regarding the notion of crisis, the book shows that the conceptualisation of crisis as either 'economic' or 'political' is misplaced. Crisis expresses the instability of the labour–capital relation on which capitalist society is based. Thus, the Argentinian crisis must be analysed as a crisis of the Argentinian state, a crisis of a particular historical form of class domination.

THE ARGENTINIAN STATE AFTER RESTRUCTURING

In Argentina, the breakdown of the social relations which sustained the populist state produced, in 1955, a process of struggle. Inward-oriented strategies became unsustainable. While the dominant class was fighting to repress, economically and politically, the working class, by changing the social relations of populism, the latter was fighting to maintain its political and economic inclusion. The outcome of this struggle was the Bureaucratic Authoritarian (BA) state.

The neo-liberal state of the 1990s has similar characteristics to the BA state of the 1970s. Both attempt to subordinate, politically and economically, the working class. While the BA state attempted to de-politicise the working class, the neo-liberal state de-politicised the economy, 'de-ideologised' politics and turned social issues into economic ones. In the neo-liberal state, the economy can no longer be a political affair, it is governed by technocrats and its main objective is to achieve efficiency rather than an equal income distribution.

The neo-liberal state is democratic but its political objectives are similar to the authoritarian state of the 1970s. While the latter dominated through political and economic repression, the neo-liberal state uses the image of political democracy as a way of legitimising economic exclusion. This is an important difference between the two forms of state domination. Unlike the BA state, the neo-liberal state uses the image of the rule of law to base its legitimacy. The neo-liberal state's legitimacy derives from the institutions of liberal democracy: an independent judiciary, parliament, local governments, individual rights. As with any other form of capitalist state all these images – political democracy, individual rights, independent judiciary, the urgent need for reforms – hide the real form of domination of the neo-liberal state: domination by exclusion. Like the BA state, the neo-liberal state has excluded a great part of its population. While the former excluded by repression, the latter excludes by the imposition of market rule.

Between the BA state of the 1970s and the de-politicised democratic state of the 1990s there was a process of struggle between those who wanted to maintain the class relations of Peronism and those who wanted to establish a new state and new class relations. The subordination of the working class and of the domestic bourgeoisie from small and medium-sized companies, and the establishment of an alliance between the powerful transnationalised and integrated bourgeoisie,[1] private foreign investors and the government are the main features of the de-politicised democratic state of the 1990s. Historically, there were two main class alliances: an alliance between the industrial and agrarian bourgeoisie, and an alliance between the 'domestic' bourgeoisie and the unionised working class. The restructuring of the 1990s has been supported by the transnationalised-integrated bourgeoisie with the exclusion of any other sector. There is no cross-class alliance. There is now no need for class collaboration.

The main aim of the neo-liberal state is to achieve economic efficiency. The problem lies in the meaning of economic efficiency. Does it mean an equal income distribution? Will economic efficiency, once achieved, provide equal opportunities for the whole population? Is efficiency understood as a tool to achieve the well-being of the whole population? Apparently not. Efficiency is understood as providing the appropriate institutional foundations for markets (World Bank, 1997). The state must provide a macroeconomic and a microeconomic environment 'that sets the right incentives for efficient economic activity' (World Bank, 1997). While the state regulates, the market is *the* allocator of resources.

The neo-liberal state of the 1990s, by imposing the power of the market, has de-politicised its management of the economy, 'de-ideologised' politics and turned social issues into economic ones. It masks its domination by exclusion with the idea of political democracy, its economic exclusion with its political inclusion. It reinvigorates the fetishised separation between 'politics' and 'economics', between the classless status of citizen and the class character of the worker. The political rights of the unemployed, under-employed, uneducated or unskilled are insufficient to transform their economic and social exclusion. In fact, the neo-liberal state has exacerbated the old contradiction between capitalism and democracy: 'capitalism is a system in which many scarce resources are owned privately, and decisions about allocating them are a private prerogative. Democracy is a system through which people as citizens may express preferences about allocating resources that they do not privately own' (Przeworski and Wallerstein, 1988). The consequences of this exacerbation have been revealed increasingly in Argentina over the 1990s.

CONCLUSIONS ON THE CRISIS OF THE ARGENTINIAN STATE

Success of the 1976 Military Dictatorship

The 1976 military dictatorship attempted to resolve the crisis of the Argentinian state by applying economic structural reform and state terrorism. The economic structural reform attempted to modify the role of the state and its class relations, while state terrorism was intended to demobilise politically the working class, and defeat the armed urban guerrilla campaign.

The state was viewed as a barrier to the resolution of the economic crisis of the 1970s. The first tool to undermine its economic role was the 1977 financial reform which liberalised the financial market. Likewise, the undermining of the industrial sector, which had been promoted by the state during the 1950s and 1960s, was another means of decreasing the direct economic role of the state. Finally, the privatisation and closing down of public enterprises was also intended to cut down the participation of the state as an actor in the economy. These measures were an attempt to restructure the state and its relation to the economy according to the monetarist approach. The ultimate objective was to give to the market the power to discipline society. Paradoxically, the state was seen as a barrier and as a tool for restructuring the economy and class relations. The power of the state was used to demobilise politically the working class and to restructure the bourgeoisie. In this sense, the military dictatorship imposed a 'state-managed liberalism', whereas the power of the state and its apparatus was used to promote or to discriminate against particular sectors.

The economic reform of 1976 modified wider class relations. In general its aim was to subordinate the working class economically. Its specific objective was to prevent a return to Peronism. To this end, by dismantling the industrial sector, the military dictatorship undermined the economic power of the industrial working class. The process of *pauperización, desasalarización* and *terciarización* increasingly subordinated the working class to market discipline.

Thus, the economic structural reform undermined the Keynesian role of the state as the regulator of the economy, and the institutionalised economic and political power of the working class. The military government thereby attempted to implement a monetarist restructuring of the state and of its class relations. In this sense, the military dictatorship intended to resolve Argentina's crisis. However, the economic reform could neither prevent high inflation rates nor reduce the fiscal deficit. Moreover, one of the features of the economic reform was the increase of external debt. By the end of the military dictatorship, Argentina had difficulty in servicing its external debt and negotiations began with the IMF. In this respect therefore the military dictatorship was unsuccessful.

Nevertheless, the 1976 military dictatorship did achieve many of its political objectives: that is, the political subordination of the working class and the elimination of Peronism, understood as an alliance between the workers and the 'domestic' bourgeoisie. The latter point is especially significant. The economic structural reform was an attempt to undermine the role of the 'domestic' bourgeoisie by promoting the concentration of capital in the biggest conglomerates at the expense of small and medium-sized companies. The study of the democratic government shows that the concentration of capital in the biggest conglomerates could not be reversed after the 1980s. The political demobilisation of the workers seemed to be temporary since, under the democratic government, the trades union movement and the working class possessed the possibility of blocking government policies. However, the economic subordination of the workers in fact lasted longer than the dictatorship itself, and thus can be considered as an achievement of the dictatorship. Likewise, the Peronist movement did not win the 1983 general elections and the Peronism of the 1990s seems to be very different from that based on an alliance between the workers and the 'domestic' bourgeoisie. Indeed, Carlos Menem has continued the monetarist restructuring of the state which seems to be the culmination of developments started by the military dictatorship.

Moreover, one of the main objectives of the dictatorship was to defeat the armed urban guerrilla movement. Through the implementation of state terrorism, the armed urban guerrilla 'disappeared' from Argentina's political scene. Indeed, the armed urban guerrilla, despite the isolated attack of 1989, did not have any significance during the 1980s. In this sense the military dictatorship achieved another political objective.

Thus, one of the conclusions of this book is that the military dictatorship, despite its inability to control high inflation or reduce the fiscal deficit, did, in fact, achieve its political objectives. Despite defeat in the Malvinas war, high inflation rates, the high fiscal deficit, and the 'horrors' of the 'dirty war', the 1976 military dictatorship achieved a 'successful' and bloody partial restructuring of social relations in Argentina. The legacy of its economic structural reform constrained the incoming democratic government. The economic legacy of the dictatorship was constituted by a huge external debt, a high concentration of capital, and the impoverishment of the working class.

The Paradoxical Legacy of the Democratic Government

The main political objective of the Alfonsín government was the consolidation of democracy. It also attempted to demobilise politically the trades union movement and the Armed Forces. It attempted to demobilise the trades union movement since the Radical party considered the movement to be a threat to democratic consolidation due to its authoritarian roots and its past record of blocking government policies. It attempted to undermine the political role of the Armed Forces and to bring them to trial due to the human rights violations committed during the military dictatorship.

Economically, the Radical government did not initially have a specific strategy to deal with the main problems that Argentina was facing. Alfonsín attempted to apply an economic strategy similar to that of the 1963 Radical government. This strategy soon proved to be unable to address the pressures facing the Argentinian economy in the 1980s.

The Radical Government's Inability to Resolve the Economic Crisis
In 1983, the economic crisis was characterised by the burden of the external debt, high inflation rates and a high fiscal deficit. The external debt not only constrained economic growth but also limited the options available to deal with the economic crisis. The external debt did not threaten democracy, but it did impose a monetarist restructuring of the state as the first step towards the consolidation of democracy. In this sense, the debt constrained the decision making policy choices of Latin American governments. The external debt crisis gave the IMF and the World Bank a significant role as regulators of the domestic economies of the debtor countries. This book demonstrates that the economic 'U-turn' of the Radical government was in large part a consequence of the pressure from international creditors to service the debt. There was no choice for a liberal democratic government other than to pay the debt and to apply an IMF plan. In response to this dilemma, the Radical government chose an alternative path: it neither fully applied nor fully rejected an IMF plan. This alternative solution confronted the government with the trades union movement which demanded a full rejection of an IMF plan, and with the international creditors who demanded a full implementation of an IMF plan. Together the two actors were able to block government policies and finally provoked Alfonsín's downfall.

The high inflation rates and the high fiscal deficit were significant features of the economic crisis. Inflation is the monetary expression of the income distribution struggle. The fiscal deficit, which caused high inflation rates, was a consequence of the burden of the external debt, tax evasion and state subsidies to the private sector. It represented the monetary expression of the appropriation of wealth by the international creditors and the wealthiest sector of Argentina's population. The government was able to control temporarily the inflation rate, but it was unable to reduce the fiscal deficit. The government did not confront the wealthiest sector of

Argentina's population and the international creditors, but it did maintain and deepen the economic subordination of the workers.

The downfall of the Radical government was in large part caused by the pressures from the international creditors and the upper bourgeoisie for the full implementation of the monetarist restructuring, combined with the barrier presented by the working class to such a restructuring.

The Strength of the Trade Unions and the Working Class

The Radical government could neither control nor demobilise the trades union movement. In this sense, the political demobilisation of the trade unions achieved by the military dictatorship was only temporary. However, the trade unions could not avoid a deepening of the economic subordination of the working class. Nevertheless, they did achieve most of their objectives: most notably the free collective bargaining legislation, the enlargement of strikers' rights, and the participation of the trade unions in the management of the Health Service Funds (*Obras Sociales*). They also achieved short-term objectives, such as many wage increases, which undermined the government's economic strategy. Thus, the trade unions, however unable to prevent a deepening in the economic subordination of the workers, proved to be able to achieve their main organisational objectives and to block government policies. Between 1983 and 1989, the strength of the trade unions was the ultimate barrier to restructuring the state and its class relations.

However, after the Peronist internal elections, the CGT's confrontational policies were neutralised by the Peronist presidential candidate who did not support the CGT strategy. Thus, the last period of the democratic government saw the exploitation of the divisions within the working class and the trades union movement as the basis upon which to secure their political demobilisation. Indeed, by dividing the *sindicalismo Peronista*, Carlos Menem achieved, during the last period of the Radical government, its political demobilisation.

The Radical Government's Success: the Political Demobilisation of the Armed Forces

The Radical government modified a historical feature of the crisis of the Argentinian state. Historically, the response to the crisis of the Argentinian state was the seizure of power of the state by the Armed

Forces. This was notably the case of the 1966 and 1976 military dictatorships. As the democratic governments of 1963 and 1973 were unable to resolve the crisis, the Armed Forces, through military coups, took office in order to impose their order. Despite the fact that the 1983 democratic government was also unable to resolve the crisis, the Armed Forces could not successfully threaten democratic stability. Alfonsín's policies towards the Armed Forces not only discredited them but also aggravated their internal divisions. This secured their political demobilisation and constituted the first step towards the consolidation of democracy. By the end of the democratic government, although the economic crisis and class conflict had deepened, the Armed Forces did not attempt to overthrow the democratic government. The Armed Forces were discredited and internally divided due to Alfonsín's policies.

The acknowledgement of the 'dirty war' through the 1985 public trial of the *Juntas Militares*, the publication of the *Comisión Nacional de Desaparición de Personas* (CONADEP) report and the outcome of the trial on the management of the Malvinas war discredited an Armed Forces already weakened by the collapse of the *Proceso*. This, together with cuts in military expenditure – which meant a drastic reduction in their industrial-military capacity and personnel – meant that the Armed Forces lost their powerful political and even economic roles. Their public image changed and they were seen from a completely different perspective; in the public's eyes they went from being the 'guardians of western values' to simple 'murderers'. Thus, the Armed Forces were no longer a political alternative. Alfonsín deepened their longer-term political demobilisation. It is essential to point out that the breakdown of the alliance between the bourgeoisie and the Armed Forces was the point of departure for their political demobilisation. However, Alfonsín, understanding the weaknesses of the Armed Forces after the collapse of the *Proceso* and attacking them exactly on the issues where they were most vulnerable – most notably, human rights violations, their own internal divisions and the defence budget – was able to modify dramatically civil–military relations. This was Alfonsín's main achievement.

RESTRUCTURING IN THE 1990s

After 16 years of democracy there is still considerable disillusionment in Argentina. Democracy and economic stability have not yet brought sustainable development. There is a high unemployment rate, increasing levels of poverty, increasing corruption and no independent Judiciary. However, nobody, after living through the horrors of a military dictatorship, can ignore the benefits of living under a democratic government: constitutional rights are no longer a dead letter in Argentina, the economically excluded majority have not been deprived of political rights. This was not the only fundamental change in Argentina's politics in the last 16 years. The state has also undergone a profound transformation.

Carlos Menem's first administration began a series of changes from the opening up of the economy to the privatisation of most public enterprises. Menem's government imposed a restructuring of the state and its class relations. During the 1980s the historical conditions for a restructuring of the state did not exist, the struggle had not yet finished and nobody could claim victory. Only after five and half years of class struggle was there a winner and a loser. The outcome of this struggle explains why Carlos Menem could impose a restructuring of the state which had been firmly opposed by the Peronist party and the Peronist trade unions during Alfonsín's government.

In fact, Carlos Menem did what Alfonsín could not. He politically demobilised the trades union movement and the Armed Forces. While the former was Menem's own achievement, the latter should be seen as a continuation of Alfonsín's policies. Menem's government was also able to stabilise the economy and to gain the trust not only of the multinational financial institutions but also of private investors. He also reformed the Constitution, after a pact with Alfonsín, allowing himself to run for another presidential term. But he will be most remembered as the architect, together with his former Economics Minister, Domingo Cavallo, of Argentina's fastest and deepest reforms of the last part of this century.

The Radical government's departure showed that the agro-industrial-financial bourgeoisie was not prepared to support a government that rejected the imposition of new rules. It also proved that while the government could survive 13 general strikes and an endless open conflict with the trade unions, it could not survive the opposition of the international creditors and the agro-industrial-financial bourgeoisie.

Carlos Menem understood this message and attempted to include the integrated bourgeoisie into his government by naming a top manager of Bunge y Born[2] as his first Economics Minister. Although this strategy failed[3] to stabilise the economy, it allowed the Peronist government to gain the support of the integrated bourgeoisie.

By 1989 it was also clear that the debt was not a political issue and that the international creditors were not prepared to support an economic strategy which would not guarantee the repayment of interest on the debt. That Argentina's economic future was highly dependent on the government's strategy towards the external debt was also beyond doubt. It was clear that repaying the debt meant the imposition of a monetarist restructuring of the state which had been expressed by the so-called 'Washington Consensus'.

Regarding the trades union movement, when Menem took office it was evident that the endless conflict between the trade unions and the Radical government had not impeded the economic subordination of the working class. This provoked divisions within the trades union movement regarding the policy of confrontation led by the CGT. This meant that the relationship between the government and the trade unions would change, there being greater trust between the new Peronist government and the *sindicalismo Peronista*. In fact, Menem did what Alfonsín tried to do in 1987: that is, neutralise the combative unions by appointing conciliatory union members to the Ministry of Labour. In October 1989, the CGT was again divided into two bodies: the pro-Menem CGT San Martín, officially recognised by the government, and the combative CGT Azopardo, isolated by the government. By dividing the labour movement, Menem achieved in a few months what Alfonsín so dearly wanted to happen: political demobilisation and government control of the trade unions.

It must be stressed that the international scene was also in transition with the Cold War nearing its end. The Alfonsín government was highly ideological with the President placing political principles over economic strategies. The confrontation between left and right was alive and kicking and the political mobilisation of civil society did not stop with the re-establishment of democracy. When Menem took office the deep economic crisis was of primary importance with political issues running second. Decisions that were simply a matter of political will for Menem were not possible for Alfonsín – for instance, the sacking of Alfredo Astiz, a symbolic figure of the 'dirty war'.

The relationship between Menem and the Armed Forces changed dramatically in December 1990. While at the beginning of his presidency he seemed to be close to the *carapintadas* movement and released 200 of them in a first amnesty, after the bloody rebellion of December 1990 Menem's government was able to defeat and dismantle the *carapintadas*. Menem could resolve the military situation because Alfonsín had previously paid the costs of dealing with human rights violations. Alfonsín paid a high political and personal cost for the trial of the *Juntas*, the CONADEP report and the dismantling of the Armed Forces' economic power. This, together with the breakdown of the historical alliance between the Forces and the bourgeoisie undermined during the *Proceso* and even more damaged with the emergence of the nationalist *carapintadas* movement, meant a profound and lasting change in civil–military relations which was an essential step towards the consolidation of democracy.

THE HISTORICAL SIGNIFICANCE OF ALFONSÍN'S GOVERNMENT

Looking back, Alfonsín's legacy seems to be much more than hyper-inflation. His historical legacy includes the consolidation of democracy, the transformation of Argentina's party political system and the establishment of conditions for the restructuring of the state and its class relations.

The consolidation of democracy was achieved through the political demobilisation of the Armed Forces and the trade unions. While the Armed Forces' case is quite straightforward, that of the trade unions is less evident. The Armed Forces were discredited after the *Proceso* and Alfonsín's policies deepened this situation. The trade unions became discredited due to their endless confrontations with the government. These confrontations did not achieve an improvement in workers' conditions and, thus, the labour movement became divided between a combative and a conciliatory line.

The year 1987 produced some crucial events. The due obedience law and the appointment of a Peronist trade unionist as Labour Minister were seen as concessions, and the Radical government was punished in the September elections. Public opinion in Argentina seemed to be tired of the power struggle between the Armed Forces, the trade unions and the government.

Gradually, the Armed Forces and the trades union movement began to lose their historically powerful role. In this sense, Alfonsín's policies, although chaotic in the short term, began to transform the party political system into one of greater stability, maturity and democracy. Historically, the Armed Forces and the trade unions have replaced the political parties and have established a perverse game: the reciprocal negation of legitimacy (Halperín Donghi, 1994a). While the Armed Forces are no longer a political alternative, the trade unions can no longer claim the exclusive political representation of the workers.

This transformation of the political party system is Alfonsín's main contribution to the consolidation of democracy. However, as stated, democracy was consolidated in a context of increasing poverty. Alfonsín's government was unable to restructure the state and avoid a monetarist restructuring of the state. Alfonsín himself opposed an economic restructuring of the state. However, the absence of an alternative to monetarism exacerbated the pressures for such a restructuring and, therefore, the outcome of the Radical government was, inadvertently, to prepare the ground for it.

Alfonsín's legacy was a feeling of hope and disillusion: the consolidation of democracy, but in the context of domination through economic and social exclusion.

NOTES

1. The term integrated means that the former divisions among the agrarian, industrial and financial bourgeoisie are no longer significant.
2. A multinational company of Argentinian origin.
3. Miguel Roig's death only six days after taking office was followed by the appointment of another Bunge y Born manager, Néstor Rapanelli. He was replaced by Antonio Erman González, a Christian Democrat, who has been Economics Minister in La Rioja during Menem's administration. After his failure to stabilise the economy and to comply with the IMF demands, Erman González was replaced by Domingo Cavallo who, in April 1991, with the launching of his Convertibility Plan dramatically restructured the economy.

Appendix:
Argentina's main economic indicators

Table A1
GDP growth (percentages)

Year	%
1976	−0.5
1977	6.3
1978	−3.3
1979	6.5
1980	1.0
1981	−7.0
1982	−5.8
1983	2.6
1984	2.2
1985	−4.6
1986	5.8
1987	1.8
1988	−3.0
1989	−4.6

Source: Argentinian Central Bank (*Banco Central de la República Argentina*), unpublished data.

TABLE A2
Inflation rates (%)

Year	%
1976	349.0
1977	160.0
1978	169.0
1979	140.1
1980	87.5
1981	131.2
1982	209.7
1983	433.6
1984	686.8
1985	385.4
1986	81.9
1987	174.8
1988	387.7
1989	4923.3

Source: National Institute of Statistics and Census (*Instituto Nacional de Estadísticas y Censos)*, unpublished data.

TABLE A3
Fiscal deficit as % of GDP

Year	%
1976	11.7
1977	4.7
1978	6.5
1979	6.5
1980	7.5
1981	13.3
1982	15.1
1983	15.2
1984	12.5
1985	5.4
1986	4.3
1987	6.4
1988	8.6*
1989	7.2*

Source: Argentinian Central Bank (*Banco Central de la República Argentina)*, unpublished data.

Note: * from Economic Commission for Latin America and the Caribbean (1990).

TABLE A4
Terms of Trade

Year	%
1976	89.5
1977	93.6
1978	91.9
1979	100.2
1980	117.7
1981	124.6
1982	105.2
1983	101.9

Source: World Bank (1989).

Note: 1970 = 100.

TABLE A5
Terms of trade (growth rates, goods and services)

Year	%
1983	−1.9
1984	16.8
1985	−18.1
1986	−5.5
1987	−9.8
1988	5.0
1989	−4.0

Source: Economic Commission for Latin America and the Caribbean (1990).

TABLE A6
Per capita GDP

Year	%
1983	1.2
1984	1.0
1985	−5.7
1986	4.6
1987	0.8
1988	−4.1
1989	−5.6

Source: Economic Commission for Latin America and the Caribbean (1990).

TABLE A7
Gross national income

Year	%
1983	0.9
1984	4.8
1985	-7.6
1986	8.7
1987	2.1
1988	-4.3
1989	-7.1

Source: Economic Commission for Latin America and the Caribbean (1990).

TABLE A8
Real wages and salaries*

Year	%
1983	22.8
1984	25.3
1985	-12.1
1986	5.4
1987	-8.2
1988	-6.1
1989	-27.9

Source: Economic Commission for Latin America and the Caribbean (1990).
Note: * Annual average variation in real wages of industrial workers.

TABLE A9
Trade balance (current US$ million)

Year	Exports	Imports	Trade Surplus
1976	3,916	3,033	883
1977	5,655	4,165	1,490
1978	6,399	3,834	2,565
1979	7,813	6,711	1,102
1980	8,020	10,539	-2,519
1981	9,143	9,430	-287
1982	7,626	5,337	2,289
1983	7,836	4,504	3,332
1984	8,107	4,585	3,522
1985	8,396	3,814	4,582
1986	6,852	4,724	2,128
1987	6,360	5,819	541
1988	9,133	5,322	3,811
1989	9,577	4,201	5,376

Source: Secretaría de Industria y Comercio Exterior (1990).

TABLE A10
Balance of payments (current US$ million)

Year	Trade surplus	Financial Service Surplus	Current Account Surplus
1976	883.1	−492.5	649.6
1977	1,409.3	−578.5	1,289.0
1978	2,565.8	680.8	1,833.6
1979	1,109.9	−920.0	536.4
1980	−2,519.2	−1,531.4	−4,767.8
1981	−287.0	−3,699.7	−4,714.0
1982	2,286.8	−4,718.5	−2,657.7
1983	3,320.0	−5,407.9	−2,437.5

Source: Argentinian Central Bank (*Banco Central de la República Argentina*), unpublished data.

TABLE A11
Balance of payments (US$ million)

Year	Balance on current account	Balance on capital account	Global balance*
1983	−2,436	−21	2,457
1984	−2,495	2,661	166
1985	−952	1,982	1,030
1986	−2,859	1,968	891
1987	−4,239	2,323	1,916
1988	−1,615	3,473	1,858
1989	−1,292	−56	1,348

Source: Economic Commission for Latin America and the Caribbean (1990).

Note: * equals the total variation in reserves (of opposite sign) plus counterpart items.

TABLE A12
External debt (US$ million)

Year	Total	Public	Private
1976	8,279	4,021	3,854
1977	9,678	6,044	3,634
1978	12,496	8,357	4,139
1979	19,034	9,960	9,074
1980	27,162	14,459	12,703
1981	35,671	20,024	15,703
1982	43,634	28,616	15,018
1983	45,069	31,709	13,360

Source: Argentinian Central Bank (*Banco Central de la República Argentina*) unpublished data.

TABLE A13
External debt (US$ million)

Year	Total	Public	Private
1984	46,171	35,527	10,664
1985	49,326	40,868	8,458
1986	51,422	44,726	6,696
1987	58,324	51,793	6,531
1988	58,303	53,265	5,038
1989	63,314	58,397	4,917

Source: Economic Commission for Latin America and the Caribbean (1990).

TABLE A14:
Total debt as % of GNP

Year	%
1980	48.4
1984	67.5
1985	84.2
1986	70.5
1987	76.4
1988	66.5
1989	121.9

Source: Organización de Estados Americanos (1992).

TABLE A15
Service payment on the total external debt (US$ million)

Year	US$ million
1981	5,391
1982	4,975
1983	6,805
1984	5,197
1985	6,089
1986	6,741
1987	6,244
1988	5,057
1989	5,237

Source: Wilkie (1993).

TABLE A16
Service payments on the interest of the total external debt (US$ million)

Year	%
1981	3,441
1982	3,581
1983	5,438
1984	4,373
1985	5,071
1986	4,302
1987	4,056
1988	3,146
1989	2,128

Source: Wilkie (1993).

TABLE A17
Interest paid as % of GNP

Year	%
1980	4.2
1984	5.8
1985	8.4
1986	5.8
1987	5.3
1988	3.5
1989	4.0

Source: Organización de Estados Americanos (1992).

TABLE A18
Military expenditure as % of GDP

Year	%
1976	3.9
1977	3.8
1978	5.1
1979	4.8
1980	4.4
1981	4.9
1982	3.5
1983	3.5
1976–83 annual averages	4.2
1984	2.3
1985	2.3
1986	2.3
1987	2.3
1988	2.1
1989	1.9
1984–89 annual averages	2.2

Source: Pion-Berlin (1997).

Bibliography

This bibliography is divided into four sections: official documents, newspapers, unpublished works and published works.

OFFICIAL DOCUMENTS

Banco Central de la República Argentina (1992) *Indicadores económicos* (Buenos Aires: BCRA).

Banco Central de la República Argentina, *Memorias anuales*, various issues.

Banco Central de la República Argentina, unpublished data.

Comisión Económica para América Latina y el Caribe (CEPAL) (1989) *Balance preliminar de la economía de América Latina y el Caribe* (Santiago: CEPAL).

Comisión Económica para América Latina y el Caribe (CEPAL) (1991) 'Nota sobre la evolución de la economía argentina en 1990', *Doc. de trabajo no. 39* (Buenos Aires: CEPAL).

Economic Commission for Latin America and the Caribbean (ECLA) (1987) *Preliminary Overview of the Latin American Economy* (Santiago de Chile: CEPAL).

Economic Commission for Latin America and the Caribbean (1990) *Economic Survey of Latin America and the Caribbean*, vol. II (Santiago: United Nations).

Honorable Cámara de Diputados de la Nación, *Diario de sesiones*, various issues.

Instituto Nacional de Estadísticas y Censos, unpublished data.

International Monetary Fund (1988) *International Financial Statistics Yearbook, 1988* (Washington, DC: International Monetary Fund).

Organización de Estados Americanos (1992) *Boletín estadístico de la OEA*, vol. II, 1–2, January–December (Washington: OEA, Departamento de Asuntos Económicos y Sociales).

Poder Ejecutivo Nacional, *Boletín oficial,* various issues.

Secretaría de Industria y Comercio Exterior (1990) *Boletín de comercio exterior* (Buenos Aires: Ministerio de Economía).

Secretaría de Información Pública, *Discursos presidenciales*, various issues.

Sociedad Rural Argentina (1992) *Indicadores*, April–June (Buenos Aires: Sociedad Rural Argentina).

Unión Cívica Radical (1983) *Plataforma electoral nacional de la Unión Cívica Radical* (Buenos Aires: UCR).

United Nations (1985) *Economic Survey of Latin America and the Caribbean* (Santiago de Chile: United Nations).

Wilkie, J. (ed.) (1993) *Statistical Abstract of Latin America*, vol. 30, part II (Los Angeles: UCLA).

World Bank (1988) *World Bank Tables 1987* (Washington, DC: World Bank and International Finance Corporation).

World Bank (1989) *Argentina: Reforms for Price Stability and Growth* (Washington, DC: World Bank).

World Bank (1992) *World Debt Tables 1992–1993* (Washington DC: World Bank).

World Bank (1997) *The State in a Changing World* (Oxford: Oxford University Press).

NEWSPAPERS, VARIOUS ISSUES

Ambito Financiero
Clarín
The Economist
Financial Times
Latin America Political Report
Latin America Regional Reports Southern Cone
Latin America Weekly Report
La Nación
New York Times
Página/12
La Voz
The Wall Street Journal

UNPUBLISHED WORKS

Alonso, P. (forthcoming) *Between Revolution and the Ballot Box. The Origins of the Argentine Radical Party, 1880–1900* (Cambridge: Cambridge University Press).

Boron, A. (1992) *La pobreza de las naciones. La economía política del neoliberalismo en la Argentina*, mimeograph.

Fontana, A. (1989) *La política militar en un contexto de transición: Argentina 1983–1989*, mimeograph.

Graziano, R. (1986) *El estado frente al endeudamiento privado externo*, mimeograph.

Minujín, A. (1991) 'En la rodada', paper presented at *Efectos de la crisis en la sociedad argentina. Los nuevos pobres*, UNICEF, Buenos Aires.

Smith, W. (1980) *Crisis of the State and Military: Authoritarian Rule in Argentina, 1966–1973* (PhD dissertation, Stanford University).

Tedesco, L. (1994) *The Crisis of the Argentinian State: Democratisation and Economic Restructuring, 1976–1989* (PhD Dissertation, Warwick University).

PUBLISHED WORKS

Abós (1984) *Las organizaciones sindicales y el poder militar (1976–1983)* (Buenos Aires: Centro Editor de América Latina).

Acevedo, M., Basualdo, E. and Khavisse, M. (1990) *¿Quién es quién? Los dueños del poder económico (Argentina 1973–1987)* (Buenos Aires: Editora/12 and Pensamiento Jurídico Editora).

Acuña, C. (1990) 'Intereses empresarios, dictadura y democracia en la Argentina actual', in *CEDES Documentos de Trabajo* (Buenos Aires: CEDES).

Acuña, C. and Smulovitz, C. (1991) '¿Ni olvido ni perdón? Derechos humanos y tensiones cívico-militares en la transición', in *CEDES Documentos de Trabajo* (Buenos Aires: CEDES).

Acuña, M. (1995) *Alfonsín y el poder económico* (Buenos Aires: Corregidor).

Alfonsín, R. (1992) *Alfonsín responde* (Buenos Aires: Tiempo de Ideas).

Andersen, M. (1993) *Dossier secreto* (Buenos Aires: Planeta).

Anderson, P. (1979) *Lineages of the Absolutist State* (London: Verso).

Argentina's National Commission on Disappeared People (1986) *Nunca más* (London: Faber).

Azpiazu, D. and Kosacoff, B. (1989) *La industria argentina: Desarrollo y cambios estructurales* (Buenos Aires: CEPAL and Centro Editor de América Latina).

Azpiazu, D., Khavisse, M. and Basualdo, E. (1986) *El nuevo poder económico* (Buenos Aires: Hyspamérica).

Balassa, B. (1986) *Hacia una renovación del crecimiento económico en América Latina* (México: El Colegio de México).

Basualdo, E. (1987) *Deuda externa y poder económico en la Argentina* (Buenos Aires: Nueva América).

Basualdo, E. and Azpiazu, D. (1990) *Cara y contracara de los grupos económicos* (Buenos Aires: Cántaro).

Basualdo, E. and Khavisse, M. (1993) *El nuevo poder terrateniente* (Buenos Aires: Planeta Espejo de la Argentina).

Beliz, C. (1988) *CGT, el otro poder* (Buenos Aires: Planeta).

Bianchi, A. *et al.* (1985) *External Debt in Latin America* (Boulder, CO: Lynne Rienner).

Bonasso, M. (1984) *Recuerdo de la muerte* (Mexico: Era).

Bonasso, M. (1997) *El Presidente que no fue* (Buenos Aires: Planeta).

Boron, A. and Faúndez, J. (1989) *Malvinas hoy: herencia de un conflicto* (Buenos Aires: Puntosur).

Bousquet, J. P. (1983) *Las locas de la Plaza de Mayo* (Buenos Aires: El Cid).

Bouzas, R. and Keifman, S. (1990) 'Deuda externa y negociaciones financieras en la década de los ochenta: una evaluación de la experiencia argentina', *Documentos e informes de investigación no.98* (Buenos Aires: FLACSO).

Branford, S. and Kucinski, B. (1990) *The Debt Squads* (London: Zed Books).

Brysk, A. (1994) *The Politics of Human Rights in Argentina* (Stanford, CA: Stanford University Press).

Cammack, P. (1985) 'Democratisation: a Review of the Issues', *Bulletin Latin American Research*, 4 (2): 39–46.

Canavese, A. and Di Tella, G. (1988) 'Inflation Stabilization or Hyperinflation Avoidance? The Case of the Austral Plan in Argentina: 1985–1987', in M. Bruno, *et al.* (1988) *Inflation Stabilization* (Cambridge, MA: MIT Press).

Canitrot, A. (1981) 'Teoría y práctica del liberalismo. Política antiinflacionaria y apertura económica en la Argentina, 1976–1981', *Desarrollo Económico*, 82 (Buenos Aires: IDES).

Canitrot, A. (1991) 'Programas de ajuste y estrategias políticas: las experiencias recientes de la Argentina y Bolivia: un comentario', *Desarrollo Económico*, 121 (Buenos Aires: IDES).

Caputo, Dante (1982) 'Balance Provisorio', in P. Waldmann and E. Garzón Valdez (1982) *El Poder militar en la Argentina (1976–1981)* (Frankfurt: Verlag Kalus Dieter Verveuert).

Carbonetto, D. (1987) *El Perú heterodoxo: un modelo económico* (Lima: Instituto Nacional de Planificación).

Cardoso, R., Kirschbaum, R. and van der Kooy, E. (1987) *Falklands: The Secret Plot* (London: Preston Editions).

Cavallo, D. and Cottani, J. (1991) 'Argentina', in D. Papageorgiou, M. Michaely and A. Choski (1991) *Liberalizing Foreign Trade*, 1 (Oxford: Basil Blackwell).

Cavarozzi, M. (1984) *Sindicatos y política en Argentina* (Buenos Aires: Estudios CEDES).

Cavarozzi, M. (1992) 'Patterns of Elite Negotiation and Confrontation in Argentina and Chile', in J. Higley and R. Gunther (eds), *Democratic Consolidation in Latin America and Southern Europe* (Cambridge: Cambridge University Press).

Cavarozzi, M. (1997) *Autoritarismo y democracia (1955–1983)* (Buenos Aires: Ariel).

Cheresky, I. (1998) 'Hay todavía lugar para la voluntad política?', in T. Di Tella (comp.) (1998) *Crisis de representatividad y sistemas de partidos políticos* (Buenos Aires: GEL).

Chudnovsky, D. (1991) *La reestructuración industrial argentina en el contexto macroeconómico e internacional* (Buenos Aires: Centro de Investigaciones para la Transformación).

Ciria, A. (1964) *Partidos y poder en la Argentina moderna* (Buenos Aires: Editorial Jorge Alvarez).

Clarke, S. (1988) *Keynesianism, Monetarism and the Crisis of the State* (Hants: Edward Elgar).

Clarke, S. (1990) 'Crisis of Socialism or Crisis of the State?', *Capital and Class*, 42, Winter: 19–29.

Comisión Económica para América Latina y el Caribe (1990) (CEPAL) *La desarticulación del pacto fiscal. Una interpretación sobre la evolución del sector público argentino en las dos últimas décadas* (Buenos Aires: CEPAL).

Corradi, J. (1985) *The Fitful Republic* (Boulder, CO: Westview Press).

Crystal, J. (1994) 'The Politics of Capital Flight: Exit and Exchange Rates in Latin America', *Review of International Studies*, 20: 131–47.

Dahl, R. (1956) *A Preface to Democratic Theory* (Chicago: University of Chicago Press).

Dahl, R. (1961) *Who Governs?* (New Haven, CT: Yale University Press).

Dahl, R. (1978) 'Pluralism Revisited', *Comparative Politics*, 10 January: 187–209.

Damill, M. and Frenkel, R. (1990) 'Malos tiempos. La economía argentina en la década de los ochenta', *Documento CEDES/46* (Buenos Aires: CEDES).

De Ipola, E. (1987) 'La difícil apuesta del peronismo democrático', in J. Nun and J. Portantiero (1987) *Ensayos sobre la transición democrática en la Argentina* (Buenos Aires: Puntosur).

De Pablo, J. C. (1989) 'Economic Policy without Political Context: Guido, 1962-3', in G. Di Tella and R. Dornbusch (eds) (1989) *The Political Economy of Argentina 1946–1983* (London: Macmillan).

De Riz, L. (1981) *Retorno y Derrumbe. El último gobierno peronista* (Buenos Aires: Hyspamérica).

De Riz, L. (1991) 'Alfonsín's Argentina: Renewal of Parties and Congress (1983-1989)', *CEDES Documentos de Trabajo* (Buenos Aires: CEDES).

del Mazo, G. (1959) *El Radicalismo* (Buenos Aires: Ed. Gure).

Di Tella, G. (1983) *Perón-Perón, 1973-1976* (Buenos Aires: Hyspanoamérica).

Di Tella, G. (1989) 'Argentina's Economy under a Labour-Based Government, 1973-76', in G. Di Tella and R. Dornbusch (eds) (1989) *The Political Economy of Argentina 1946–1983* (London: Macmillan).

Di Tella, G. and Dornbusch, R. (eds) (1989) *The Political Economy of Argentina 1946–1983* (London: Macmillan).

Di Tella, G. and Rodríguez Braun, C. (1990) *Argentina 1946–1983: The Economic Ministers Speak* (Oxford: Macmillan).

Diaz Alejandro, C. (1969) *Devaluación de la tasa de cambio en un país semi-industrializado. La experiencia de la Argentina 1955–1961* (Buenos Aires: Instituto Di Tella).

Diaz Alejandro, C. (1970) *Ensayos sobre historia económica argentina* (Buenos Aires: Amorrortu).

Dorfman, A. (1983) *Cincuenta años de industrialización en la Argentina 1930-1983* (Buenos Aires: Ediciones Solar).

Dornbusch, R. (1989) 'The Latin American Debt Problem: Anatomy and Solutions', in B. Stallings and R. Kaufman (eds) (1989) *Debt and Democracy in Latin America* (Boulder, CO, San Francisco and London: Westview Press).

Dornbusch, R. (1990) 'Panel Discussion on Latin American Adjustment', in J. Williamson (ed.) (1990) *Latin American Adjustment: How Much Has Happened?* (Washington: Institute for International Economics).

Dornbusch, R. and De Pablo, J. (1988) *Deuda externa e inestabilidad macroeconómica en la Argentina* (Buenos Aires: Sudamericana).

Drake, P. (1989) 'Debt and Democracy in Latin America, 1920s–1980s', in B. Stallings and R. Kaufman (eds) (1989) *Debt and Democracy in Latin America* (Boulder, CO, San Francisco and London: Westview Press).

Edwards, S. (1997) *Crisis y reforma en América Latina* (Buenos Aires: Emecé).

Escudé, C. (1989) 'De la irrelevancia estratégica de Reagan y Alfonsín: hacia el desarrollo de un "realismo periférico"', in R. Bouzas and R. Russell (eds) (1989) *Estados Unidos y la transición argentina* (Buenos Aires: Legasa).

Escudé, C. and González de Oleaga, M. (1996) 'La política exterior de Alfonsín: lecciones de una sobredosis de confrontaciones', *UTDT Working Papers no. 31* (Buenos Aires: Universidad Torcuato Di Tella).

Fanelli, J. and Chisari, O. (1989) 'Restricciones al crecimiento y distribución del ingreso: el caso argentino', *Documentos CEDES/27* (Buenos Aires: CEDES).

Fanelli, J. and Frenkel, R. (1989) 'Argentina's Medium Term: Problems and Prospects', *Documentos CEDES/28* (Buenos Aires: CEDES).

Fanelli, J. and Frenkel, R. (1990) *Políticas de estabilización e Hiperinflación en la Argentina* (Buenos Aires: CEDES and Editorial Tesis).

Fanelli, J. *et al.* (1990) 'Growth and Structural Reform in Latin America, Where We Stand', *Documentos CEDES/57* (Buenos Aires: CEDES).

Fayt, C. (1967) *La naturaleza del peronismo* (Buenos Aires).

Ffrench-Davis, R. *et al.* (1986) *Mas allá de la crisis de la deuda* (Buenos Aires: GEL).

Fisher, J. (1989) *Mothers of the Disappeared* (Boston: South End Press).

Fontana, A. (1984) 'Fuerzas Armadas, partidos políticos y transición a la democracia en la Argentina 1981–1982', *The Helen Kellogg Institute for International Studies, Working-paper*, 28 (Notre Dame, IN: University of Notre Dame).

Fontana, A. (1986) 'De la crisis de Malvinas a la subordinación condicionada: conflictos intramilitares y transición política en Argentina', *The Helen Kellogg Institute for International Studies, Working-paper*, 74 (Notre Dame, IN: University of Notre Dame).

Fontana, A. (1987) 'La política militar del gobierno constitucional argentino', in J. Nun and J. Portantiero (eds) (1987) *Ensayos sobre la transición democrática en la Argentina* (Buenos Aires: Puntosur).

Fontana, A. and Llenderrozas, E. (1992) 'Decisiones políticas en tiempos de crisis', in R. Frenkel *et al.* (1992) *Argentina. Evolución macroeconómica, financiación externa y cambio político en la década de los 80* (Madrid: CEDEAL).

Fraga, R. (1989) *La cuestión militar* (Buenos Aires: Centro de Estudios para la Nueva Mayoría).

Fraga, R. (1990) *Prensa y Análisis Político* (Buenos Aires: Centro de Estudios para la Nueva Mayoría).

Fraga, R. (1991) *La cuestión sindical* (Buenos Aires: Centro de Estudios para la Nueva Mayoría).

Freedman, L. and Gamba-Stonehouse, V. (1990) *Signals of War: The Falklands Conflict of 1982* (London: Faber & Faber).

Frenkel, R. (1979) 'Decisiones de precios en alta inflación', *Desarrollo Económico*, 75.

Frenkel, R. (1980) 'El desarrollo reciente del mercado de capitales en la Argentina', *Desarrollo Económico*, 78.

Frenkel, R. (1988) 'Extensión de contratos y efectos ingreso. Aspectos de la dinámica inflacionaria en economías indexadas', *Documentos CEDES/26* (Buenos Aires: CEDES).

Frenkel, R. *et al.* (1992) *Argentina. Evolución macroeconómica, financiación externa y cambio político en la década de los 80* (Madrid: CEDEAL).

Frenkel, R., Fanelli, J. and Sommer, J. (1988) 'El proceso de endeudamiento externo argentino', *Documento CEDES/2* (Buenos Aires: CEDES).

Galleti, A. (1961) *La política y los partidos* (Buenos Aires: Fondo de Cultura Económica).

Gamba, V. (1987) *The Falklands/Malvinas War* (London: Allen & Unwin).

Garfunkel, J. (1990) *59 semanas y media que conmovieron a la Argentina* (Buenos Aires: EMECE).

Gaudio, R. and Thompson, A. (1990) *Sindicalismo Peronista/Gobierno Radical. Los años de Alfonsín* (Buenos Aires: Fundación Friedrich Ebert and Folios Ediciones).

Gerchunoff, P. (1989) 'Peronist Economic Policies, 1946–1955', in G. Di Tella, and R. Dornbusch (eds) (1989) *The Political Economy of Argentina 1946–1983* (London: Macmillan).

Gerchunoff, P. and Dieguez, H. (1984) 'La dinámica del mercado laboral urbano en la Argentina, 1976–1981', *Desarrollo Económico*, 93.

Gillespie, R. (1982) *Soldiers of Perón, Argentina's Montoneros* (Oxford: Clarendon).

Godio, J. (1989) *El movimiento obrero argentino* (Buenos Aires: Legasa).

Godio, J., Palomino, H. and Wachendorfer, A., (1988) *El movimiento sindical argentino* (Buenos Aires: Sudamericana).

Goldthorpe, J. (1978) 'The Current Inflation: Towards a Sociological Account', in J. Goldthorpe and F. Hirsch (1978) *The Political Economy of Inflation* (London: Martin Robertson).

Guadagni, A. (1989) 'Economic Policy during Illia's Period in Office, 1963–6', in G. Di Tella and R. Dornbusch (eds) (1989) *The Political Economy of Argentina 1946–1983* (London: Macmillan).

Haggard, S. and Kaufman, R. (1989) 'The Politics of Stabilization and Structural Adjustment', in J. Sachs (ed.) (1989) *Developing Country Debt and Economic Performance*, I: *The International Financial System* (Chicago, IL: University of Chicago Press).

Haggard, S. and Kaufman, R. (1995) *The Political Economy of Democratic Transitions* (Princeton, NJ: Princeton University Press).

Haggard, S. and Webb, S. (1993) 'What Do We Know about the Political Economy of Economic Policy Reform?', *The World Bank Research Observer*, 8, 2: 143–68.

Hall, P. (1986) *Governing the Economy* (Oxford: Oxford University Press).

Halperín Donghi, T. (1994a) *La larga agonía de la Argentina peronista* (Buenos Aires: Ariel).

Halperín Donghi, T. (1994b) *Argentina en el callejón* (Buenos Aires: Ariel).

Heyman, D. (1991) 'From Sharp Disinflation to Hyperinflation, Twice: The Argentine Experience, 1985–1989', in M. Bruno *et al.* (1991) *Lessons of Economic Stabilization and its Aftermath* (London and Cambridge, MA: MIT Press).

Hilt, E. and Pastor, M. (1993) 'Private Investment and Democracy in Latin America', *World Development*, 21(8): 489–507.

Holloway, J. (1992) 'Crisis, Fetishism, Class Composition', in W. Bonefeld and R. Gunn and K. Psychopedis (1992) *Open Marxism*, II (Boulder, CO: Pluto Press).

Holloway, J. and Picciotto, S. (1977) 'Capital, Crisis and the State', *Capital and Class*, 2: 76–101.

Huntington, S. (1993) *The Third Wave. Democratization in the Late Twentieth Century* (Norman: University of Oklahoma Press).

Iglesias, E. (1990) 'From Policy Consensus to Renewed Economic Growth', in J. Williamson (ed.) (1990) *Latin American Adjustment: How Much Has Happened?* (Washington, DC: Institute for International Economics).

James, D. (1988) *Resistance and Integration. Peronism and the Argentine Working Class, 1946–1976* (Cambridge: Cambridge University Press).

Jessop, B. (1990) *State Theory* (Cambridge: Polity Press).

Kahler, M. (1990) 'Orthodoxy and Its Alternatives: Explaining Approaches to Stabilization and Adjustment', in J. Nelson (1990) *Economic Crisis and Policy Choice: the Politics of Adjustment in the Third World* (Princeton, NJ: Princeton University Press).

Karl, T. (1990) 'Dilemmas of Democratization in Latin America', *Comparative Politics*, 23(1): 1–21.

Katz, J. and Kosacoff, B. (1989) *El proceso de industrialización en la Argentina: Evolución, retroceso y prospectiva* (Buenos Aires: CEPAL/CEAL).

Kiguel, M. and Liviatan, N. (1991) 'The inflation–stabilization cycles in Argentina and Brazil', in M. Bruno *et al.* (1991) *Lessons of Economic Stabilization and its Aftermath* (London and Cambridge, MA: MIT Press).

Kosacoff, B. (1989) 'Desarrollo industrial e inestabilidad macroeconómica: La experiencia argentina reciente', in D. Azpiazu and B. Kosacoff (1989) *La industria argentina: desarrollo y cambios estructurales* (Buenos Aires: CEPAL and Centro Editor de América Latina).

Krasner, S. (1978) *Defending the National Interest* (Princeton, NJ: Princeton University Press).

Laclau, E. (1973) 'Peronism and Revolution', *Latin American Review of Books*, 1.

Landi, O. (1978) 'La tercera presidencia de Perón: gobierno de emergencia y crisis política', *CEDES Documento de trabajo*, 10.

Lázara, S. (1988) *Poder militar, origen, apogeo y transición* (Buenos Aires: Legasa).

Lázara, S. (1997) *El asalto al poder* (Buenos Aires: Tiempo).

Lessard, D. and Williamson, J. (1987) *Capital Flight and Third World Debt* (Washington, DC: Institute for International Economics).

Lewis, P. (1992) *The Crisis of Argentine Capitalism* (Chapel Hill: University of North Carolina Press).

Linz, J. and Stepan, A. (1996) *Problems of democratic transition and consolidation* (Baltimore, MD: Johns Hopkins University Press).

López, E. (1987) *El último levantamiento* (Buenos Aires: Legasa).

López, E. and Pion-Berlin, D. (1996) *Democracia y cuestión militar* (Buenos Aires: Universidad Nacional de Quilmes).

Lowenthal, A. (1983) *The Peruvian Experiment Revisited* (Princeton, NJ: Princeton University Press).

Luna, F. (1958) *Alvear* (Buenos Aires: Editorial Libros Argentinos).

Luna, F. (1973) *De Perón a Lanusse* (Buenos Aires: Emecé).

Luna, F. (1982) *El 45* (Buenos Aires: Editorial Sudamericana).

Luna, F. (1983) *Golpes militares y salidas electorales* (Buenos Aires: Sudamericana).

Machinea, J. (1990) 'Stabilization under Alfonsín's Government: A Frustrated Attempt', *Documento CEDES/42* (Buenos Aires: CEDES).

Machinea, J. and Fanelli, J. (1988) 'Stopping Hyperinflation: The Case of the Austral Plan in Argentina: 1985–1987', in M. Bruno *et al.* (1988) *Inflation Stabilization* (Cambridge, MA: MIT Press).

Mainwaring, S., O'Donnell, G. and Valenzuela, S. (eds) (1992) *Issues in Democratic Consolidation* (Notre Dame: University of Notre Dame Press).

Majul, L. (1990) *Por qué cayó Alfonsín* (Buenos Aires: Sudamericana).

Majul, L. (1992) *Los dueños de la Argentina* (Buenos Aires: Sudamericana).

Mallon, R. and Sourrouille, J. (1975) *La política económica en una sociedad conflictiva* (Buenos Aires: Amorrortu).

Manzetti, L. and Dell'Aquila, M. (1988) 'Economic Stabilization in Argentina: the Austral Plan', *Journal of Latin American Studies*, 20: 1–26.

Maronese, L., Cafiero de Nazar, A. and Waisman, V. (1985) *El voto Peronista '83: perfil electoral y causas de la derrota* (Buenos Aires: El Cid Editor).

Matsushita, H. (1983) *Movimiento Obrero Argentino, 1930–1954* (Buenos Aires: Siglo XX).

McGuire, J. (1992) 'Union Political Tactics and Democratic Consolidation in Alfonsín's Argentina, 1983–1989', *Latin American Research Review*, 27(1).

Meller, P. (1990) 'What Washington Means by Policy Reform', in J. Williamson, (ed.) (1990) *Latin American Adjustment: How Much Has Happened?* (Washington, DC: Institute for International Economics).

Miliband, R. (1969) *The State in Capitalist Society* (London: Weidenfeld & Nicholson).

Miliband, R. (1973) 'The Capitalist State: Reply to Nicol Poulantzas', in J. Urry and J. Wakeford (1973) *Power in Britain* (London: Heinemann Educational Books).

Miliband, R. (1983) 'State Power and Class Interests', *New Left Review*, 138 (March–April).

Minsburg, N. (1987) *Capitales extranjeros y grupos dominantes argentinos* (Buenos Aires: Centro Editor de América Latina).

Moncalvillo, M. and Fernández, A. (eds) (1986) *La renovación fundacional* (Buenos Aires: El Cid Editor).

Moneta, C. *et al.* (1985) *La reforma militar* (Buenos Aires: Legasa).

Mora y Araujo, M. (1986) 'The Nature of the Alfonsín Coalition', in P. Drake and E. Silva (eds) (1986) *Elections and Democratization in Latin America, 1980–1985* (San Diego: University of California).

Morales Solá, J. (1990) *Asalto a la ilusión* (Buenos Aires: Planeta)

Morales, J. and McMahon, G. (1996) *Economic Policy and the Transition to Democracy* (London: Macmillan).

Mosley, P. (1987) 'Conditionality as Bargaining Process: Structural-Adjustment Lending, 1980–1986', in *Essays in International Finance*, 168 (Princeton, NJ: Princeton University Press).

Neier, A. (1990) 'What Should Be Done about the Guilty?', *The New York Review of Books*, 37(1) (February).

Nelson, J. (1990) *Economic Crisis and Policy Choice: The Politics of Adjustment in the Third World* (Princeton, NJ: Princeton University Press).

Nelson, J. (1993) 'The Politics of Economic Transformation', *World Politics*, 45: 433–63 (April).

Nelson, J. *et al.* (1989) *Fragile Coalitions: The Politics of Economic Adjustment* (New Brunswick, NJ: Transaction Books).

Norden, D. (1990) 'Democratic Consolidation and Military Professionalism: Argentina in the 1980s', *Journal of Interamerican Studies and World Affairs*, 32(3): 151–76 (Fall).

O'Brien, P. and Cammack, P. (eds) (1985) *Generals in Retreat* (Manchester: Manchester University Press).

O'Connell, A. (1988) 'La coordinación de los deudores latinoamericanos: el Consenso de Cartagena y el Grupo de los Ocho', *Estudios Internacionales*, XXI, (83) (July–September).

O'Donnell, G. (1978) 'State and Alliances in Argentina, 1956–1976', *Journal of Development Studies* 15(1): 3–33.

O'Donnell, G. (1988) *Bureaucratic Authoritarianism: Argentina, 1966–1973, in Comparative Perspective* (Los Angeles: University of California Press).

O'Donnell, G. (1994) 'Delegative Democracy', *Journal of Democracy*, 5(1), January: 55–69.

O'Donnell, G., Schmitter, P. and Whitehead, L. (eds) (1986) *Transitions from Authoritarian Rule. Comparative Perspectives* (Baltimore, MD, and London: Johns Hopkins University Press).

Obschatko, E (1988) 'Los cambios tecnológicos', in Barsky *et al.* (1988) *La agricultura pampeana* (Buenos Aires: FCE/CISEA/IICA).

Orsatti, A (1983) 'La nueva distribución funcional del ingreso en la Argentina', *Desarrollo Económico*, 91.

Ostiguy, P. (1990) *Los Capitanes de la Industria. Grandes empresarios, política y economía en la Argentina de los años 80* (Buenos Aires: Legasa).

Palermo, V. (1990) 'Programas de ajuste y estrategias políticas: Las experiencias recientes de la Argentina y Bolivia', *Desarrollo Económico*, 119.

Palermo, V. and Novaro, M. (1996) *Política y poder en el gobierno de Menem* (Buenos Aires: Norma).

Pastor, M. (1990) 'Capital flight from Latin America', *World Development*, 18(1): 1–19.

Peña, M. (1973) *El Peronismo, selección de documentos para la historia* (Buenos Aires).

Peralta-Ramos, M. (1987) 'Toward an analysis of the structural basis of coercion in Argentina: the behavior of the major fractions of the bourgeoisie, 1976–1983', in M. Peralta-Ramos and C. Waisman (eds) (1987) *From Military Rule to Liberal Democracy in Argentina* (Boulder, CO and London: Westview Press).

Perina, R. (1983) *Onganía, Levingston, Lanusse: Los militares en la política argentina* (Buenos Aires: Editorial Belgrano).

Petras, J. and Brill, H. (1988) 'Latin America's Transnational Capitalists and the Debt: A Class-Analysis Perspective', *Development and Change*, 19: 179–201.

Petrecolla, A. (1989) 'Unbalanced Development, 1958–62', in G. Di Tella and R. Dornbusch (eds) (1989) *The Political Economy of Argentina 1946–1983* (London: Macmillan).

Pilbeam, K. (1992) *International Finance* (London: Macmillan).

Pion-Berlin, D. (1991) 'Between Confrontation and Accommodation: Military and Government Policy in Democratic Argentina', *Journal of Latin American Studies*, 23: 543–71.

Pion-Berlin, D. (1997) *Through Corridors of Power* (University Park, PA: Pennsylvania State University Press).

Potash, R. (1969) *The Army and Politics in Argentina, 1928–1945* (Stanford, CA: Stanford University Press).

Potash, R. (1971) *El ejército y la política en la Argentina* (Buenos Aires: Sudamericana).

Poulantzas, N. (1973) 'The Problem of the Capitalist State', in J. Urry and J. Wakeford (1973) *Power in Britain* (London: Heinemann Educational Books).

Poulantzas, N. (1978) 'Towards a Democratic Socialism', *New Left Review*, 109 (May–June).

Przeworski, A. and Wallerstein, M. (1988) 'Structural Dependence on the State on Capital', *American Political Science Review*, 82, 1 (March).

Puiggrós, R. (1957) *Historia crítica de los partidos políticos* (Buenos Aires: Editorial Argumentos).

Puiggrós, R. (1968) *La democracia fraudulenta* (Buenos Aires: Editorial Jorge Alvarez).

Ranis, P. (1991) 'View from Below: Working-Class Consciousness in Argentina', *Latin American Research Review*, 26(2): 133–56.

Remmer, K. (1986) 'The Politics of Economic Stabilization', *Comparative Politics*, 19 (1), October: 1–24.

Remmer, K. (1989) *Military Rule in Latin America* (Boston: Unwin Hyman).

Remmer, K. (1991) 'The Political Impact of Economic Crisis in Latin America in the 1980s', *American Political Science Review*, 85(3): 777–800.

Rock, D. (1975) *Politics in Argentina 1890–1930: the Rise and Fall of Radicalism* (Cambridge: Cambridge University Press).

Roett, R. (1984) 'Democracy and Debt in South America: A Continent's Dilemma', *Foreign Affairs*, 3: 695–721.

Romero, L. A. (1995) *Breve historia contemporánea de la Argentina* (Buenos Aires: Fondo de Cultura Económica).

Rouquié, A. (1983a) *Poder militar y sociedad política en la Argentina* (Buenos Aires: EMECE).

Rouquié, A. (1983b) 'Argentina: The Departure of the Military – End of a Political Cycle or Just Another Episode?', *International Affairs*, 4 (Autumn).

Russell, R. (1988) 'Un año de política exterior: las relaciones con Estados Unidos, América Latina y Europa Occidental', in R. Perina and R. Russell (1988) *Argentina en el mundo 1973–1987* (Buenos Aires: GEL).

Russell, R. (1990) 'Argentina: una nueva política exterior?', in H. Muñoz (ed.) (1990) *El desafío de los noventa* (Caracas: Nueva Sociedad).

Sachs, J. (1988) 'Comprehensive Debt Reduction: The Case of Bolivia', *Brookings Papers on Economic Activity*, 2: 705–13.

Sachs, J. (1989a) 'New Approaches to the Latin American Debt Crisis', *Essays in International Finance*, 174 (Princeton, NJ: Department of Economics, Princeton University).

Sachs, J. (1989b) *Development Country Debt and the World Economy* (Chicago: University of Chicago Press).

Sachs, J. (1990) 'Social Conflict and Populist Policies in Latin America', *Occasional Papers*, 9 (San Francisco: International Center for Economic Growth).

Sánchez de Losada, G. (1985) 'La nueva política económica', *Foro Económico*, 5.

Schvarzer, J. (1983) 'Cambios en el liderazgo industrial argentino en el período de Martínez de Hoz', *Desarrollo Económico*, 91.

Schvarzer, J. (1985) *La experiencia argentina de renegociación de su deuda externa: limitaciones y perspectivas*, mimeograph (Buenos Aires: CEDES).

Schvarzer, J. (1986a) *La Política Económica de Martínez de Hoz* (Buenos Aires: Hyspamérica).

Schvarzer, J. (1986b) 'De la deuda externa al Plan Austral', in EURAL (1986) *Crisis y regulación estatal: dilemas de política en Europa y América Latina* (Buenos Aires: GEL).

Schydowlsky, D. (1986) 'The Tragedy of Lost Opportunity in Peru', in J. Hartlyn and S. Morley (eds) (1986) *Latin American Political Economy: Financial Crisis and Political Change* (Boulder, CO: Westview).

Sguiglia, E. (1992) *El Club de los Poderosos* (Buenos Aires: Planeta).

Skocpol, T. (1980) 'Political Response to Capitalist Crisis: Neo-Marxist Theories of the State and the Case of the New Deal', *Politics and Society*, 10: 155–201.

Skocpol, T. (1985) 'Bringing the State Back In: Strategies of Analysis in Current Research', in P. Evans, D. Rueschemeyer and T. Skocpol (eds) (1985) *Bringing the State Back In* (Cambridge: Cambridge University Press).

Smith, W. (1985) 'Reflections on the Political Economy of Authoritarian Rule and Capitalist Reorganization in Contemporary Argentina', in P. O'Brien and P. Cammack (eds) (1985) *Generals in Retreat* (Manchester: Manchester University Press).

Smith, W. (1989) *Authoritarianism and the Crisis of the Argentine Political Economy* (Stanford, CA: Stanford University Press)

Smith, W. (1990) 'Democracy, Distributional Conflicts and Macroeconomic Policymaking in Argentina, 1983–1989', *Journal of Interamerican Studies and World Affairs*, 32(2): 1–42.

Solimano, A. and Serven, L. (1993) 'Debt Crisis, Adjustment Policies and Capital Formation in Developing Countries: Where Do We Stand?', *World Development* , 21(8): 127–40.

Sourrouille, J., Kosacoff, B. and Lucángeli, J. (1985) *Transnacionalización y política económica en la Argentina* (Buenos Aires: CET/CEAL).

Stallings, B. and Kaufman, R. (eds) (1989) *Debt and Democracy in Latin America* (Boulder, CO, San Francisco and London: Westview Press).

Stepan, A. (1978) *The State and Society: Peru in Comparative Politics* (Princeton, NJ: Princeton University Press).

Stiles, K. (1987) 'Argentina's Bargaining with the IMF', *Journal of Interamerican Studies and World Affairs*, 29(3), Fall: 55–85.

Thorp, R. and Whitehehead, L. (eds) (1987) *Latin American Debt and the Adjustment Crisis* (London: Macmillan).

Torre, J. C. (ed.) (1988) *La formación del sindicalismo peronista* (Buenos Aires: Legasa).

Torre, J. C. (1989) *Los sindicatos en el gobierno 1973–1976* (Buenos Aires: Centro Editor de América Latina).

Torre, J. C. (1990a) *La vieja guardia sindical* (Buenos Aires: Sudamericana).

Torre, J. C. (1990b) *El gobierno de la emergencia en la transición democrática: de Alfonsín a Menem*, mimeograph (Buenos Aires: Instituto Di Tella).

Torre, J. C. (1993) 'The Politics of Economic Crisis in Latin America', *Journal of Democracy*, 4(1): 104–16.

Torre, J. C. (1995) *El 17 de octubre* (Buenos Aires: Ariel).

Unamuno, M., Bárbaro, J. and Cafiero, A. (1984) *El Peronismo de la derrota* (Buenos Aires: CEAL).

Verbitsky, H. (1987) *Civiles y militares* (Buenos Aires: Legasa).

Verbitsky, H. (1990) *La educación presidencial* (Buenos Aires: Editora/12 and Puntosur).

Villar, D. (1971) *El Cordobazo* (Buenos Aires: La Historia Popular).

Villareal, J. (1985) 'Los hilos sociales del poder', in E. Jozami, P. Paz and J. Villareal (eds) (1985) *Crisis de la dictadura argentina* (Mexico: Siglo XXI).

Waisbord, S. (1991) 'Politics and Identity in the Argentine Army', *Latin American Research Review*, 26(2): 157–70.

Waldman, P. (1981) *El Peronismo* (Buenos Aires: Hyspamérica).

Williamson, J. (ed.) (1990) *Latin American Adjustment: How Much Has Happened?* (Washington, DC: Institute for International Economics).

Williamson, J. (1993) 'Democracy and the "Washington Consensus"', *World Development*, 21(8): 1329–36.

Wynia, G. (1992) *Argentina. Illusions and Realities* (New York: Holmes & Meier).

Index

Agosti, Orlando E. 25, 66, 121
agricultural sector
  Austral plan 117
  military dictatorship (1976–83)
    31–2
Alchourón, Guillermo 117
Alderete, Carlos xxiv, 119–21, 153
Alemann, Juan 57
Alemann, Roberto 16, 48, 50, 145
Alfonsín, Raúl
  and Armed Forces xxii, 62, 64–5,
    68–70, 121–7, 162–5, 175–6
  Austral plan 103–15
  democratisation 62
  economic legacy 149–53
  election victory (1983) 54–5
  external debt crisis 84–7, 89–95,
    150–1
  historical significance 179–80
  Radical party leadership xxv(n5)
  resignation 148–9
  and trade unions xxi, 62, 70–81,
    118–21
  United States support for 137–8,
    139–40
  and Welfare State xxvi(n9)
*Alianza Argentina Anti-Comunista –
  Triple A* 11, 19, 25, 26
Alvear, Marcelo T. de xxv(n5)
Anaya, Jorge 66, 121, 131(n23)
Angeloz, Eduardo 143
Aramburu, Pedro 6, 10
'Argentinian Revolution' (1966) 17–18

Arguindegui, Jorge 67
Armed Forces
  and Alfonsín xxii, 62, 64–5, 68–70,
    121–7, 162–5, 175–6
  anti-Peronism xix, xxv–xxvi(n7)
  crisis 51, 60(n32)
  legislation 159–60
  and Menem 178–9
  military rebellion (1987) 125–7
  military rebellions (1988) 158–61
  political role xix–xxii, 6–12
  'self-cleansing' 65–70
  wages 105–6
  see also military dictatorship
arms, purchase of 45–6
Astiz, Alfredo 179
Austral plan xxiii–xxiv, 79, 80, 81, 96,
  103–9
  failure of 109–15
  and trade unions 115–21
Australito plan 112–21

Baker, James 137, 139
balance of payments 185
Balbín, Ricardo xxv(n5), 6, 53
Baldassini, Antonio 74
Baños, Jorge 162
Barreiro, Ernesto 125
Barrionuevo, Hugo 75, 77, 99–100(n9)
Bignone, Reynaldo 49, 51, 52
Black Monday 141–5
Bolivia, New Political Economy 84,
  101(n20)

Borda, Osvaldo 74
Borras, Raúl 64
Brady, Nicholas 139
Bretton Woods system xvii
Brodershon, Mario 95
Bureaucratic Authoritarian state (BA) 9, 169–70

Cáceres, Isidro 160–1
Cafiero, Antonio 132, 135, 154–5, 166(n4)
Camdessus, Michel 137
Cámpora, Héctor 11
Canitrot, Adolfo 95
capitalist state, conceptualisation 168–71
Capitanes de la Industria 120, 130(n20)
carapintadas 125–7, 159–61, 163–5
Caridi, General 158, 160–1
Cartagena Consensus 90–1
Casella, Juan Manuel 75, 77, 99(n8)
Castillo, Ramón 2
Cavaliere, Armando 119
Cavallo, Domingo 39, 52–3, 139–40, 148, 166(n6), 177
class struggle 168
Colombres, Ricardo 66
Comisión Nacional sobre Desaparición de Personas (CONADEP) 66, 176
Conable, Barber 136
concertación social 75–7, 79–81
Confederación General del Trabajo (CGT) 6, 129–30(n17), 132
  Austral plan 115–21
  confrontation with government 72–9, 153–8
  divisions of 2, 3, 9, 72, 178
Conferencia Económica y Social (CES) 116–18
Consejo Supremo de las Fuerzas Armadas 66–9
Cordobazo 9–10, 18
crisis
  economic (1975–76) 19–20
  of the state xvi, xviii–xix, xxii, 11–12, 20–1, 168–9

debt
  external debt crisis xx, 42–6, 57, 82–7, 89–95, 150–1, 174

foreign debt 16
democracy, transition to 51–3
desaparecidos 25–6, 64, 66, 67
Dessa, Ted 97
devaluation 30, 31
Di Pietro, Hugo 6
'disappeared, the' *see desaparecidos*
disciplinamiento social xiii, xxiv(n1), 12, 23, 24, 31, 56, 98, 152, 165
'due obedience' xxiii, 65, 67, 69, 126, 163, 164

economic indicators 181–8
economy
  1955–66 14–17
  Alfonsín's legacy 149–53
  'Argentinian Revolution' (1966) 17–18
  Austral plan 103–15
  Black Monday 141–5
  crisis of 1975–76 19–20
  external debt crisis xx, 42–6, 57, 82–7, 89–95, 150–1, 174
  Menem's policies 146–9
  military dictatorship (1976–83) 26–31, 55–7
  normalisation 24, 58(n3)
  Peronism 12–14, 18–20
  Primavera plan 132, 135–9
  Radical government 82–98, 133–53, 174–5
elections (1983) 54–5
elections (1987) 113
elections (1989) 138, 146
'electoral fraud era' 2
Estenssoro, Paz 84, 101(n20)
Europe, trade with Argentina 86
exports, industrial exports 36, 59–60(n20)
external debt
  crisis *see* debt
  tables 186, 187

Falkland Islands *see* Malvinas
Favaloro, Rene 66
Federación Obrera Regional Argentina 2
Fernández Long, Hilario 66
Ferreyra Aldunate, Victor 97
financial reform, military government 30

Firmenich, Mario 66
fiscal deficit 150, 182
foreign investment 14–15, 17–18, 59(n10)
free collective bargaining 75–6, 153–4
Frondizi, Arturo xxv(n5), 6–7, 15–16

Galimberti, Rodolfo 66
Galtieri, Leopoldo 49, 50, 66, 121, 131(n23)
García, Alan 86
García Vázquez, Enrique 89, 145
Gattioni, Bishop Carlos 66
Gorriarán Merlo, Enrique 66, 161–2
Graffigna, Omar 66, 121
Grinspun, Bernardo 63, 78–9, 81, 89, 94–5, 98, 133
Gross Domestic Product (GDP) 149, 181, 183
Grupo de los 15 119, 120, 132, 153–5
Grupo de los nueve 130(n20)
Grupo de los Ocho 145, 166(n12)
Grupo de los Once 78, 80, 100(n12)
Grupo de Oficiales Unidos (GUO) 2
Grupos Económicos Nacionales (GEN) 23, 36, 37, 38–9, 45, 56–7
guerillas
    attack by (1989) 161–3
    removal of 19, 23, 25, 55, 68–9, 173
Guido, José María 7, 16

heterodox economic plan 96–7, 100–1(n19), 101(n32)
human rights violations 51–2, 54
    punishment of 64, 65–70, 121–4, 176
hyper-inflation 146–9, 156–7

Illia, Arturo xxv(n5), 7–8, 16–17
import substitution industrialisation (ISI) 14–15
industrial exports 36, 59–60(n20)
industrial labour market 40–2
industry
    foreign investment 14–15
    under military dictatorship 32–40
    under Peronism 14
inflation
    annual rates 28, 182
    Austral plan 103, 110
    hyper-inflation 146–9, 156–7

political aspects 87–8, 129(n1)
international economic order xvii
International Monetary Fund (IMF)
    Austral plan 104, 111, 113
    debt to 82–7, 89–95, 111, 129(n2), 134, 174
    restructuring xx, 46

Junta Militar 24–5, 51–2
    punishment of 65–70

Keynesianism xvii–xviii
Klimovsky, Gregorio 66
Krieger Vasena, Adalbert 9, 17–18, 22(n8)

labour market, industrial sector 40–2
Lambruschini, Armando 66, 121
Lami Dozo, Basilio 66, 121, 131(n23)
Lanusse, Alejandro 10
Levingston, Roberto 10
Lima, Vicente Solano 11
Lonardi, Eduardo 6
looting 147
López Rega, José 11, 19
Luder, Italo 52, 54

Machinea, José Luis 95, 137, 140, 143–4
McNamara, Robert 97
Madres de Plaza de Mayo 25–6, 64
Malvinas war xxi, 49–51, 176
Martínez de Hoz, José A. 25, 26–7, 30, 33, 38–40, 47, 48, 58(n5)
Massera, Emilio E. 25, 66, 121
Menem, Carlos
    and Armed Forces 179
    economic policies 146, 148, 154–5, 173, 177–8
    presidential candidate 135, 139–40, 146, 162, 166(n4)
    restructuring 177–9
    and trade unions 132, 156, 175, 178
Menéndez, Luciano 25
Meyer, Marshall 66
Miguel, Lorenzo 118, 119
military coup (1930) 1–2
military coup (1943) 2
military coup (1955) 5, 6, 8, 14
military coup (1966) 8, 17
military coup (1976) 12, 24

military dictatorship (1966–73) 9–10, 17–18
military dictatorship (1976–83)
  agricultural sector 31–2
  collapse of 47–53
  consequences of xx–xxii, xxiii
  economic policy 26–31, 55–7, 171–2
  external debt 42–6
  industrial sector 32–40
  juridical framework 24–5
  state terrorism 25–6, 64, 65–70
  success of 171–3
military expenditure 188
military rebellion (1987) 125–7
military rebellion (1988) 158–61
monetarism xvii–xviii, 87–8
Montoneros 19, 25
Mucci, Antonio 73–4
Muldford, David 137, 139

national corporations *see Grupos Económicos Nacionales*
neo-liberal state 169–71
Nevares, Bishop Jaime de 66
Nicolaides, Lt General 51
normalisation, economy 24, 58(n3)

Obregón Cano, Ricardo 66
Onganía, Juan Carlos 7, 9–10, 159
orthodox economic plan 100–1(n19)

Pardo, Hector 66
Patrón Costas, Robustiano 2
Perdía, Roberto 66
Perón, Eva 4
Perón, Juan Domingo
  arrest and release (1945) 3–4
  death 11, 53
  and Frondizi 6
  presidency 4–5, 11, 18–19
  and trade unions xxvi(n8), 2–3, 4–5, 19
  and working class 4–5
Perón, María Estela Martínez de 11, 19
Peronism xix, xxv(n6), 6, 7–8, 12–14, 54–5, 173
Peronist party
  election campaign (1989) 139–40
  leadership elections 135
Peru, debt repayment 86

Pianta, General 67
Polo, Luis 125
poverty 40–1, 60(n27), 157
Prebisch, Raúl 89
price indices 149–50
Primavera plan 132, 135–9, 155
private sector, debt 45
privatisation 36–7, 108–9
public investment 59(n19)
Pugliese, Juan Carlos 145, 146
Punto Final law 123–4, 127
purchasing power 152

Rabossi, Eduardo 66
Radical government
  and Armed Forces 64–70, 121–7, 175–6
  economic policy 82–98, 103–21, 133–53, 174–5
  objectives 62
  and trade unions 70–81, 115–21, 153–8
  see also Alfonsín, Raúl
Radical party xix, xxv(n5), 54–5
Rico, Aldo 125, 158–9, 163–4
Ríos Ereñú, Eduardo 125
Rodrigo, Celestino 19–20
Rodríguez, Jesús 146
Rodríguez, José 119, 120
Ruiz Guiñazú, Magdalena 66

Sábato, Ernesto 66
Sapag, Elías 67, 69, 75, 99(n6)
Schultz, George 137, 139
Seineldín, Mohamed Ali 160–1
Semana Santa rebellion 125–7
Sigaut, Lorenzo 47–8
sindicalismo Peronista xxi–xxii, xxvi(n11), 5, 132, 175
Social Pact 18–19
social relations xv–xvi
Sourrouille, Juan Vital 78, 80, 95–7, 107–8, 112, 120, 143
state
  Bureaucratic Authoritarian (BA) 9, 169–70
  capitalist state 168–9
  concept of xiv–xvi
  crisis xvi, xviii–xix, xxii, 11–12, 20–1, 168–9

neo-liberal 169–71
Strassera, Julio 123
strikes 29–30, 31, 48, 76–7, 79, 117, 118, 119, 153–6

tax system 114
terms of trade 183
terrorism, state terrorism 25–6, 64, 65–70
Tonelli, Ideler 153
trabajo a desgano (work to rule) 29–30
trade
balance of 184
international 13–14
see also exports
trade unions
and Alfonsín xxi, 62, 70–81, 118–21, 175
and Armed Forces 6–7, 9–10
and *Austral* plan 115–21
concertación social 75–7
confrontational policy 153–8, 175
membership 42
Peronism xix–xx, xxi–xxii, 2–3, 4–5, 19
strikes 29–30, 48
transnational companies 39
Triaca, Jorge 74, 119
Tróccoli, Antonio 97

Ubaldini, Saúl 74, 79, 130(n17), 153
unemployment 38, 152, 157

Unión Cívica Radical del Pueblo 6, 7
Unión Cívica Radical Intransigente 6
Unión Sindical Argentina 2
United States
relationship with Argentina 86
support for Alfonsín 137–8, 139–40

Vaca Narvaja, Fernando 66
Valle, Juan José xxv–xxvi(n7)
Videla, Jorge R. 25, 31, 35, 66, 121
Viola, Roberto 47–9, 66, 68, 121

wages
1960s 15–16, 16–17
annual variations 27–8, 40, 151, 184
decreases 156–7
increases 18, 105–6, 109–10, 118, 120
minimum wage 76, 100(n10)
'Washington consensus' 83–4, 178
working class
and Perón 4–5
under Alfonsín 157–8, 175
under military dictatorship 40–1, 57
World Bank
Plan Primavera support 136–41
structural adjustment 46

Yrigoyen, Hipólito xxv(n5)